The Battles That Created England 793-1100

The Battles That Created England 793-1100

How Alfred and his Successors Defeated the Vikings to Unite the Kingdoms

Arthur C. Wright

FRONTLINE BOOKS

First published in Great Britain in 2022 by
Frontline Books
An imprint of
Pen & Sword Books Ltd
Yorkshire – Philadelphia

Copyright © Arthur C. Wright 2022

ISBN 978 1 39908 798 8

The right of Arthur C. Wright to be identified as Author of this work has been asserted by him in accordance with the Copyright, Designs and Patents Act 1988.

A CIP catalogue record for this book is available from the British Library.

All rights reserved. No part of this book may be reproduced or transmitted in any form or by any means, electronic or mechanical including photocopying, recording or by any information storage and retrieval system, without permission from the Publisher in writing.

Typeset by Mac Style
Printed in the UK by CPI Group (UK) Ltd, Croydon, CR0 4YY.

Pen & Sword Books Limited incorporates the imprints of Atlas, Archaeology, Aviation, Discovery, Family History, Fiction, History, Maritime, Military, Military Classics, Politics, Select, Transport, True Crime, Air World, Frontline Publishing, Leo Cooper, Remember When, Seaforth Publishing, The Praetorian Press, Wharncliffe Local History, Wharncliffe Transport, Wharncliffe True Crime and White Owl.

For a complete list of Pen & Sword titles please contact

PEN & SWORD BOOKS LIMITED
47 Church Street, Barnsley, South Yorkshire, S70 2AS, England
E-mail: enquiries@pen-and-sword.co.uk
Website: www.pen-and-sword.co.uk

Or

PEN AND SWORD BOOKS
1950 Lawrence Rd, Havertown, PA 19083, USA
E-mail: Uspen-and-sword@casematepublishers.com
Website: www.penandswordbooks.com

For John, who made it all possible.

Contents

Introduction		ix
Chapter 1	The Bolt from the Blue	1
Chapter 2	The Rude Awakening	6
Chapter 3	The Plague of Locusts	13
Chapter 4	The Irresistable Force	19
Chapter 5	Pro Aris et Focis	24
Chapter 6	Going a-Viking	31
Chapter 7	A Glorious Summer	37
Chapter 8	Supporting Success	44
Chapter 9	The "Hot Trod"	51
Chapter 10	Mastering the Waters	57
Chapter 11	A Subtle Strategic Legacy	64
Chapter 12	Inheriting Both Sword and Strategies	72
Chapter 13	Unity of Purpose	77
Chapter 14	Problems of Integration	84
Chapter 15	So to a Famous Victory	90
Chapter 16	Revenge is Sweet	97
Chapter 17	Confusion	100
Chapter 18	Gradual Collapse	105
Chapter 19	Duty, Defeat and Heroism	108

Chapter 20	A New Economic Model	116
Chapter 21	Chaos, Cowardice and Cupiditas	122
Chapter 22	From Atrocities to Despair	126
Chapter 23	The Kingdom Overrun	132
Chapter 24	The Real Millennium	138
Chapter 25	Deceit and Despair	143
Chapter 26	Turning the Tables	148
Chapter 27	The Weakness of the English Crown	152
Chapter 28	A Winter's Tale	157
Chapter 29	Fulford and Stamford	164
Chapter 30	The Affair of England	172
Chapter 31	Harold's Strategic Genius	177
Chapter 32	The Jaws of Defeat	180
Chapter 33	The Master Stroke	183
Chapter 34	A Kingdom by Default	186
Chapter 35	The Abhorrent Vacuum	190
Chapter 36	Axholme and Stafford	194
Chapter 37	Maintenance of the Aim	201
Chapter 38	Fresh "Bones" for the Kingdom	207
Chapter 39	Crisis, Attrition and Oath	211
Chapter 40	The Power of the Crown	215
Chapter 41	Anglo-Norman Security	221
Chapter 42	The Communal Achievement	226
Index		231

Introduction

In the popular imagination, I fear, the warfare of the 'Dark Ages', the long period dividing Romans from Normans, is not only obscure but unstructured and unimaginative. Battles and conflicts lacked witnesses in most cases and they lacked contemporary evidence and analysis in every case, which tends to relegate them to bloody slogging matches whose participants are imagined as superheroes hacking one another down in a series of individual contacts. Germanic mythology encourages the perception of alpha male legends and inevitably all such battles are divorced from the means of waging warfare as the chroniclers recording them had no concept beyond Divine Will. All this is unfortunate as not all battles require locations or slaughter, the means of obtaining victory are much more subtle than this, and also because, then, the true panorama of history, of failures and successes, is lost in a repetitive and unedifying series of disasters and miseries and so divorced from the important social context.

All too often the particular period of this book, the ninth, tenth and eleventh centuries, is presented as a disjointed series of events and invasions lacking coherence or historical structure: sadly too much emphasis has been (and often still is) laid on political constructs that have no relevance beyond the very recent past, certainly they did not exist in this period or for centuries afterwards. The common error of planting present perceptions onto the remote past has therefore denied us the unfolding, if often hesitant, process of unification presented by the several texts of the *Anglo-Saxon Chronicle*, unification that simultaneously gave birth to ideas of common identity and purpose, this in spite of the necessary fusion of several ethnicities. Yet such is the continuous and coherent story that was set down in the *Chronicle*, all unwittingly, by our ancestors.

It is therefore not at all surprising if, by comparison, we see the military and social structures, the disciplines and well-documented organisation of the Roman legions, as a separate world of efficiency whose illumination was snuffed out by 'barbarians at the gates'. A rolling fog of ignorance then, apparently, obliterated our historical landscapes until we come to the Norman superheroes who relit both records and culture. This is apparently the view of some writers, whilst others regret the demise of an apparently democratic, but weak and disorganised, bucolic. Yet in spite of this fog of ignorance, we do, from time to time, stumble on amazing and physical treasures, such as Sutton Hoo or the Staffordshire Hoard and then we wonder how this 'Dark Age' could have produced such sophistication. What we fail to ask ourselves is why such ability was not duplicated in other spheres of 'Dark Age' human activity. Well, I think that if we understood these several centuries of conflicts and their battles a little better, we might throw just a little more illumination on the whole indistinct social panorama.

In AD 410 the Emperor Honorius, in need of even more troops to shore up his tottering empire, issued his famous rescript of the Lex Julia de Vi Publica and withdrew all regular garrisons from Britannia Superior and Britannia Inferior, and with them went all effective civil administration and records. From now on these far-flung provinces were empowered, for the first time, to permit ordinary citizens to bear military arms and to organise themselves into militias. From this point onwards and for many centuries to come Britain (before too long to become England) left behind what semblance she had enjoyed of recorded events, of history; she entered the realms of romance and phantasy. Traditionally we have called these centuries 'the Dark Ages', for lack of any proper illumination, though their span has somewhat diminished in recent history as modern historians attempt to move the goalposts back to the same end of the field under the light of archaeology.

With the removal of the Roman Army, civil government, administration and bureaucracy ended, for there was no one to train specialists, co-ordinate or pay these servants and a very different society then emerged with the fusion of older and newer societies. Some historians have represented this as a 'golden age' of bucolic egalitarianism set in a rural idyll, others have lamented the end of urban civilisation, whilst popular imagination has revelled in those visions of genocide, rape and arson that sell novels. In truth we know nothing certain about it from written records, hence 'Dark Ages', but we have a 'pick-and-mix' mass of snippets on which to hang a slowly emerging archaeological picture. Perhaps too often the one colours the interpretation of the other as devotees of one cause (or 'religion') attempt to reinforce the historical structure that their personal educational path has provided (or political consideration dictated) by daubing archaeology over the gaps.

What finally emerges on the Anglo-Saxon pages of our history books is a society (for few scholars have the courage to argue for mixed societies when facts are so scarce) displaying both wealth and sophistication and no longer reflecting what we had taken to be the Anglo-Saxon bucolic. Instead we see a sudden illumination, though one lacking spotlights, which causes us to look more carefully at the available evidence, and we see a landscape in both physical and political evidences whose emergence is difficult to explain. It is, however, still a world very different from the one that was to follow.

My own appraisal is that this post-Roman period became a highly structured, hierarchical and formal world where even conflicts had become generally 'limited', which is to say that warring factions tacitly agreed to minimise the social and economic damage done to their essential local economies when settling aristocratic differences through fairly formalised warfare. After all, no one benefits from inheriting a vacant desert, a wasteland. To make such a reciprocal political structure function there must have been rigid social distinctions and hierarchies, and the obvious wealth of these kingdoms (as revealed by archaeology) reinforces such a supposition. One other feature is also important, this world of formal kingdoms and codes was now a Christian world and this also predicates social rigidity and aristocratic fusion with the Church. The Church needed aristocratic assistance and the aristocracies needed Divine intervention in their affairs.

Much to the joy of novelists, this happy world of aristocratic entertainment was now brought to an end, at first by a dramatically isolated interruption but then by one that quickly escalated to a continuing disaster. Wave after wave of determined raiders, with no scruples about limiting warfare, descended on the hapless aristocratic and the religious houses, and on their kingdoms. Their success was due to mobility, determination and appreciation of the Anglo-Saxon social structure, but also to the development of a strategic plan (though historians seem to have overlooked this last!) and these things served them well – until King Alfred discovered their formula. After that came a brief *modus vivendi*.

From this point the, now not quite so dark, 'Dark Ages' progressed through and into further internecine rivalries, rather as before, to a point where further raiders and invaders descended on the English (as they now were). Once again we are told of the affinity these new raiders had with the former (but now settled) invaders, though no one told these former Danish raiders (now inhabitants) that all they had to do was show their party badge. These new 'Vikings' (meaning 'pirates') have become the stuff of romantic fiction as adventurous, well-groomed, skilled seamen and international traders whose swashbuckling activities inspire certain sections of modern society. In reality murderers, rapists, arsonists, iconoclasts, slavers, psychopaths and thieves in heterogeneous gangs, they are held up as worthwhile role models for modern youth, a triumph of romance over reality.

These new raiders proved to be determined and deadly adversaries, yet the evolution of defences and systems enabled the English to fight back. For a while England next became a Danish province under Cnut until the Breton kingship of Edward restored a sort of identity, if not complete unity, to the thirty-four shires that now comprised the kingdom. These 'Viking wars' were therefore centuries of grief, hardship and even of catastrophe but they eventually forged and unified an England in *one* kingdom, one that was then capable, under Norman kingship, of defending itself against all comers, all attempted invaders and invasions. How this finally came about, how they achieved such ultimate defensive unity, is largely outside the scope of this book, but I have written about it elsewhere.[1]

This present book, therefore, details the evolution from heterogeneous Anglo-Saxon kingdoms and their internal conflicts, through various battles and invasions, to the point where one amorphous (if not invariably united) kingdom acquired the capacity to best all comers, *after* the Norman Conquest. In so doing these different peoples themselves acquired a new identity, so this is the process by which an English national identity became possible in succeeding centuries as old rivalries and kingdoms now fused together.

So we will speak of 'battles which made England' though, in fact, battles on their own solve nothing because they create nothing. War is the totality of the means employed to achieve political success, so our overview of these conflicts must necessarily include their social and political matrix. Battles are fought, won and lost, on a wide variety of battlefields and not all of them were (or are) soaked with blood, yet, hopefully, they do all (whatever their precise nature) facilitate a sort of catalytic progress.

For a substantial part of this book my principal guide has been the *Anglo-Saxon Chronicle*, in fact a collation of surviving accounts and texts, our only source of reasonably reliable event reportage. Of course, this *Chronicle* has been the historian's standard template for this period and, if we make allowances for oral distortion and mythological excursions, it does seem to be pretty accurate when compared with other sources and comprehensive when the several versions are collated. However, even the apparently factual matrix has generally lacked cohesion, often appearing as a jumble of events lacking linkage by accurate context and also that catenation that creates a continuous narrative. After all, in a world that does not readily obey the laws of chronology and also has components that seem to float in space and time, life (as illustrated by such 'history') becomes not what one might suppose should be reality, which is to say that instead it becomes what individuals want to imagine. That is why the period is such a favourite with novelists and politicians.

So I have attempted to remedy this lack of context and analysis by recreating a complementary matrix of landscapes, topography and communications for our *Chronicle*'s commentary. In this I have been assisted by *Domesday Book*, our only nearly contemporary statistical overview. I have tried to set events in a scenery of *their* likely world, rather than one implanted on what we see in reality today. Using this as our foundation, we can fit other pieces of archaeological and philological evidence into a narrative, one that will allow us to deduce, then analyse and put in train, events that may finally present a more illuminating picture, hopefully to disperse a little more of the fog of history.

Note

1. Arthur C. Wright, *English Collusion & the Norman Conquest* (Frontline, 2020), in particular Chapters 8 and 9 and the focus on the Salisbury Oath Taking of 1086.

Chapter One

The Bolt from the Blue

Looking out across the Ouse, towards the mainland, on a beautiful morning early in June 793, with the divine blessing of a waxing sun to warm the zephyrs dancing over these waters and the caresses of such airs creating myriads of tiny bright jewels to dazzle the eyes, the holy brothers of the Abbey of 'Lindisfarena' offered heartfelt praise to Almighty God with a solemn *Te Deum Laudamus* while remembering their blessed founders, Saints Aiden and Cuthbert.

Was there another place in Northumbria so rewarded with holy calm and isolation, one so isolated from a wicked world, a world that was only briefly connected to their island when the tides uncovered the Causeway? This island was a place conducive to that prayer and meditation that grants revelations of divine vision to the truly dedicated among God's elect. Indeed, in winter, so cold and windswept, making one so mindful of the power of the Almighty yet so kind in the present season to the faithful, replete with Divine Grace, a place untroubled by the ordinary affairs of men, a place where one could continually pray for Divine Intervention on behalf of those generous patrons who supported Mother church. Moreover, the cares that one had here and the seasonal privations (sent by God) the relentless 'offices' of the Rule of St Benedict, which left so little time, day or night, for sleep and other comforts, these things were the prelude to admission into that blessed realm beyond the sky where the elect offer continual praise and adoration to the Almighty Father, Son and Holy Ghost (and which they in turn design to accept), where former monks become blessed souls, men who had escaped those torments of Hell that would afflict all other men until the Glorious Resurrection and Day of Doom, Domesday, brought final judgement to both the quick and the dead. Such was the great promise of the monastic life, given in return for privations and humility, the ultimate translation to glory.

This place was *medicata insula*,[1] the healing isle, and its gardens, tended by both lay brothers and slaves, provided abundant vegetables, while the surrounding waters teemed with fish of all kinds, shellfish and thousands of seabirds to provide good eating, including eggs. Grateful mainlanders over the waters sent gifts of kine and swine (when tide and regimen permitted them), wheat, barley and oats, beer for the brothers and wines for the Father

Abbot and his table, all given in return for the brother's prayers for Divine intervention in their husbandry and local politics.

That mainland world, *the* world, was one that the brothers had renounced, the one they had escaped from, a world of unceasing manual labour (for most men and women) and yet, for many a world more attractive than coenobitic celibacy on an isolated rock. Yet, for some, this island was instead an assurance of security in a strictly communal life and also in the world to come. In this Northumbria of hierarchical society, there was a small and kingly elite, each member of higher society with their own mead-hall hearth troop (retainers), where the privileged lived in considerable opulence, secure in the knowledge that the Christian God was their protector and decider of destinies. These Anglo-Saxon elites made wars on one another, from time to time, and so secured (or lost) treasure as booty, acquiring captives, slaves and territory thereby. The slaves and the territory then provided new resources to those men who ploughed and, by and large, kings and their major landholders and retainers were careful to limit such depredations for it was a 'do-as-you-would-be-done-by' world that, in this way, mostly kept in balance. The majority toiled and that was the reason to preserve them, a small group of warriors fought, nominally as 'protectors', and another minority prayed and offered insurance against both natural and artificial misfortunes, and kings sat above them all. Indeed for some in the landholding elite, the Church had *now* become so attractive that they also aspired to become abbots and to found their own monasteries and, as such, why the Rule (of the two Saints Benedict) need not be so arduous as in the older established conventual houses. Moreover, no Christian dared to interfere with the Church and its establishments, which conferred some real earthly immunity. Indeed, the Council of 'Clofesho' held in 803 was directed against such secular lordship of monasteries, aiming to correct the inherent danger contained in the Ismere Charter of Æthelbald of Mercia in 736, but as long as Anglo-Saxon society remained reasonably secure such sinecures remained very tempting.[2]

So, God was in his Heaven and all was right with the world of kingdoms and conventual houses and their several peoples. And on this June morning far away on the horizon of the German Ocean watchers saw four sails. Nothing strange there, maybe they were looking for the Farne Islands, maybe their heading would change northwards to Berwick or even the Firth of Forth. Ships did not normally approach from the north-east, that was the only strange thing about it, most ships came coastwise from the south. As the day wore on so the ships wore southwards, then by rounding the east of the island, then passing Guile Point, it became clear that they were not seeking the Farnes at all. Reports to the Father Abbot would have been puzzling, Lindisfarne was not an 'emporium', a port-and-market, yet if they came from the north-east well, he might have reasoned, they could be carrying a valuable cargo of furs and ivory, he had heard of such traders. Perhaps, the Brother Almoner or some manciple was sent to the waters' side to enquire their purpose, welcome them and commence negotiations for port fees? Brothers returned to their devotions, lay brothers and slaves to their tasks.

Those ships did not lose way as they approached the beach below the abbey, instead they drove straight for it. Over bows and quarters, into the waters, tumbled screaming heathen warriors, armed to the teeth. The porte reeve never stood a chance. Perhaps four 'sokes', ship loads of warriors, probably as surprised as the monks were to see them, as surprised to discover such a community, slaughtered the brothers as they ran. They burst into the church and massacred monks at the altar, they rounded up some worthwhile human specimens for slaves and butchered every other living soul, stripping the place of anything of intrinsic value then setting fire to the rest. The library also went up in flames.

With the causeway flooded by the tide, there was nowhere for the monastic community to run to and no one on land who could defend them. Those who had been spared, for thraldom (in Norway most likely), went to the ships and rowed away to a miserable future, leaving behind them the smoking ruins of a famous monastery filled with charred and dismembered cadavers, some undoubtedly tortured to death as offerings to the pagan gods. Anyone watching from the land that night would have seen a vision of Hell and carried to them on the summer air the smell of burning flesh, the screams of the damned and the drunken revelry of demons.

What but contempt could these raiders have for a foolish community that chose to live, defenceless, in such an isolated place, trusting in a god who had no powers? Christendom was rocked to the core, how could God have permitted such an outrage, what Divine purpose could this serve? We should not underestimate the blow to the Church: who could believe in an Almighty who was powerless against such heathens and their gods? This had not been a sinful community, so whose wickedness did such a sacrifice expiate? Well, at least their agonies had ended in translation to the Blessed Realms.

Well to the south in County Durham lay the community of Jarrow Monkwearmouth, the Abbey of St Paul of Tarsus, whose most famous son (brother) had been the Venerable Bede, generally acclaimed by modern historians as 'the father of English History'. Well, this is not quite accurate for (in truth) he was the father of English ethnology, turning Gildas's polemaic (*De Excidio et Conquestu Britanniae*) into an ethnic structure. Not quite an Autolycus, nor yet the writer of *The Winter's Tale*, he was nevertheless, a collector of 'unregarded trifles', the sort of statistical information that other holy authors discarded. His *History of the English Church and Peoples* not only included, as it should, a most instructional hagiography, a fine collection of saintly miracles working in and among the English kingdoms and illustrating the power and supremacy of the One True God (head), it also added more than a smattering of secular stories. The sources of these and the current accuracy of their statistical inclusions we can never know, but some seem to have been quite venerable. Jarrow had a superb library after his death and, maybe, before but, of course, there were no mechanics by which to gather, let alone verify, store or collect casual reportage and oral traditions. The Venerable Bede could only write what he had read and what he believed, and his beliefs included a dazzling array of miracles. These latter were probably never witnessed by him and one also doubts that he verified his secular additions. Yet we should commend his statistics, even if these were gathered from various and outdated sources. For these alone he stands out as an historian, rather than for his perfect Latin.

Somewhere over the cold, northern waters, it seems, some miserable exile spoke too freely, about the rich library, beautiful volumes and stained glass windows of this famous abbey, for a year after the sacking and destruction of Lindisfarne, in AD 794 several ship sokes of heathen pirates entered the River Tyne and sailed or rowed all the way to Jarrow. Saint Paul was of no more avail than Saint Cuthbert had been, thereby at least demonstrating the parity of English saints with holy apostles; the convent was massacred and burnt to the ground, the library destroyed – except for the hacksilver from the bindings of holy books. The beautiful glass was shattered into tiny fragments by barbarians who had no idea how it was made and away they sailed with their treasure and their slaves to tell the tale of weak and defenceless communities, ripe for the plucking. Penetrating deep inland this time, they still do not seem to have been opposed. If the powers of the saints had now failed, then it must be the Will of God and how (then) could men prevail? Events were indeed to show that the Divine Purpose had changed.

As is the way with such events, the chroniclers were quick to find retrospective portents; hurricanes, fiery dragons in the sky and famine had (they claimed) all foretold disasters. For two hundred years there had been nothing like this, but the more inland minsters and monastic houses probably felt reasonably secure under the protection of God and of earthly princes. No one knows where these 'heathens' came from but Norway seems a possibility as for two generations we hear no more and maybe these raids had been as much the results of lucky navigation as anything else? As yet we have no firm evidence of Norwegian shipbuilding and sailing abilities at this date. Then, in 835, all of a sudden, 'heathens' returned in force.

Chapter Two

The Rude Awakening

When we look at the Staffordshire Hoard and the Sutton Hoo treasure we might wonder why such wealth, of which only these tiny samples remain to us, had not attracted other peoples before the ninth century? The answer, I suspect, is far from simple. In the first place the Migration Period and then the Heptarchy (as we conveniently divide our 'Dark Age') were characterised by vigorous martial activity, at least in their initial stages. Some historians have suspected that population pressures in the emerging Scandinavian kingdoms, as well as the need for younger sons to gain status through warrior deeds, obliged migrants to fight for land. Recent research has indeed shown that Norwegian influence was, overall, stronger in England, with Swedish groups largely exploring and raiding eastwards into Europe instead, though not all 'Vikings' were Scandinavians.[1] In Norway, the 'bondir', or free-farmer, was the principal social unit and for him and his sons, bound by Odal rights.[2] It was essential to acquire slaves, 'thralls', with which to work the land and also to breed, though slavery and slaving was important in every region of Europe.

However, the principal threat, as far as it can be ascertained for lack of reliable information, first came in the ninth century from Denmark, and here we do see dynastic developments. While the present monarchy can only trace their ancestry from Gorm the Old early in the tenth century, there is evidence that consolidation into kingdoms in Denmark (including Schleswig-Holstein) was occurring by the late eighth century. The first period of the final 'Danevirke' earthwork belongs to the period 650–808, and surely this must indicate the influence and power of kingship?[3] Simultaneously, developments in shipbuilding were producing vessels like the Oseberg Ship, buried c.834 but in service probably before c.800. Surviving Norwegian ship evidence indicates a similar technological development for them, though navigation must have presented, at least initial, problems. It seems likely that the vessels that made Lindisfarne in 793 were 'lucky' adventurers, though the attack on Jarrow seems to display some more accurate course-laying. For some time afterwards the Norwegians seem to have turned their attention to Scotland and then to Ireland, the 'Kingdom of the Isles', leaving the Anglo-Saxon kingdoms alone.

Notes

1. 'Medicata insular' from 'Medcaut', Nennius' Old Welsh Name for the Island in his *Historia Brittonum*, a derivation suggested by Richard Coates and Andrew Breeze, q.v. Andrew Breeze 'Medcaut the Brittonic Name of Lindisfarne' in *Northern History* (2008) vol. 42, pp.187–188. The reference might be to the influence of a medical herbarium or to an infirmary?
2. Q.v. *Anglo-Saxon Kingdoms, Art, Word, War*, eds. Claire Breay and Joanna Story (British Library, 2018), catalogue entries 44 and 38.

Of course, we cannot be sure that in 835 we are dealing with Danes alone, our *Chronicles* are not so accurate or discriminating. Yet it is surely no coincidence that King Horik I of Denmark, a very warlike character, shook off his joint kingship with Harold Klak in 823 and from then (to his demise in 854) was sole monarch? Coincidentally, the Oseberg Ship was buried, with its royal occupant, *c.*834. It seems that pressures on Danish society were possibly strong at this time. As an eminent scholar has put it, 'overpopulation in select classes of society is a very different matter' to overpopulation in the absolute sense, so we cannot equate piratical attacks with demographics and should look elsewhere.[4] In Scandinavian populations where a free kindred, land and warrior prowess were the trinity of status, then the lack of one of these elements (say land) could be compensated by raising the profile of the others. Moreover, wealth speaks for lack of status in any sociological model. These, I fancy were the real motivations.

So the two main driving forces for Danes, and perhaps for Norwegians, were probably increased skill in shipbuilding (and management) and the need to increase the compound of wealth with status. The key to the latter, certainly in the eighth and early ninth centuries, was not the fortuitous discovery of unlimited gold and silver – for there are now and were then few dragon's hoards to discover and, besides, even when markets exist they can glut – no, the key to wealth was slaving. Every freeman's homestead relied on supplies of slaves, so those surplus to personal or family needs could be traded (even universally) as high-value goods.

Of course, it is an agreed feature of this 'Danish' period of activity in the ninth century that territorial gain was *not* the primary motivation, rather the earlier incursions moved from one form of exploitation to another. This seems explicable in terms of raids intent on gathering captives and securing both loot and provisions, with slaves subsequently traded (either on the spot or sent abroad) and the victors living 'high on the hog' until both provisions and domestic slaves became exhausted. Within this period of acquired ease, secured by an initial terror, would be opportunities for raiders to both continue raiding (from a secured base) and also to process the metallurgical spoils of war, perhaps often for resale. In this way we can account for the evidence of trading activity.

There were no overwhelming climate, population or religious questions forcing these peoples to seek a new world, the lure was quite simply easy money and the freedom to do as they chose. To claim that the 'great army' came in 865 complete with entourage of wives and children occupying good warrior space and leaving rowing benches without oarsmen, likewise that they deliberately imported merchants and craftsmen to 'improve' the backwards Saxons, does stretch credulity to the limits. Nevertheless, I have seen it proposed. Every oar was needed for motive power and every one a warrior, if a ship was to be safely sailed and the war band secure. Vikings were *not* the creators of industries and founders of trading centres, they came instead to plunder them. They were terrorists, pirates and slavers who needed every man to pull his weight at an oar or in the attack. Theirs was not a 'works outing', though it may have provided an apprentice scheme for juvenile arsonists, rapists and murderers at times, instead each venture was a dangerous business proposition requiring enormous initial expenditure by the leader of a war band, harsh discipline and total commitment and, even then, things did not always 'go their way'.

This pattern of social organisation was very different from that of the Anglo-Saxon kingdoms, often smarting or restless under Mercian hegemony by *c*.800 but still hierarchical, structured, limiting warfare largely to the political sphere, wary of the Church, careful not to destroy the essential economic foundation of agriculture or even the now emerging trading links. Such a world acknowledged that there were those not engaged in the classical occupations of farming and fighting, so (by derivation) by this date establishing 'emporia', a name derived from the Greek *emporos*, or 'one who comes to land'. These centres of long-distance trade gave rise to specific mention in the Laws of Wihtraed of Kent (*c*.695), a kingdom dominated by the importation of eastern and Continental luxuries and producing glass, brooches, metalwork and very possibly specialised weaponry (from the Weald),[5] but such resources also existed elsewhere and would obviously make tempting targets for raiders who were certainly outside the general 'gentleman's agreement' of Anglo-Saxon kingship.

Kings and senior clerics controlled this lucrative trade for, indeed, it was they who both generated and acquired the high-value, high-status goods so traded. These were neither flea nor farmer's markets, there was no need for international trade in everyday products and commodities for everyone produced their own. Thus merchants coming ashore and the vendors coming to meet them were, alike, traders in luxuries and well able to pay the 'taxes' or port dues levied by kings and by senior clerics who controlled the emporia. Such places and such ostentation do not remain secret and along with stories of the luxuries so traded would emerge the wealth of Anglo-Saxon England in minerals: gold, silver, copper, tin, lead, iron and the ability to extract and use them.[6] Not only products but also the metals themselves and even their artisans would each have their value. It is a picture of rich kingdoms and rich churches with apparently no need of defensive preparations but with local concentrations of wealth on the coasts, and a land teeming with an unwary peasantry. Over the waters, others in very different societies were watching.

In the year 835, the 'heathens', as our *Chronicles* style them, returned with a vengeance, the pejorative telling us that these were new and unknown peoples. They thought outside the straitjacket of 'limited warfare' and so targeted secular *and* religious properties alike. The Anglo-Saxon kingdoms were never to be the same again though, of course, no one at the time knew that this was to be a significant step in the creation of an 'England' for such raids appeared to be individual calamities and each individual kingdom was, at first, counting its own costs.

These 'heathen men ravaged Sheppey', so they had been bold enough to enter the Thames estuary and, in what was to become a familiar pattern, they seized an island (Sheppey) as a base and a strand (place of safe maintenance and beaching for ships) and from behind natural defences (the Swale and marshes) terrorised adjacent Kent and, no doubt, intercepted shipping bound for the Londonwic emporium. Here they could command the Essex shore and the Medway, maybe as far as Reculver with its distinctive minster, though Thanet and Canterbury might have been more strongly defended and, for the present, safer. Anyway, it was a clever choice of location that speaks of a careful, military intelligence-gathering process.

The next year the focus changed to the West Country and these raids were probably of Norwegian origin as they came from Ireland: twenty-five ships' companies, perhaps 700 to 1,000 men, landed on the north coast of Somerset, so commanding all other shipping passing along the Bristol Channel. Here they met King Ecgbryht, the king of Wessex, at Carhampton on the edge of Exmoor. Ecgbryht was an experienced commander who had acquired Surrey, Sussex, Kent, Anglia and Mercia – to become 'Bretwalda' or 'High King'. He had also pacified Northumbria and North Wales, no mean feats, yet here at Carhampton the heathen force, probably supported by Brythonic elements from further west, 'held the battlefield' in spite of 'great slaughter' all round. Maybe the king's gesiths had become too used to limited warfare but it is also likely that the raiders had made clever use of the ethnic divide between Anglo-Saxons and residual Damnonian tribes in Cornwall and Devon in order to recruit allies, and that they also made clever use of the terrain.

The *Chronicle* names Carhampton, yet at the time this was not so much a place name as a hundred (a division of the shire) and the raiders could actually have landed at 'Mynydd', Minehead, so as to take command of North Hill and watch for approaching forces. Their actual strand may have been at Porlock Bay, 'Port Loc' or 'the enclosure by the harbour', where they could rely on natural defences in the form of marshes between strand and land, and also high ground from which to scan the Brendon Hills.

Though their initial purpose was almost certainly slaving, for the new 'Viking' settlements in Ireland needed workers, the discovery of Taunton monastery (which pre-dated 904) and Bridgwater would have been a bonus. They could command the north Somerset coast and all passing shipping as well as Exmoor and the wooded country beyond. If this surmise is correct, then a battle fought with, by now familiar, marshland defences behind them would allow the raiders a chance to fall back in need, so as to place the marshes before them while they gained their ships on the shingled strand. So they would have both 'held' the field *and* escaped with their captives, leaving their Damnonian allies to face their fate. Thus we hear that, though they 'held the field' (got away), there was also 'great slaughter' on both sides.

Taking stock of the events of 836 and the successful formula practised then, two years later 'a great ship force' (presumably from Ireland) landed somewhere in Cornwall and united with the Damnonian tribes. Some writers have represented this as an altruistic Viking support of the Cornishmen challenging oppression by Ecgbryht, but this is to implant modern concepts onto the past (once again); rather we should see it as a convenient liaison offering increased manpower in exchange for freedom from enslavement. The Vikings were targeting further inland and so they also needed local guides. It proved to be a regrettable experiment. They seem to have attempted to march overland from Cornwall into Devon but King Ecgbryht was prepared and met them at Hingston Down, where he put to flight 'the Britons and the Danes' (if Danish they were).

This place is generally accepted to be Hingston Down ('Hengestdun' or 'Stallion's Hill') on Dartmoor near Gunnislake and Tavistock, on the Tamar, and the obvious site would be Kit Hill. This suggests that on this occasion the raiders had overreached themselves by fighting inland and without a fallback position. Maybe some depopulation of the coastal areas had now forced them to march inland looking for slaves, or perhaps this area was already mining tin (as it was later famous for doing) and so had an obvious community of sturdy workers and booty. Perhaps King Ecgbryht had learned at Carhampton that he needed to draw them on and into a battlefield of his own choosing, while his position as 'high king' would place many more gesiths and thanes at his command than one kingdom alone could normally muster.

In 840, it was the turn of Horik's Danes to return, this time targeting the rich emporium of 'Hamwic' (Southampton), with thirty-seven ships' companies, well over 1,000 warriors. Ealdorman Wulfheard met them and took the victory 'with great slaughter' but his own death, soon after, may have been the consequence. It seems that the Danes had made the mistake of attacking on land and without a fallback position. Then more Danes landed at Portland and in the reversion to the 'island model', they were successful for they killed Ealdorman Æthelhun and 'held the battlefield'. Clearly these attacks had relied on commercial intelligence and they also aimed to dislocate the Channel trade with France.

Now emboldened, in 841 pirates struck not only at Lindsey but also at East Anglia, then at Kent where Ealderman Harebryht was killed in Romney Marshes. Yet again we see the use of marshy habitats combined with mobile amphibious forces. The raiders now had the measure of their victims and they also had a good intelligence network, perhaps established as innocent traders using the emporia. So in 842 they returned to make murderous attacks not only on Londonwic and the Thames but also Rochester and the Medway, thence to the emporium of Quentovic (south of Boulogne), the Continental link with this Thames mouth and Thanet trading empire. Here we see them controlling both sides of the narrows in the Channel and bringing all such trade to a halt. These expeditions were obviously as concerned with booty as with slaves, though emporia no doubt included slave markets and in this I think we can suspect the hand of King Horik, seeking luxuries and providing ready markets for them at his court in Denmark.

Not that the Norwegian Vikings in Ireland had given up, for in 842 some thirty-five ships' companies returned to the Bristol Channel, landing once again at Carhampton, territory they already knew and which had worked to their advantage before. King Æthelwulf of Wessex marched against them and though the raiders 'had the power of the battlefield', they do not appear to have enjoyed outright victory. Returning home to lick their wounds, they then reappeared two years later, presumably searching for slaves and perhaps heading for Bridgwater. So in 845, Ealdormen Eanulf and Osric, and Bishop Ealstan, with the men of both 'Sumersaete' and Dorset, met them at the mouth of the Parrett and 'made great slaughter ... and took the victory'. Again the *Chronicle* seems to identify them as Danes, but I think we should separate out both the origins and the strategies of the Irish and the Danish raiders. These pirates had succeeded in uniting the hearth troops of two shires in rapid response, even before their king could join them, no doubt due to the emphasis on slave taking, which drew these Vikings dangerously beyond familiar territory and, perhaps, further up than the mouth of the river, maybe as far as Bridgwater, only to be trapped when they attempted to sail out again. Over on the east coast the lure was, at least equally, the emporia. However, we should not make the mistake of thinking that the two, separate, camps did not communicate.

Notes

1. A. Margaryou, 'Population Genomics of the Viking World', *Nature* (16 September 2020) – research conducted by Erske Willerslev and Jette Arneborg, also reported in *National Geographic* (2020).
2. H.R. Loyn, *The Vikings in Britain* (1977), pp.26, 48.
3. Ibid., pp.16–17.
4. Ibid., p.26.
5. Arthur Wright, *Domesday Book Beyond the Censors* (2017), pp.79–86.
6. 'Stallion's Hill' is the usual interpretation but the highest point of Hingston Down is actually Kit Hill ('birds of prey Hill'), which also sounds an ominous name given their association with slaughter.

Chapter Three

The Plague of Locusts

So for six years there was, apparently, peace. We hear of no raids during this period but in fact several Danish warlords were gathering strength and possibly plotting with the Irish Vikings. As in 1066, 1068 and 1084,[1] fleets do not assemble themselves overnight, but as Anglo-Saxon England is not generally thought to have belonged to the new shipbuilding cartel (we will return to this later), so it seems that England's kingdoms may have missed the signs.

The onslaught came in 851 when Irish Vikings returned to Devon. Sadly, we have little information about this (which may indicate its ferocity) but at an unknown place named 'Wicganbeorg' these raiders met Ealdorman Ceorl and the men of Devon, who made great slaughter and took the victory. Perhaps once again, the raiders made the mistake of straying too far inland?

What no one expected was an almost simultaneous attack on the east coasts and this time it was an army in a fleet. Some 350 ships, we are told, if anyone had the skill and courage to count them, entered the mouth of the Thames: perhaps 10,000 to 13,000 warriors! They entered Kent and sacked Canterbury, then they put King Brithwulf of Mercia to flight and entered Surrey, so King Æthelwulf of Wessex brought up his West Saxon army to meet them at 'Acled' (or 'Aclea'). Here this king made great carnage and had the victory. The Danes seem to have made the mistake, once again, of striking overland and so into unfamiliar territory, whereas the locals (at least) were on their own ground. Still, 'it is an ill wind ...' and Æthelwulf's focus on the eastern shires left the Irish raiders in the West Country free to over-winter in Devon. The West Saxons needed time to recover, it seems.

Obviously, the attack on the Thames and Kent had been timed to take advantage of the recovery of the emporia. Though the remnants of their army were able to take ship again – no doubt they had left a garrison on their old haunt, Sheppey – they were not sufficient to attempt more at the southern end of the Wantsum Channel than the rounding of Thanet and (perhaps) the North Foreland. No doubt reasoning that the Wessex army was now guarding the area adjacent to London, these ships made for Sandwich, and if that *is* the route they chose in the hope of retrieving something in the way of luxuries and slaves, well, here they were met on land by King Æthelstan of

Kent, bent on vengeance, and ealdorman Ealhere, apparently *on* the waters! Somehow the English *had* acquired a fleet and they handled them so well that they took nine ships and put the rest of the Vikings to flight. This is the first reference we have to the employment of sea power by the Anglo-Saxons and it suggests that historians may have been mistaken about Anglo-Saxon shipbuilding and sailing capabilities.

These several defensive movements look very like co-operation, resulting in concerted attacks by defending forces wherever the 'heathens' came ashore. Both sides had now made supreme efforts, the one to attack (from two, widely separated, bases), the other to defend (by strategic planning). The raiders had underestimated their adversaries and had failed to adhere to their own, formerly successful, formula. I think that the English commanders had decided on the establishment of bases, so that Æthelstan of Kent was defending his most valuable location, the Isle of Thanet. In so doing he obliged the Danish army to move out of Kent but, equally, he was ready for them on his southern coast when they either rounded the North Foreland or sailed through the Wantsum Channel. If the latter was their route, then it would have been a simple matter to block their exit at Sandwich and so force them to come ashore and fight. I commend this possibility as the most likely tactical disposition.

The Isle of Thanet, as it then was, was an attractive target to raiders. Both graves and chance archaeological finds attest the wealth and importance of its emporium. Reciprocal tidal currents from the north Kent shore (including the sea-mark of Reculver) to the Essex and Suffolk inshore coastline, due to the disparity between high and low-tide timings, made it an ideal destination.[2] It was both an ideal destination and an ideal distribution point for Continental imports, for by crossing into the Thames mouth, ships could avoid the strong currents in the narrowest part of the Channel, the South Foreland, and also the Goodwin Sands; they could enter the north end of the Wantsum in order to berth safely and then by following the channel of the Wantsum emerge at Pegwell Bay and the Sandwich Flats. From here the return passage to France was easier than in the opposite direction. Vessels from Quentovic (Boulogne) could be carried to any point between the North and the South Forelands by prevailing westerlies but the North Kent shore provided more sheltered sailing for vessels with only limited ability to wearship or make effective way. As to the onwards distribution of goods, it was either by sea, to Londonwic, to Essex or to Suffolk, or overland into and beyond the rich kingdom of Kent. It was the foundation of its kingdom's wealth in trade.

Two years later, in 853, a 'heathen force' once again landed on Thanet, only to be met by ealdormen Ealhere and Hutha commanding the men of both Kent and Surrey. The result seems to have been bloody and not wholly satisfactory for both ealdormen were killed, though the raiders retired. Well, if they could not have Thanet then such Danish pirates from Ostend and further north could always intercept ships in the mouth of the Thames. In 855, 'heathen men' over-wintered on their old haunt, the Isle of Sheppey. King Æthelwulf does not appear to have been too concerned and left them to the men of Kent while he went to Rome 'in great state' and there took a whole year's holiday! Soon after his return he died and his sons divided the kingdoms that had been his: Æthelbald took Wessex and Æthelberht Kent, Essex, Surrey and Sussex. Then, in 860, Æthelbald died and so his brother received all the kingdoms. If this was the 'dream ticket', he was soon to receive a rude awakening.

This apparently peaceful interlude may well have masked clandestine activities. Apparent toleration of the men on Sheppey seems to imply some sort of *modus vivendi* and we should not assume that all raids were mindless acts of terrorism. This lacuna could well have been employed in trading with Kent and Essex, so allowing these 'traders' to reconnoitre the Thames approaches. Later we are told that Danes built a defended strand at Shoeburyness, directly opposite to Sheppey, which may well have been the highest part of Foulness Island. I suggest that the outpost on Sheppey was taking time to explore the coasts of Anglia in some detail, just for future reference. By encouraging international trading, all the English kingdoms were weakening their security, giving access to inland waterways and increasing Danish knowledge of inland navigation together with insights into the wealth of kingdoms and their strengths and populations. Originally their attacks on monastic communities had been chance encounters but now they were building a gazetteer. The rise of a European commercial economy is thought to have begun in the late eighth century and Kent and Thanet do seem to have been at the forefront, due to the influence of many factors.[3] However, trade also takes many forms, including slave and pirate markets, and provides unforeseen opportunities.

Well, in 860 'a great ship force' entered the Solent and Southampton Water, making their way to Winchester, the very capital of the Kingdom of Wessex. The Ealdormen Osric and Æthelwulf, with the men of Hampshire and Berkshire, put them to flight and had the battlefield. Once again striking inland had been the pirates' weakness, traversing unknown territory beyond the emporium of Hamwic. Now strangers who landed were no longer greeted with enquiries as to their intent, such as we read of in *Beowulf*. Now such sightings were instead the signal to gather forces and oppose them with as many men as possible. They were no longer regarded as honest traders if they 'came to port' but instead were presumed to be hostiles.

However, over in Kent the 'heathen force' on Sheppey had apparently been presumed to be honest traders, and by now they knew the shorelines well and the country round-about. Now they made their next descent on Thanet and the men of Kent made a truce with them and promised tribute, so they had made good use of their time. They may have remained on Thanet for some time but eventually they broke this truce and 'in the night' they stole up and then proceeded to ravage east Kent. We are not told of any defensive actions and, indeed, there is now a brief gap in our records that suggests disaster.

Then in 866 came a great 'heathen force' to Anglia, no doubt well briefed by their (now) local pilots and guides, and this army made winter quarters somewhere: it was preparing to stay. The Anglians made peace with them and, ominously, they then began to gather horses. Æthelred succeeded to the throne of Wessex and no one knew what the intentions of these invaders were, though clearly they now knew parts of the land as well as knowing the coasts.

Well, this time they did not intend to tramp into a trap inland, no, their tactics had changed to include faster-moving horsemen, light cavalry who could scout and skirmish; now they marched north and on Northumbria, crossing the Humber to York, no doubt shadowed by their fleet sailing northwards along the east coast. So in 867 they also had amphibious forces. Apart from their clever strategy of moving together from Anglia to Lindsey and beyond, why choose Northumbria? Well, the Northumbrians were embroiled in a civil war, one that offered a third party considerable potential for intervention. Obviously these 'heathens' knew this entire coast and its politics very well, so they may have been from what is now northern Holland as well as from Denmark.

The account we have is confused but it seems that late in this year, perhaps after the great army, or 'force' as it is called, had established itself, the Northumbrians finally decided to oppose them. The result was that both the rival kings were killed and the Northumbrian forces slaughtered. Of course, we know equally little about the political situation in Denmark at this time, all we know is that descendants of the line of Godfred exercised some sort of kingship. Moreover, though we suspect that the Swedish Ynglinga dynasty had once had links with East Anglia, their kingships remain obscure.[4] Whether Irish Vikings had rounded Land's End and into the Channel, to reach East Anglia or, equally possible, had crossed from the Mersey overland to march on York and join this 'force' we cannot know, but it was a very powerful intervention, wherever its components came from. The apparent pre-planning, let alone the preparations to assemble such an army and fleet, do strongly suggest strategic and political direction. This was no serendipitous raid by thugs in different gangs, each under their own local leader, it was a properly planned and financed invasion involving combined forces and components under a single direction.

So, having made short work of the Northumbrians and, by their very size, perpetually in need of supplies and booty, the 'force' now entered Mercia to take up winter quarters at Nottingham in 868. Here they set up a defended camp so that when King Æthelred and his brother Alfred, arrived with the West Saxon army, intending to reinforce King Burhred of Mercia, they found 'the force' established and well fortified (in what is now the Lace Market district) and there was no heavy fighting. There was no point to be served by wasting lives and no way of prosecuting a winter siege, just as frontal assaults against earthworks were also impossible. Some sort of peace was made with the Danes and, no doubt, some sort of tribute paid in order to buy time. Just too bad for the inhabitants of Nottingham and its region; the invaders lived as they pleased and with the spring, with supplies exhausted, they decamped and sailed, marched and rode back to York, where they remained for the rest of 869.

Let us pause for a moment to muster the facts and review the change of strategy. No longer in independent gangs of freebooters targeting the known wealth of emporia (including their slave markets, for they undoubtedly had them) and then retiring with their spoils, this was now a combined and organised criminal organisation of vast size. They descended like a plague of locusts, devouring and destroying all in their path, living a luxurious lifestyle and taking whatever they wished, then moving on. No doubt booty and slaves were sent back, to 'home', at intervals and the pregnant captives discarded to seek the compassion of any surviving relatives; in truth, wherever they descended became a true pirate hell, like Cartagena in the seventeenth century.

The dominant trade was undoubtedly slaves for there was a constant need for them in Ireland, Scandinavia and the Baltic and slave markets existed in England and on the Continent, yet the formation of a heathen army strongly suggests that the new objective was not personal slaving but wholesale activity aimed at the Dublin market and elsewhere. Violence and deracination were mixed with a concept of dishonour, and captives from more formalised military activities no doubt helped rebalance the obvious emphasis on female captives.[5]

Worst of all, the heathens had graduated from taking advantage of natural defences to building defensive works and such fortifications, though not elaborate by later standards, were, in their novelty, baffling to contemporaries. A ditch, bank and stockade, when well defended, was an effective obstacle against attackers devoid of siege weapons, a standing force or commissariat, or even the skill required for such assaults, and so the poor captives were perforce abandoned to their fates. The formidable determination required for frontal escalation was a world apart from the limited and 'gentlemanly' field warfare of the older Anglo-Saxon kingdoms. Furthermore, these 'heathen' warriors now included mobile scouts and reconnaissance and the longer 'the force' remained in one place the more it acquired essential 'local knowledge'. The invasion had now entered an entirely new phase and the Anglo-Saxons were not prepared.

Notes

1. Arthur C. Wright, *Decoding the Bayeux Tapestry* (2019) and also *English Collusion and the Norman Conquest* (2020), when we know these preparations took several years to accumulate the necessary shipping and chandlery and so could not be kept secret.
2. Arthur Wright, *Fools or Charlatans: The Reading of Domesday Book* (2014) p.381.
3. Q.v. Michael McCormick, *Origins of the European Economy: Communications and Commerce AD 300–900* (CUP, 2002).
4. Loyn, *The Vikings in Britain* (1977), pp.15 and 17–18 in particular.
5. On the subject of slaving see Ben Raffield, 'The Slave Markets of the Viking World: Comparative Perspectives on an Invisible Economy' in *Slavery and Abolition, a Journal of Slave and post-Slave Studies* vol. 40, no. 4 (2019) pp.682–705. Also Raffield, Price and Collard, 'Polygymy, Concubinage and the Social Life of Women in Viking-Age Scandinavia' in *Viking and Medieval Scandinavia* vol. 13 (2017) pp.165–209.

Chapter Four

The Irresistable Force

Terror was not their only effective harbinger, for they were also increasing their skill to collect intelligences. So in 869 they sat tight in York, maybe making plans and gathering information as well as sending shipments of captives over the seas. Then in 870 they marched back into, and through, Mercia to enter Anglia. Here they took Thetford, then an important city, for their new winter quarters, no doubt replete with slaves and loot from Mercia but in need of provisions for their vast host. 'Wintersetls' were essential during those months when ships lay inactive because of inclement weather. Indeed, it is not unlikely that by now, given their success, they were attracting less desirable elements of Anglo-Saxon society to themselves to swell their numbers and provide important information.

King Edmund of Anglia marched against them and probably got no further than Eye, a short distance from Thetford, where at 'Hægelisdun' (possibly Hæleð – dun on the Dove) he was defeated and captured. It is said that he refused to apostatise (what else would the Church say of a saint) and so, like St Sebastian, he was tied to a tree and shot full of arrows before being beheaded. His saints day is 20 November, which may approximate to the date of the battle.[1] Almost immediately he was declared to be a saint and martyr, and a century later Abbo of Fleury wrote his encomium. For centuries afterwards he remained the patron saint of England with a splendid shrine at Bury St Edmunds.

Perhaps it was the reign of terror now unleashed on eastern England that convinced contemporaries that King Edmund was a martyr who had died in defence of his peoples. 'The force' now burned Peterborough to the ground, destroyed the monastery and slaughtered abbot and monks, then they set about all the other Church properties they could find, looting and burning, and ate Anglia bare. There can be little doubt that every outlaw who could now joined them and also that the slave transports must have been crammed full by the spring. Then, flushed with their success, 'the force' rowed, rode and marched west, to Reading.

This was a confederation of Scandinavian pirates, though the majority may have been Danes and Frisians. The leaders are said to have been Ivar the Boneless, youngest son of Ragnar Lodbrok, and one Ubba, sometimes described as Ivar's brother and sometimes as a Frisian 'earl'. One reason given for their leadership is that they were sworn to revenge on King Ælla of Northumbria, who had cast the captive Ragnar into a pit of snakes to die. As to Ivar's intriguing name, some have suggested that it meant 'legless', which sounds ridiculous, so one scholar has suggested a later scribal error, one that turned the title *exosus*, or 'the hated', which seems appropriate, into *ex-osus*, or 'no bones'.[2] I also like the hypothesis that his men thought him lacking in sexual prowess. No doubt such a psychological problem would make his mood swings very difficult to predict.

Well, the year 871 proved to be a disaster for Wessex for in this year 'the people fought nine battles against the force in the kingdom south of the Thames, besides those to which Alfred, the king's brother, ealdormen and thanes often rode to, which no one counted'.[4] If recent years had seemed disastrous, Domesday was now about to be unleashed on Saxon England, for the raiders had established their hold on the land and held it by terror, by numbers and by a strategy of co-operation and combination. We might say they were no longer fortuitous hunter-gatherers, they had become exploitative farmers.

The nature of warfare had changed dramatically for the old, established, feuding, Anglo-Saxon kingdoms. Social structures that had served such units for centuries were not immediately capable of concerted and unified action, and there was no one who could give such direction. Consequently, while they could engage with smaller-scale attacks on their individual kingdoms, once the raiders combined and once they had at least general 'local' knowledge, it was extremely difficult to organise a joint defence force. The invaders also had the advantage of amphibious forces and so, once they had established their beachhead, were able to deploy and then roll over any opposition they encountered. Had there been a coastal watch and defence organised then combined Saxon armies might have stood a chance, though the very nature of such 'household' and gesith formations, even when calling out a 'fyrd', made gathering into effective combinations a slow process.[5] The invaders, of course, once ashore could operate as one homogenous mass or they could divide into their constituent war bands in order to sweep whole districts.

In the past we have been told that these so-called 'Danes' had now evolved from sporadic raiders to colonisers, bringing their families to settle, people seeking a better life. There is, however, *no* evidence of any mass population movement from Scandinavia and nothing more than a few Scandinavian place names scattered among many English ones, to attest this supposed resettlement.[6] As has been observed elsewhere, the occurrence of Danish names in one kingdom and not in the other suggests that before Bernicia and Deira had been united as Northumbria these place names had already been applied, that is *before* our Viking period.[7] No, we must look elsewhere for the social picture. It was (in fact) one of political entrepreneurism, exploitation of the weak, the practical demonstration that 'might is right' (as Demosthenes put it), certainly that might guaranteed land rights. Not that the invaders sought anything more than temporary territorial rights; their ambitions were not to 'conquer' territory, as has sometimes been claimed, but to acquire 'dominium' without the burdens of 'proprietas', power without the additional burden of responsibilities and obligations. Once an area had been exhausted of assets, drink and food they moved on to pastures new. Later they were to acquire a territory of their own and with it fixed habitations, but not quite yet.

Now they were able to move from location to location, exploiting as they went until that area was exhausted. For its inhabitants this represented temporary servitude without amelioration; for the invaders it represented a promised land, the ultimate achievement of slavery, a privileged class living off the sweat of others by the exercise of terror. The weaknesses of these Anglo-Saxon kingdoms had been their rivalries, together with a rigid class, or caste, system; things that underpinned Church and aristocracy by keeping the toiling masses in their place. At the lowest level of serfdom and slavery there was, nevertheless, still the terror of being displaced, mutilated and rendered homeless by the 'new masters', for most of the invaders who chose to settle (unlike the ancient kingships) had no need to protect the peasantry at all – they could move on to newer, greener pastures when the immediate lifestyle failed. Yet for some Danes it seems, for perhaps a slowly increasing number, this invasion offered the lure of good land for the taking, women and slaves ('thralls') for the taking and loot for resale or for processing, for there are always people prepared to trade with known thieves. These were the elements who eventually settled and apparently integrated rapidly with the Saxon inhabitants, as we will see, the suggestion being that many who did so were actually from Ireland and Francia and not Danes.[8]

So it was that in 871 'the force' rode to Reading, in the Kingdom of Wessex, and as two Danish 'earls' rode upcountry with their war bands they were met at Englefield, on the west side of Reading, by ealdorman Æthelwulf. Here he had the victory, killing the 'earl' named Sidrac. It seems that these forces were both vanguards, as this was still early in January, for four days later King Æthelred and his brother Alfred also came up with a large body of warriors and attacked those who held Reading. There were heavy casualties on both sides and ealdorman Æthelwulf was killed, so 'the power of the battlefield' went to the Danes under Halfdan Ragnarsson.

Reinforcements were now arriving on either side and, four days later we are told, Æthelred and Alfred took the field once again, this time meeting 'the whole force' at Ashdown, possibly modern Ashe in Hampshire, just north of Winchester, though other historians have suggested the Berkshire Downs. Here it seems that the 'heathen' army divided into two 'vans' or wings, one of them commanded by 'kings' Basecg and Halfdan and the other by Danish 'earls'. Æthelred took on the 'royal' wing and killed Basecg while Alfred took on the Danish 'earls'. The fighting lasted until well into the night and with very heavy casualties all round, as is often the case in such confusion, the outcome was undecided. Exhaustion and darkness had taken their toll.

Having command of Reading, the Danes could now sail reinforcements up the Thames so, together with their mounted warriors, they were capable of outflanking an infantry army and we find Æthelred and Alfred falling back westwards onto their own lines of communication so as not to be surrounded by a pincer movement. A fortnight later, on 22 January, they met 'the force' at Basing and here they lost to the Danes. It seems that the enemy were now intent on taking Winchester, the ancient capital of Wessex, so two months later they met them again at a place called 'Macredun', which has been suggested as 'Morton' or Morden in Wiltshire, which, if accurate, would suggest that Winchester had already fallen for it is on the edge of Salisbury Plain. Here the Danes again divided into two vans or wings and although both were put to flight and great slaughter attended a long drawn-out battle, by their persistence the Danes took the victory. It sounds as though the *Chronicle* is creating a 'Persian version', though they do also say that a large 'summer fleet' sailed into Reading, so reinforcing the enemy, to the disadvantage of the West Saxon defenders of Wessex.

We see now that the whole nature of this warfare had changed, for instead of being a series of 'heavyweight' contests it had now become a war of movement, with battles based on a particular tactical disposition mimicking the ancient Roman *alae*. Reading between the lines, we may also guess that King Æthelred had been grievously wounded, perhaps the reason for seceding 'Macredun'? Anyway, in April 871 he died. His sons were too young to succeed and lead and so, according to a pact previously made by the brothers, Alfred became King of Wessex. In May, with a now diminished army, he encountered 'the whole Force' at Wilton, just west of Salisbury, and though it was a lengthy engagement the outcome was inevitable and he lost. Nevertheless, he retained sufficient reputation with his adversaries to be allowed to sue for peace and there was no alternative. Things looked black for Wessex and for all the Anglo-Saxon Kingdoms.

Notes

1. Q.v. *The Book of Saints* by the Benedictine Monks of St Augustine's, Ramsgate (London, 1921).
2. Robert Fergusson, *The Hammer and the Cross* (2009).
3. Anne Savage trans in *The Anglo-Saxon Chronicles*, Phoebe Phillips editions (1983).
4. Q.v. Nicholas Higham, *The Blackwell Encyclopaedia of Anglo-Saxon England* (ed. M. Lapidge, 1999 and 2001), p.136.
5. For the origins of the select and general 'fyrds' and the limited defensive nature of some groups of freemen, also the evidence to be gathered from 'fyrdwite' payments and definitions of 'thegnage', 'cornage' and 'drenage' see C. Warren Hollister, *Anglo-Saxon Military Institutions on the Eve of the Norman Conquest* (Oxford, 1962), pp.29–35.
6. Q.v. Michael Lapidge (ed.) *The Blackwell Encyclopaedia of Anglo-Saxon England* (1999 & 2001), pp.136 and 369; also Martin Ryan in Nicholas Higham and Martin Ryan, *The Anglo- Saxon World* (Yale, 2013 & 2015), pp.284 and 286–289.
7. Q.v. Ken Buckingham in *Wiðowinde* 194 (2020) for a very well-reasoned analysis of 'Bee/By' names and other supposed Viking colonisation indicators.
8. Q.v. Shane McLeod, *The Beginning of Scandinavian Settlement in England: the Viking 'Great Army' and Early Settlers, c.865–900, studies in the early Middle Ages* (2014).

Chapter Five

Pro Aris et Focis

We have now seen how rivers functioned at this period much as railways were to do in later warfare. In 871 'the force' took Reading, a point (on the Thames) with several marshy islands (at this time), and then they struck westwards, presumably following the River Kennet from its confluence with the Thames at Reading. This would lead them to Newbury and even to the Vale of Pewsey, depending on the draught and beam of their craft. Waterways were the logistic lifeline, bringing in men and supplies, but they also provided foraging on either bank and the possibility of slaves, which could then be transported back to London. The terror, therefore, was particularly concentrated along the catchments of viable rivers and, in this case, maybe as far as Marlborough.

We do not know how well the Roman network of roads had survived by this time, how comprehensive it was, and certainly the density proposed by Margary[1] and by Bishop[2] must have been sadly diminished, but coincidence alone suggests that major roads were influential in determining Anglo-Saxon and maybe later battle sites.[3] Roads as well as rivers seem now to have played their part. Ermine Street would have assisted the push westwards, supplementing the river route and carrying traffic to Gloucester, intersecting the Fosse Way in the process. The Fosse Way was the great road from Exeter to Lincoln and itself intersected Watling Street, the London to Chester road, at High Cross. Ermine Street ran from Cambridge to York via Gainsborough and Doncaster and Wool Street linked Cambridge to Colchester. The Peddar's Way ran from the north edge of the Wash to Chelmsford, and as far as we can tell the prehistoric Icknield Way was also probably in use and partly in parallel with the Peddar's Way. Yet roads involved perils for invaders, local knowledge encouraged ambush of enemies and, unless in a large and dense body of men, little retreat was possible. Standing off into midstream on a river was a far more secure way to travel and more economical of casualties; it was also easier to transport 'gains' in this way!

Well, for those who promote the 'immigration' theory, the results of this year are singularly disappointing for the Danes did not take over the kingdom, neither did they leave settlers in the south and west. No doubt they accepted a hefty 'tribute' but they then retired to Reading and from thence to winter quarters in London, leaving Wessex badly mauled but intact. The *Chronicle* tells us that in 871 the Danes lost nine 'earls' and a 'king', titles generally reserved for their nobility, so they actually suffered considerable loss, even though nominally victorious. This tenacity of Wessex and its ability to bounce back and re-engage is remarkable. Just what had made it possible?

Terror, of course, can be its own worst policy. It does not make friends and when applied to a whole society has the disadvantage that it is indiscriminate. Unlike the earlier inter-kingdom conflicts, these Viking/Danish attacks (we may use either title) did not respect the essential sustainers and creators of wealth, the peasantry, without whom no army could survive and this was because the Danes were aiming to exploit, not husband, wealth and resources. That is why, having despoiled one place, they then moved to another, why they chose cities with trading centres, such as York, Nottingham, Thetford, London and Reading, why they appear to have targeted Winchester, where maximum rewards were located, and all these were places offering them defensive possibilities during the inactive winter months.

As this pattern emerges we also see Anglo-Saxon resistance increasing. *Pro aris et focis* (for land and the hearth) is a powerful stimulation: ordinary inhabitants now stood to lose their land and sustenance, hearth and home, maybe liberty as well. Warfare was no longer a matter of 'companions', gesiths from the mead-bench with some sort of levy of free spearmen to swell the ranks, it now behove every able-bodied man to protect his wife, children, livelihood and possessions by joining in communal defence, for alone and against such numbers no man stood a chance. Without fresh shieldmen to swell the ranks, Æthelred could never have sustained the defence of his kingdom for so long. Society was now united as never before and we may suspect the beginnings of a breakdown of the old, rigid social hierarchy.

On the other hand, 'the force' had no need to exhaust itself for it had no larger territorial ambitions, either to acquire land or to defend territory. Living easy and turning a steady penny were their objectives. A determined resistance could be 'managed', for there were always softer targets elsewhere, and control of a marketplace like London provided a certain amount of trade and not just sales of slaves. Recycled loot or hacksilver could be used to purchase luxuries from the bolder foreign traders. Losses from engagements would be filled by new recruits, both from Frisia-Scandinavia and also, undoubtedly, from renegade Saxons eager to share in the freebooting lifestyle, and these last would bring local knowledge with them, including knowledge of roads, tracks and locations connecting places.

For Wessex there now seems to have been a period of rest and recuperation, time for Alfred to rebuild his forces, which suggests (perhaps) some respect

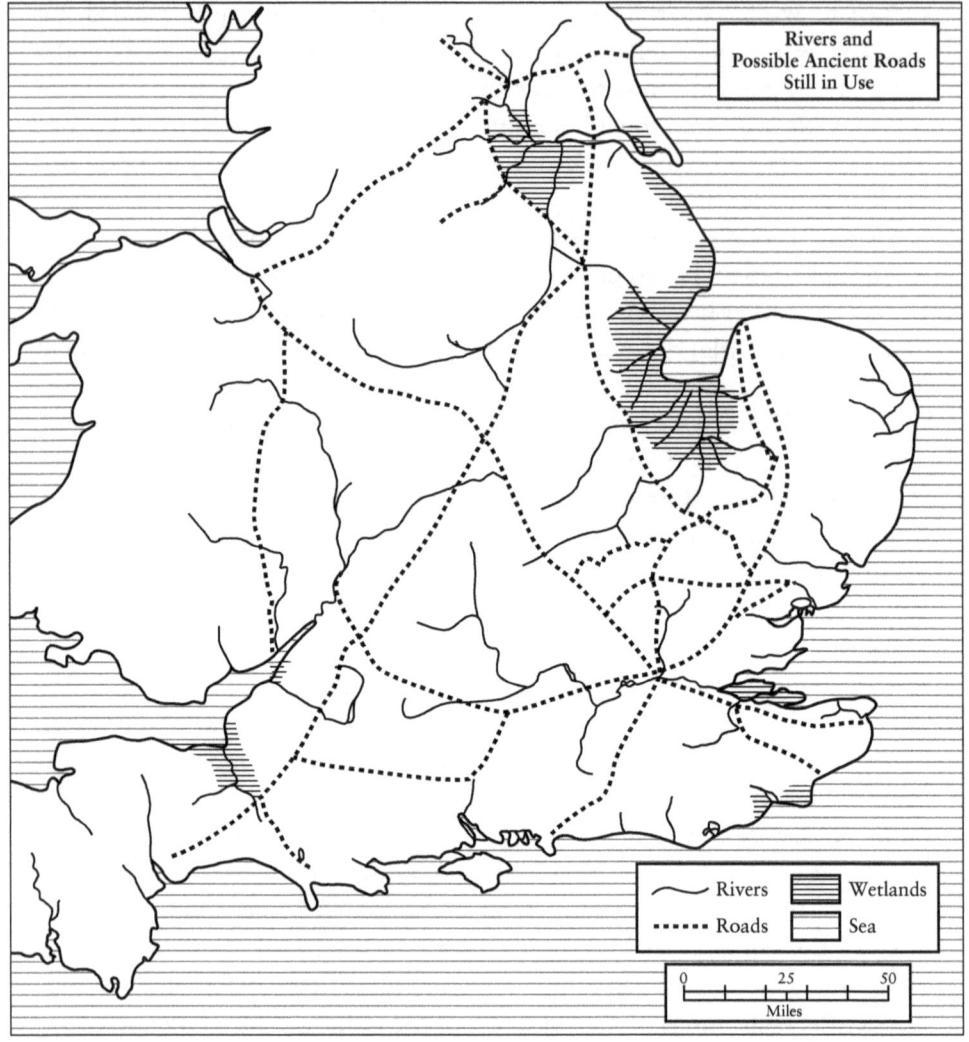

Map 1: Rivers and Possible Ancient Roads Still in Use.

for his skill in 871 as well as the payment of regular tribute. In 872, therefore, 'the force' attacked Mercia yet again, and so they were also forced to make peace and pay tribute. The following year 'the force' went into Northumbria and then retired to winter quarters at Torksey on the western edge of Lincolnshire and, once again, the Mercians made peace and gave tribute. This place was a substantial town by 1066 and may have been so already. What is more, the Fosse Dyke (an old Roman canal) connected Torksey and the Trent with Lincoln and the Witham, which this camp effectively covered.

Here, on the Trent at Torksey, midway between Gainsborough and Lincoln, the Vikings (true to form) chose a virtual island in the marsh, a site

> **Map 1: Rivers and Possible Ancient Roads Still in Use**
> There may, of course, have been others but these are the roads for which we appear to have evidence such as the Ickniend Way, the Peddar's Way, Wool Street, Watling Street, the Fosse Way, Ermine Street and Ermin Street. Rivers are obvious highways.

covering some 64 acres with stranding for ship repairs and maintenance. Here they built a camp for (it has been proposed) maybe 2,000 to 3,000 warriors, artisans and slaves, and they seem to have set up as merchants. Excavators, in 2012, could find no certain defences other than the surrounding marshlands but they did find major evidence of metal working in both base and precious metals, coins dating from the eighth century, up to 872, some of them cut up, with hacksilver and evidence of weighing. The conclusion was that the camp's economy was based on hacksilver, working and reworking loot and even attempting to forge coins.[4] The presence of Arab silver dirhams also suggests to me that Viking traders from the Baltic, whose connections also extended eastwards and down to the Mediterranean, were there to purchase slaves; I think this rather more likely than Arab traders sailing into the Trent to purchase large amounts of hacksilver or provisions.

Of course, this was certainly not the main wintersetl but only the trading and manufacturing post, for there assuredly were more than 2,000 warriors, even if they were all here at Torksey. Presumably this Great Heathen Army (*mycel hæpen here*), or at least their fleet, had entered the Trent via the Humber estuary and they could then dominate the whole course of the river, raiding on either bank, Lincolnshire or Nottinghamshire, even down to Newark, where the Trent and the Witham again converged at the Vale of Belvoir. The Torksey camp was undoubtedly a hive of industry and commerce but it should not be viewed as the total Viking presence and more recent research has revealed an overall extent of 136 acres.[5] Visiting trading ships would need to be escorted to it and, despite winter weather, parties of raiders could operate safely on the Trent. No doubt other Viking marauders and foragers struck out overland. The temporary inhabitants of Torksey Island had nothing to fear from local forces but the marshes surrounding the island would make it an effective prison for slaves, so we might also view it as a slave market, while both male and female collaborators can be expected along with unscrupulous Saxon traders.

Once again the lure of unprotected trading centres beckoned and so, with the spring, 'the force' left Lindsey (and Torksey) to enter the River Tame from the Trent, perhaps working on intelligences and reconnaissance gained during the winter months. Local knowledge was important. Tamworth, the seat of Mercian Kingship since King Offa's day, was now sacked and

King Berghred driven out, 'and they overcame all the land'. With that accomplished, replete with loot and captives, they used the Trent to make wintersetl at Repton, from where they could despoil Staffordshire, Derbyshire and Nottinghamshire, perhaps even as far as Leicestershire. Nevertheless, fighting seems to have been hard and maybe disease also struck: Repton has been excavated and has yielded some important evidence for it proved to be more than an artisan enclave and trading post.

The first and obvious site here was excavated between 1970 and 1980 by those famous archaeologists Martin Biddle and Birthe Kjolbye-Biddle and comprised a 'D'-shaped and heavily ditched enclosure whose 'gatehouse' was formed by the inclusion of the existing Anglo-Saxon, stone, church within the vallation.[6] This priory-church, dedicated to St Wystan, was a royal mausoleum and cult site and the 'God's acre' so enclosed could never have accommodated more than a tiny fraction of 'the force'. Neither was there much of a strand on the waterfront opposite the church: a 20ft bluff faced the river, whose rise in winter rains would have more than covered the tiny beach located below the bluff.

Once again the main wintersetl was elsewhere and, by good fortune, archaeology has turned up further sites at Repton. Close by the church site, in the vicarage grounds, have been found the workshops along with the sites of (probably temporary) structures.[7] At Foremark, just to the east of this, have also been located items comparable to those uncovered at Torksey and this location is very close to Heath Wood, which has many Scandinavian burial mounds.[8] Indeed, Foremark would offer a far better strand on which to beach and maintain ships. Neither here nor at Torksey was there any need for Viking detachments to feel threatened, they simply required comfortable quarters and processing facilities, though having these sites in close proximity would ensure mutual support in need.

So what of the church site and its defended acre of ground? Well, for a start, it served for burials, pagan burials. The Biddles discovered the body of a man buried with a sword, a sure indication of rank and status, and also a silver Thor's hammer amulet. This warrior had sustained serious injuries in the form of a blow to the head and spear or sword thrusts through the eye and into the brain, and a deep cut inside the left thigh caused by crude emasculation. Next to him lay a younger man who had also died violently. Were they related, was this a family tragedy and burial? Recent work by Cat Jarman has concluded that the older man was between 30 and 40 years of age when cut down and the younger man between 17 and 20 years of age. Both bodies appeared to be Danish but with possible connections to the Irish Sea region and they were certainly related, so possibly father and son.[9] Theirs had been high-status burials, with the 'father's' missing member replaced by a boar's tusk prosthetic, in order to render him whole in the next life.

Even more tantalising evidence was found adjacent to the church for in a (by then) disused chamber, possibly once a chapel, lay almost 300 bodies, predominantly male. These had filled the ancient chamber and over them a mound had been raised, so they had not been mere captives. Due to disarticulation and disturbance, opinions vary as to the nature of their deaths, though the predominant favourite is that they died in battle and the state of disarticulation suggests that they may have lain exposed to carrion feeders for some time. However, any warrior's greatest enemy has always been disease and cantonments act as breeding grounds for fatal distempers, so we cannot altogether rule out an epidemic. Nevertheless, however it was they died, they were honoured with a ceremony and laid beside their leader, so this site had some significance for the invaders.

What purpose did this enclosure and its church serve? The obvious conclusion is that it was intended as a citadel, what later generations would call a 'castle'. As such, the church building would serve as the hall house for the commanders of this mixed force, presumably with their hearth companions camped within the earthwork, but I think that the church also served another purpose that winter.

Repton Church is a remarkable structure and a remarkable survival. It was built early in the seventh century and so was old even by 874, a rare and highly defensible stone building and one containing a splendid crypt, the original site of a royal mausoleum. Clearly in 874 the monks received some warning of their enemy's advance for they removed the holy relics before 'the force' arrived. Of all the plunder taken by this great army, the most valuable would be human, so I suggest that the crypt of Repton Church served as an ergastulum, a slave captives' prison, for the highest-value individuals, for the 'special deliveries' and, maybe, for some held to ransom. Here they would at least be secured from most of the drunken and licentious soldiery outside.

The Heath Wood site, overlooking the Trent and its plain to the north, is situated close to the Foremark site and comprises the most significant Viking cremation site yet discovered in England. In all there are fifty-nine barrows raised over either the sites of complete pyres or, in some cases, apparently the sites of cremation material, brought from elsewhere. Of those properly excavated, we appear to have evidence not only of funeral feasting but of ritual sacrifice, in one case a hound and a horse.[10] Most remarkably, this horse appears to have been imported with his master, an exceptional cargo at this date and indicative of a *very* high-status individual, in my opinion. Moreover, this site seems to have remained in use for some years after the 'great army' had moved on, so it is possible that the jumble of bodies in the mausoleum also represents more than the casualties from one season. Resistance seems to have been increasing in Mercia.

The defiled church remained abandoned for some time after the Danes had departed. It would, of course, have been necessary but difficult to reconsecrate it but perhaps it also enshrined some tragic memories and ghosts in its now empty crypt-mausoleum? Eric Fernie has presented a convincing argument for serious structural damage inflicted by the Vikings, necessitating the rebuilding of the structure and, in particular, the reconstruction of the crypt in the early tenth century.[11] The present floor level in the crypt is possibly rather higher than before, obscuring part of the bases of the later columns supporting the vaulting and, as far as I am aware, it has never been excavated. I wonder what secrets the original floor might one day yield?

Notes

1. I.D. Margary, *Roman Roads in Britain* (3 vols, 1955–73).
2. M.C. Bishop, *The Secret History of the Roman Roads of Britain* (2014 and 2019).
3. Q.v. N.J. Higham, *The Kingdom of Northumbria A.D. 350–1100* (1993).
4. Dawn Hadley & Julian Richards, 'The Winter Camp of the Great Viking Army, AD 872-3, Torksey, Lincolnshire' in *Antiquaries Journal* vol. 96 (2016), pp.23–67. Also 'Viking Torksey, Inside the Great Army's Camp' by the same authors in *Current Archaeology* 281 (2013), pp.12–19. Also see Samantha Stein, *Understanding Torksey, Lincolnshire: A Geo-Archaeological and Landscape Approach to a Viking Overwintering Camp* (Sheffield University thesis, 2014).
5. Q.v. Dawn M. Hadley and Julian D. Richards, *The Viking Great Army and the Making of England* (2021), p.91.
6. Biddle & Kolbje-Biddle, 'Repton and the Vikings' in *Antiquity* 66 (1992), pp.36–51.
7. Report by Phoebe Western in the mailonline (August 2020), Excavations by Cat Jarman.
8. Cat Jarman in *Current Archaeology* 352 (2019), also ibid., 184.
9. Ibid.
10. Q.v. Hadley and Richards (2021), pp.163–172 for a full analysis and observations.
11. Eric Fernie, quoting Harold Taylor and the Biddle's, 'The Eastern Parts of the Anglo-Saxon Church of St Wystan at Repton: Function and Chronology' in *The Antiquaries Journal* vol. 98 (2018), pp.95–114.

Chapter Six

Going a-Viking

'Going a-Viking', so it seems, was not unlike the 'triangular trade' of the eighteenth century. In the latter, English ships were only the carriers, of course, but their crews suffered similar wastage to the whaling fleets; perhaps half of any crew might die of fever caught from the wretched 'cargo' but those who returned home shared in the profits of the venture, most of which went to the entrepreneurs who financed the ships and the masters who sailed them. So it was with Vikings, though unlike the 'triangular trade' they had also to capture their prisoners. Nevertheless, there was profit to be had for the risks undertaken and also booty to be acquired at the same time. There was also the life of (relative) luxury for the warriors, who lived off the land and enjoyed its plenty.

Of course, generations of historians have preferred to present an entirely different picture, one of romantic 'supermen', a portrayal spiced with sex and violence but in no way involved with murder, rape, torture, enslavement, arson, robbery and destruction. The value of the human flesh has been downgraded by historians and the bullion value inflated, so that every man among many thousands of Vikings might be supposed to have taken home with him the equivalent of many thousands of pounds. Yet the quantity of valuable goods accidentally lost by the occupants of the camp at Torksey (alone) shows how the country was now being rapidly stripped of all valuables, valuables not easily replaced and how careless these 'nouveau riche' pirates had become. This rate of attrition could not be maintained. As we shall see later on, vast sums of money were sometimes their collective reward but they were certainly not invariable, even at this early date and (anyway) the lion's share always went to the pirate's leaders. It has also been convenient to forget the absolute Scandinavian dependence on slavery, thraldom and the reliance on slavery in Anglo-Saxon England's kingdoms.[1] We have no outright records of Saxon kings selling their slaves to Danish raiders but we should surely suspect such dealings? Indeed, when 'tribute' was paid, surely human beings would have formed part of the value? They were not only high-value commodities, it was a good way of getting rid of convicted criminals and debtors.

Naturally, as sometimes happened to the Barbary pirate slavers of the seventeenth century, the snatching of more valuable social members might also result in rescue attempts at sea, when sparsely defended 'transports' might be outclassed and outsailed by alert locals. No doubt return journeys to Scandinavia used their human cargoes as rowers, but that also meant that every oarsman (or person) was not a defending warrior. When we hear of Saxon vessels prevailing, we should perhaps suspect attempts at rescue on the high seas. And, as we shall see, once England began to organise its defences, then it became more profitable for the raiders to remove 'operations' to the Continent. In the meantime, actually settling down in the English kingdom would surely have been a dangerous prospect for individual Danish pirates: two can play at arson, murder and enslavement!

So our picture is not at all 'black and white'. Danish leaders needed compliant Saxon rulers, Viking recyclers needed local and international customers for their products, holding captives (and even books)[2] to ransom required negotiation and he who had the power, called the tune. Especially important, the ships *must* have been maintained, not only to ensure amphibious operations but also to convey the highest-value goods to the best markets overseas. Very soon it seems likely that slaving became *the* important commercial activity of such raiders.

As we have seen, these Vikings had become victims of their own success. Having rapidly graduated from lightning raids to despoiling the emporia, they had effectively 'killed off' the emporia. Not only would merchants and traders hesitate to come and trade with the English kingdoms, what would they come for? Kings, nobles and especially the Church were the sponsors of the emporia; remove them and their wealth and there was no patronage. Equally serious for the Church, close the emporia and a *very* valuable source of income, the port dues, would have been eliminated. The profitable raiding of the earlier period had given way to perpetual parasitism: no longer content to return home with loot and captives, the 'new formula' of the *mycel hæpen here* was draining the Saxon kingdoms of treasure, for nothing is inexhaustible. Of course, terror could be increased in order to ensure compliance but a large army requires massive provisions and its warriors require some intrinsic reward, something beyond carnal pleasures, for in many cases individuals would (eventually) be looking to returning home, both rich and glorious. In such circumstances the only option would be to increase output in the captives' sector. Consequently, English resistance must often have increased, forcing contingents of raiders to seek out fresh fields of human commodities, fields offering less and less well-organised resistance, for assuredly the Saxon kingdoms were now attempting to meet force with force, hence the Viking raids on Northumbria, which evidence a decided shift of focus.

By bringing together hoard and find spot evidence, Dawn Hadley has concluded that Little Carlton, Risby Cross Roads, Swinhope and Binbrook on the Lincolnshire Wolds, all accessible from Barton Street or Ermine Street, were visited by parts of the 'great army'. Other places were also visited, such as Catton in Derbyshire and on the Trent, not far from Repton.[3] I think that these were probably local holding points where slaving parties delivered their captives for onward shipment by road and/or river, all conveniently converging on the Humber, from where the slave markets of the Baltic and Scandinavia were accessible, rather than their being depots for foraging parties. Foraging did not require a stay of any duration, rather a 'blanket' approach. However, slaving would require successive sweeps in order to net the best 'goods', though tribute might also have been paid at such outposts.

In order to ensure continued tribute, the Danes now installed their own puppet king in Mercia, the *Chronicle* calls him 'an unwise thane', and he swore them oaths, gave hostages and promised to assist 'the force' when so required. Then they left Repton–Foremark and Halfdan ('Healfdene') took a contingent into Northumbria to fight Picts and the men of Strathclyde, not such a wealthy country but probably less well organised for defence and populated by hardly agriculturalists. He then made his wintersetl by the Tyne, no doubt preparatory to offering a spring 'shipment'?

Meanwhile, Guthrum, Oscytel and Anwynd took their men to Cambridgeshire and stayed there with a large force. The Fens and the vast expanse of the Wash were ideal territories, allowing amphibious raids on Lincolnshire and Norfolk as well as offering a natural inland harbour at Ely with easy passage to Denmark and Frisia. Freebooters could sail from the Wash to terrorise the coasts of Anglia and Essex or they could move inland using the River Nene. This threat to Wessex seems to have galvanised Alfred, who had now (if not before) gathered a ship force. Maybe it was in the Thames that he met seven Danish ships, but wherever it was, he took one and put the rest to flight.

This now put Wessex back into the picture and so in 876 'the force' stole into Wareham 'past the West Saxon troops', presumably because they had already reconnoitred the Isle of Purbeck, Brownsea Island and Poole Harbour and saw this ideal site: an island in the marshes formed by the rivers Frome and Piddle. Now Alfred made peace with them: they gave important hostages and so, presumably did he and all swore oaths on a holy ring. Apparently they had not done this before for anyone and they then promised to leave the kingdom. However, some of 'the force' had acquired horses and this contingent then stole away, under cover of night, to head for and secure Exeter, so that they could there join with shipborne forces. It sounds as though the Danes had been confined to Wareham and that the site of the accord was Dorchester, just along the Frome, and that they were prepared to do anything in order to escape. Their island refuge, we should note, had in this case now been made into their prison, a neat reversal of events.

Of course, Alfred rode as hard as he could with his mounted men for Exeter, but the headstart was too great and he did not overtake the Danes. Sure enough, the ship force, the main army of this Danish 'force', now set sail in order to meet their land force at Exeter, but they had not counted on the weather. As they rounded Purbeck, presumably Durlstan and St Aldhelm's Heads, they ran into an almighty storm and are said to have lost 120 ships, perhaps 4,000 men or more. It sounds as though they left the shelter of Swanage Bay on the tidal race, sailing wide of Peveril Point (to miss the Peveril Ledges) and the Old Harry Rocks may have stretched further out to sea at this time, offering some sort of lee, straight into the teeth of a sou'westerly that either drove them back onto Handfast Point or the Old Harry Rocks. Or they were sheltered until clearing Anvil Point and then found themselves forced towards the quarry shore and Dancing Ledge, then into the south-east stream and race off St Aldhelm's (St Alban's) Head. Here there is a 4-mile underwater ledge that throws up furious breaking waves on the tidal lee, especially when against wind and tide. Low freeboard Scandinavian vessels making no more than 5 knots under oars would swamp easily in a beam sea. There was no possibility of 'crabbing' in such ships, though some may have been driven astern. If so, those who avoided this deadly lee-shore might well have been blown back even onto The Needles (Isle of Wight)! At a guess, they were attempting to sail westwards in October or early in November, which sounds as though Exeter was their intended wintersetl.

Nevertheless, the mounted Danes, who had arrived first, surprised the burgh at Exeter, occupying it before Alfred's army arrived. That, of course, now left them trapped within the burgh and vastly inferior in numbers to the Wessex men outside. Others, probably the remaining garrison at Wareham, now gave Alfred all the hostages he asked for and swore him great oaths in order to reach a *modus vivendi*. Given assurances, this garrison now evacuated and made for Mercia. Once in Mercia they were in no condition to plunder an already depleted resource, so their leaders resorted to land division, a common enough substitute throughout history for payment. Some land they gave to their puppet king Ceolwulf and some they shared among themselves. In Northumbria, Healfdene was in a similar predicament for lack of loot and so he also began to share out land to his troops. Necessity had now radically altered the Danish strategic concept, substituting land for portable wealth. The problem now was for these new landowners to hold on to their property and live off it, simultaneously disinclining them to further extensive raiding.

So in 877–878, though it was midwinter (Christmas time), the contingent trapped within the burgh at Exeter were desperate enough to steal quietly out, after twelfth night, and ride north-east, making for Chippenham. There was obviously no point in them striking out for the Channel coast, nor yet the Severn, so presumably they had managed to receive some secret intelligences while invested and now they sought to unite with a force advancing from Mercia along the old Fosse Way. Having succeeded, they established themselves at Chippenham and, the *Chronicle* says, many people fled 'over the sea'. Alfred's forces were now exhausted, it was difficult to keep an army in the field for so long – summer, autumn and winter – without a fully-fledged commissariat, for Wessex men could hardly live off their compatriot's lands. Alfred had been wrong-footed by attrition and had lost the initiative for the present.

Now it was King Alfred's turn to go on the run: with only 'a little company' he disappeared into woods and moors, to play guerrilla and 'tip and run', the Danish game, while his subjects made the best accommodation they could with the invaders. Once again built defences, the burgh at Exeter, had proved the salvation of a theoretically outnumbered force. So this brief period is usually characterised by dramatic writers and novelists as King Alfred surviving alone while pursued by a ruthless and numerous enemy. It is the 'Alfred cake' scenario with the Danes ensconced at Chippenham (which also had a burgh) and supposedly terrorising his kingdom. No doubt there is some truth in this last presumption but what has not been remarked before, I think, is the complete change in Saxon behaviour that emerges now in Wessex. It is as though Alfred has had inspiration.

Of course, there was no concept of nationality at this date – not until the nineteenth century – so the ordinary inhabitants of Wessex were predictably indifferent as to who was king, they simply lived and worked in a kingdom and wished to be left alone. They supported whoever it was that promised them security. The hearth troops and thanes, of course, needed to be loyal to their king both as an ethic and out of self-interest, but there was really nothing to stop them changing sides if they so desired. I suspect that at this point in Alfred's reign, 877–878, his thanes and their retainers had been in the field for too long and needed to return to their own estates in order to check affairs 'at home'. Prolonged sieges were just not possible in such circumstances. Yet the removal of all obstacles left the pirate freebooters an open field and they, given the shortage of booty, were looking for slaves. These precious commodities could be marketed for bullion or set to work on the newly apportioned Danish estates. Added to the misery of requisition and its attendant threat of starvation, suddenly the peasantry were also involved in active defence – for self-preservation.

The primary duty of any ruler is defence. It is a social and economic imperative, not an ethical one. The mass of peasantry looked to their king, also to their thanes, for relief from such apprehensions but, for the present, the king needed warriors. Thanes might return after a spell at home, ealdormen would do their best to recruit, but losses in battle and to campaign diseases could not be made up overnight. Peasants are not instant warriors; even when eager to enlist and even when given instruction they can really only offer mass. Yet the economic motivation of the invaders was now all too obvious for anyone to doubt that one system of serfdom was better than another. These incursions were not like the old jockeyings of Mercia, Wessex, Anglia and Kent for they now involved the whole spectrum of society and, moreover, a society sustained by deep-seated religious beliefs quite contrary to the incomers and their renegade recruits. Surely, in spite of all reverses, God was ultimately on the side of the Christian kingships, it was in His interest to intervene!

In the winter of 878, Ubba, brother of Healfdene, was also in Devon. He came with twenty-three ships, perhaps 1,000 men, to raid and slave, and here he was slain along with forty bodyguards and 800 warriors. Asser tells us that ealdorman Odda's army had been trapped in the hill fort at 'Cynwit' but that in a lightning dawn sortie they overpowered the Danes. The standard called 'The Raven' was also taken here and there can be no doubt that this success was due to strong royal influence *and* a new determination within the shire. The Danes did *not* exercise absolute power from their base at Chippenham. Landholders large and small were, (with a few exceptions who departed overseas) prepared to rally to the king's cause and to the defence of their tenantry, and the tenantry were determined to resist enslavement.

Notes

1. Q.v. Loyn, op. cit. (1977) pp.15, 28, 53, 83. Also Lapidge, op. cit. (1999 and 2001), p.423, article by David Pelteret.
2. e.g. The Stockholm Codex Aureus (National Library of Sweden MSA 135), alias the 'Canterbury' Codex, marginalia to the Gospel of St Mathew, which declares that Ealdorman Alfred and his wife Wærburh ransomed books from the heathen army and gave them to Christchurch, Canterbury in the late ninth century.
3. Q.v. Hadley and Richards, op. cit. (2021), pp.120–128.

Chapter Seven

A Glorious Summer

More recently some writers have been critical of Alfred's achievements, pointing out that his real and outright victories were few and his troubles many. This is an assessment I cannot endorse. Maybe the *Anglo-Saxon Chronicle*, our main source, does tend to present a 'Persian version' at times, distorting events to suit the propaganda objective (as many historians still do), nevertheless, whether or not we accept that there are nine or ten 'Principles of War', I would submit that Alfred was an exponent. The real problem is that so many historians, past and present, have failed to understand the events we are now attempting to piece together. The traditional interpretation of this period has been far too simplistic and lacking in analysis.

Impossible as it is, at this remove, to judge with any accuracy the abilities of commanders, it has to be admitted that the most stubbornly determined resistance of all the kingdoms to the *mycel hæthen here* was presented by Wessex. Even after defeats, King Alfred seems to have continued to raise forces so, inevitably, there had to be dramatic social changes that made this possible, even if we cannot clearly discern them today. Also, he knew when to press an engagement and when to be circumspect and economical of his resources, and that is important in warfare. Of course, he involved Divine intervention, but he did not rely on it, which was (in itself) no doubt a revelation to his people in a world where it was the usual excuse for failures.

I also think that the invaders had trapped themselves within their policies to some extent 'killing the goose that laid the golden egg' and maybe they had also grown a little complacent. Perhaps individuals, now obliged to contemplate land owning rather than brigandage, began to relish the prospect of status, wealth and slaves within an unresisting landscape, with all being theirs for the taking, rather than peripatetic violence and debauchery. Such a dichotomy would explain why they subsequently split into two parts, one satisfied with its achievements and the other restive for pastures new and riper. If so, the 'remainers' were to receive a sudden shock, for two sides of any conflict can resort to burning homesteads and murdering their occupants. To become a part of the landscape, a man needed some guarantee of security and had to live in harmony with his neighbours.

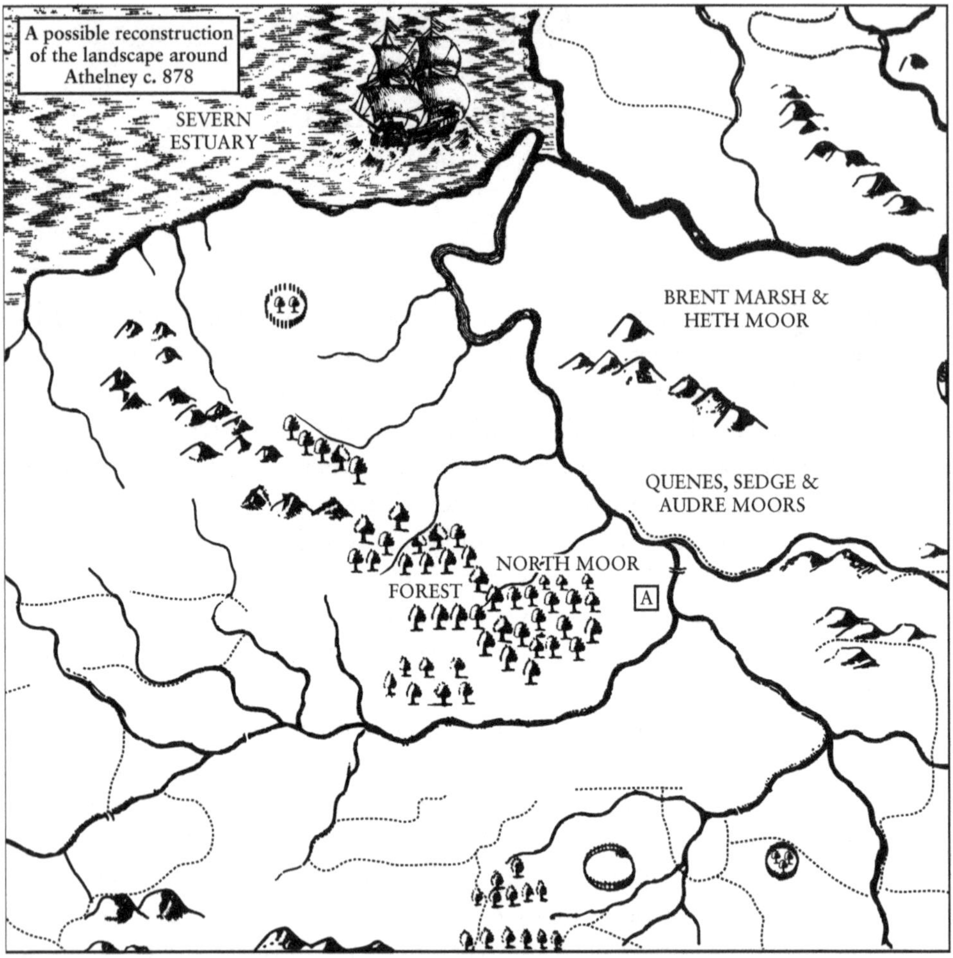

Map 2: A Possible Reconstruction of the Landscape Around Athelney, c.878.

So when we hear that King Alfred and his hearth troops built a fort on the Isle of Athelney, in the Somerset Levels, we should not think of it as a hideaway, a 'funk hole' but as a well-chosen wintersetl. If he did burn some cakes it was probably because he had a strategic vision.[2] The Danes would have had no difficulty finding the place had they followed the Fosse Way south to the Parrett, yet they did not feel secure enough to make the attempt; neither side felt secure enough to lay prolonged siege to a strong fortification and this one *was* strong. It lay at the confluence of the rivers Tone and Parrett and to the east of this island in among rivers and marshes, was East Lyng, a fortified burgh in its own right. This probably acted as the main barracks for Alfred's troops as the two sites were linked only by a narrow causeway, the Balt Moor Wall, which is, today, a dyke or embankment bearing a pathway

> **Map 2: A Possible Reconstruction of the Landscape Around Athelney, c.878.**
> This map uses Speed's map of 1610 as a base but omits the settlements that had formed by then in order to emphasise the desolate terrain of the undrained Somerset Levels in 878, also showing the hills and estimated tree cover. Yeovil lies south-east of here with the River Parrett as a convenient highway. Athelney is marked 'A'.

along its crest. This conjoined strongpoint was as formidable as any other we know about at this time.

Thus by 878 it was the men of Wessex who were occupying a defensive chain covered to the north-east by marshes and moors and to the north-west by a heavily wooded area (later a royal forest and Petherton Park), one close enough to Taunton to be effective, a development that turned the tables on the Danes. Neither readily accessible on foot nor by boat and to a man carrying 40–50lb of mail, a shield, helmet and sword, impassable, this was an excellent base for operations. Marshes and fens not only provided natural defences they also provided wild provisions (eels, fish and birds); moreover islands provided elevated fields of vision over wide expanses of flat terrain, while bird flocks offered early warning of attempted surprise attacks during daylight and, by their alarm calls, also at night. In this particular case, access was gained only along an exposed causeway with nowhere on which to make more than the narrowest of fronts by an attacking column. Further provisions could be found in the woodlands to the west, which stretched to the Quantocks.

From this fastness, Alfred's flying columns, following the Parrett eastwards to Yeovil and then operating as the Danes had done hitherto, could extend out into the Dorset Downlands and even Cranborne Chase, the latter compartmentalised no doubt (as in a later period) with heaths and woodlands and very much 'wilder' than in recent centuries.[3] Indeed, even in 1086 Dorset was 41 per cent 'pasture and woodland', with a further 14 per cent unrecorded and presumably worthless to agriculture because so much infertile land overlay the Eocene sands and gravels that extend west from the New Forest: a very wild aspect indeed and one so useful to guerrillas.[4] This belt of useful covers, dotted with such circumvallate ancient hill forts as Bradbury Rings and Knowlton Henge, ran from the Cerne Valley to Morden Bog and Wareham Forest and then blended naturally into the New Forest. 'Woods and inaccessible moors' provided a baseline from which to strike on a wide front and northwards (at anywhere) from Chippenham and to the Vale of the White Horse.

It occurs to me that King Alfred might also have been concerned to prevent the Danes extending to the south-west. Chippenham was only a short distance from the Fosse Way yet they seem to have made little or no attempt to venture southwards along it and to enter Somerset or to take Bath. Whether they knew of the wealth of the Mendip Hills is impossible to say but the rugged Carboniferous landscape of the Cheddar Gorge area and its wild undergrowth would have been a very dangerous landscape for ignorant marauders to enter and we have seen how risk-averse these 'seamen' tended to be. Athelney was a prudent strategic choice for a stronghold if one wished to defend the Polden and the Mendip Hills.

King Alfred was combining local knowledge (and, no doubt, local skills) with the strategic paradigm of the enemy, leaving them powerless to advance on him over such terrain, unable to invest his Athelney stronghold yet also incapable of knowing where the next raid would come from. In the seventh week after Easter, the king rode to Ecgbryht's Stone, said to be on the (south-) east of Selwood Great Forest but just possibly to the west (the Latin *oriens* and *occidens* being phonetically similar), and there all the fighting men of Somerset, Wiltshire and Hampshire came to meet him.[5] The only men missing were the few who had been wealthy enough to flee overseas, we are told; presumably those with disposable wealth? Clearly there had been considerable preparations for an offensive made during the spring.

This army then camped overnight, presumably surrounded by the southern fringes of Selwood Forest and the Yeovil marshes, before moving on via the woodland cover of Sherborne to the Iley Oak, but exactly where 'Iglea' or 'Æcglea' was we do not know.[6] Dr Kelly has suggested an island in the River Wylye, possibly by the bridge at Brixton Deverill, which would perhaps be the Wylye Oak.[7] Here they again halted for the night. As Ecgbryht's Stone was in my opinion probably somewhere in the vicinity of Yeovil and South Cadbury, 'Stone' being shown to the north of Yeovil on John Speed's map of 1610, this would represent a march of perhaps 20 miles as the crow flies. It looks as though Alfred was following a route to Wincanton, through Selwood Forest and Penselwood, to then meet up with a route similar to the modern A350, thus traversing Selwood Forest northwards, making use of cover rather than following the more open and obvious Fosse Way for any distance. On the other hand, instead of making for the Wylye, he could have marched over what is now Longleat to Frome and then east to Westbury and so on to Edington. Either way, the avoidance of the Fosse Way strongly suggests that the Danes were on the defensive rather than the offensive and apprehensive of an English attack. Alfred sought surprise and I suggest that he had a definite tactical plan in mind, as we shall see.

Presumably from 'Iglea' they sent out parties to reconnoitre their enemy's position and reactions, for with Exmoor as his backyard when at Athelney, Alfred would have had a plentiful supply of ponies with which to equip his raiders and his scouts. Maybe the army now advanced cautiously for another 5 miles or so, as this would enable them to take possession of Scratchbury and Battlesbury hill forts, camps that would offer commanding views eastwards and northwards over Salisbury Plain. Chippenham would then have been 20 miles away, as the crow flies, with Edington only 6 miles away to the north. Alfred was an acclaimed hunter and here we certainly see him stalking his prey.[8]

By now the Danes probably knew of their approach and so the two armies met at Edington, near Westbury, 'Ethandun', and King Alfred's Wessex army took on 'the whole force' and put them to flight. The actual site of 'Ethandun' has been claimed as Bratton Camp and that is where the commemoration stone and plaque stand today.[9] However, I agree with Dr Kelly that Piquet Hill seems to be the more likely site, supposing that the royal army took up the vantage point on this hill, which would even offer them reverse-slope cover for many of their troops and so encourage an overconfident enemy to make a frontal attack upslope. A 'gentleman's agreement' to meet on the flat plain seems (to me) most unlikely, especially when such care had been taken to camouflage the army's approach and ensure surprise.

Given that Alfred's Wessex army may have had a considerable mounted element (as I have proposed) then an advanced guard could well have secured Piquet Hill before the Danes at Chippenham were really aware of the major threat. Tentatively, I suggest that while the main part of the army rested on the reverse slope, the mounted men might then have made a feint, so drawing the Danes into a long, infantry approach uphill until they encountered the Wessex army in position, when the mounted men would retire around the flanks. So battle was joined and it went well for Alfred and his army.

'The force' apparently broke and ran, making for Chippenham, and Alfred rode after them with his army in pursuit. The survivors made the shelter of the burgh and here they were besieged for fourteen nights. Being desperate, they then gave hostages and great oaths that they would leave. I suspect that Alfred had also taken some important prisoners for it was promised that 'King' Guthrum, of East Anglia, would receive Christian baptism. This was agreed and three weeks later Guthrum was obliged to travel to Aller in the Somerset Levels, there to receive baptism. Here, today, they display an undoubtedly Saxon bowl font that, it is claimed, is the very font used in this ceremony. Guthrum then took the name Æthelstan and Alfred stood godfather to him.

Then followed the 'loosing of the Chrism' ceremony, which was held at Wedmore, nor' nor' west of Glastonbury, and they feasted for twelve nights and presumably, exchanged gifts. Thus was made 'the Peace of Wedmore' and the surviving members of 'the force' left Chippenham, going north to Cirencester for the winter and, no doubt, teaming up with Danes from Mercia. With the Thames at their disposal, it is no surprise to hear that this new 'force' next descended on Fulham. Guthrum's men, we are told, finally returned to Anglia, sharing it out, while the freebooters at Fulham were probably joined by dissidents from elsewhere. Now they had to decide what to do next and where to go in the face of a victorious and strong English army.

I have drawn attention to Alfred's use of mounted men, indispensable for guerrilla warfare when in open country and away from water courses. As yet the Vikings were mainly focused on following waterways, presumably for lack of local knowledge inland, but we shall see that in the years to come they laid increasing emphasis on being 'horsed'. They too could learn from their enemy. Battles were invariably infantry affairs, even when at sea, but horses not only allowed more rapid movement and movement over more difficult terrain, they were also essential troop carriers allowing infantry to arrive fresh for the fight. No sensible commander wants to commence an engagement with exhausted troops, and pedestrian progress was slowed by the weight of armour and accoutrements to be carried. Horses made good military sense.

In the First World War, determined attempts were made to improve the stamina of infantry when carrying full kit by intensifying route marches but, in the end, experience showed that men could only become accustomed to so much foot slogging and weight-carrying while remaining useful. We should imagine our Saxon and Viking warriors to be much the same, burdened with byrnies weighing 30lb or more, plus helmets, shields, swords, spears and sustenance and yet only equipped with turnshoes, a totally inadequate type of footwear for sustained or rough marching. Horses also relieved heavily armoured men of the need to don armour before commencing an engagement or, alternatively, carried the armour for them when acting as pack animals. So, optimally, well-mounted warriors could move faster when in full readiness and so fall on unprepared enemies and communities, provided they knew the local roads, tracks and byways. This was, I believe, the advantage that Alfred perceived but it also led, ultimately, to Viking raiders amassing geographical and topographical awareness and then themselves acquiring horses. We shall see this develop as we continue our story.

Notes

1. 'The truth-loving Persian does not dwell upon the trivial skirmish fought near Marathon …'
2. Douglas Horspool, *Why Alfred Burned the Cakes* (Profile, 2006).
3. Q.v. Oliver Rackham, *The History of the Countryside*, p.136.
4. Ibid., pp.291 and 335.
5. Dr Paul Kelly, *King Alfred: A Man on the Move* (2019) discusses the possibilities at length on pp.68–72.
6. *The Anglo-Saxon Chronicle* and Asser's *Life of Alfred*.
7. Q.v. Dr Paul Kelly, 'The King Alfred Blog', also see Kelly op. cit. (2019), pp.79–86.
8. Q.v. Simon Keynes & Michael Lapidge, *Alfred the Great, Asser's Life of King Alfred and other contemporary sources* (Penguin, 1983).
9. Once again Dr Kelly discusses the possibilities in some detail: op. cit. (2019), pp.85–87.

Chapter Eight

Supporting Success

The 'force' that met Alfred at Ethandun in 878 was no longer the entirely freebooting *mycel hæpen here* of 871 for elements had already begun to settle in Northumbria, Anglia and Mercia, fragmenting due to their own success and excesses. Some of them would now have been keen to return to lands in Anglia and settle down, and this could have impaired their ardour for battle. Nevertheless, Alfred's achievement was significant for he seems to have taken on the most significant remaining portion of that scourge. His response was carefully planned and prepared, from what we can see, and it brought both short-term and long-term benefits. Those elements of Danish contingents who now wished to settle and enjoy the 'fruits of their labours' had to reach a *modus vivendi* with a morally reinforced Wessex on their borders. Now the Danish settlers had themselves become as vulnerable as the dwellers in the Anglo-Saxon kingdoms, perhaps more so, and it behove them to become circumspect.

Now the freebooters at Fulham, having a reduced capability and, maybe, under pressure from apprehensive settlers, found their own freedom of movement curtailed together with a risk of summary justice, so they decided on a different course of action. En masse, they now went overseas to Frankland, to Ghent, and there they stopped for a year gathering more ne'r-do-wells. By 881 they were sufficiently reinforced and fought a major battle with the Franks. Being then victorious and horsed, they continued on their European tour and out of our story for a brief while.

Of course, there were others always ready to try their hands, newcomers who could not believe that the old order could change and maybe youngsters keen to prove their prowess. So it was that in 882 King Alfred took his ships to sea to fight with four ship's companies, taking two ships, killing many pirates and receiving the surrender of the remaining vessels. Perhaps predictably, some three years later, half of 'the force' that had gone abroad returned and descended on Rochester, besieged the city and built themselves a burgh. Here they remained until Alfred arrived to dislodge them, when they retired first to their ships and then whence they had come. They did not wish to risk battle.

King Alfred is often credited as being the 'father of the Royal Navy', and he was certainly employing ships for defence for he sent a ship force to cover East Anglia and to the mouth of the Stour, where they met sixteen Viking ships. It seems that, in spite of Guthrum's conversion, this 'King of Anglia' could not exercise complete control over his peoples. The English ships fought the Viking ships, seized them all and killed their crews. However, while returning with their spoils, presumably with crews divided in order to man the captured vessels and so unable to either make speed or resist effectively, they met a large Viking ship force. This sounds as though it was at the mouth of the Thames, always a lucrative route to London. Predictably the Danes now had the victory.

So 'the force', or some of it, was in East Anglia before removing themselves to the Seine. King Alfred occupied the City of London, a 'square mile' still defended by the old Roman walls, a notable strategic development. Ealdorman Æthere was given command and, we are told, 'all the English turned to him' (King Alfred): he clearly wished to consolidate his power and position. Nevertheless, those people subjected to the Danish settlers, the eastern bloc later known as 'the Danelaw' and stretching from York to Anglia, remained independent of Wessex.

It is impossible to say what Guthrum's influence was on his peoples, Æthelstan as we should now call him, but in 890 he died. He is said to have been buried at Hadleigh, Suffolk.[1] Two years later 'the force', having been bested on the Continent, decided to return to England to try their luck once again, hoping for the enervating effects of peace. They sailed up the Lympne, also called the Limen and now known as the Rother, having entered at New Romney (which in 1287 or before changed to Rye) at the eastern end of the Andredes Weald, itself a vast tract of sparsely populated woodlands and scrublands. The Lympne and Limen was a large river mouth, one possibly covering what is now the Walland Marsh according to Dr Kelly's excellent analysis of the evidence.[2] Four miles inland, presumably at Appledore, they came to a burgh in a wetland, which was only half-built and apparently occupied by 'peasants', so they had no difficulty securing it. The *Chronicle* credits them with 250 ships, maybe 8,000 men or more; a formidable force.

Fortunately, they seem to have missed a great prize, perhaps as a consequence of entering unknown territory in an attempt at surprise. What they seem to have missed were the Wealden industries that lay to the west, around Battle and Robertsbridge. I have speculated about these elsewhere and will return to them later.[3] The only possible reason for the English to build a burgh here would be to protect something further up and maybe deeper in the Weald, but the Danes do not seem to have asked such an obvious question. Had they instead taken the western branch of the Limen, to Tenterden, things might have been very different. As it was, this 'force' was apparently only seeking a secure base from which to strike due north and join an attack on London, probably by intercepting any Wessex army that might attempt its relief by advancing eastwards. There had apparently been careful planning for concerted action and the terror was about to start all over again. This, it appears, was the plan.

During the lacuna of the late 880s England, Wessex had waxed prosperous again and this had not gone unremarked. First came 'the force' to Appledore, living off the fertile lands to the north of that location, strengthening the burgh they had taken and striking north for the Medway and Thames, in effect amputating Kent. Meanwhile, Hæsten arrived in the Thames with eighty ships, perhaps another 2,500 men, and so he built himself a burgh at Milton Royal, Milton Regis (Sittingbourne), covering the approach to Sheppey and any road over the Long Reach. This was an old Viking favourite as an island strand. As they had begun to do at Repton, the Vikings were now reinforcing their strands and marshy fastnesses with burghs. Now the combined Danish 'forces' could together hold a line across Kent and predate the Thames estuary, also the Anglia–Thanet seaway and the Dover–Quentovic (Boulogne) route, and London was certainly within their power.

The problem for King Alfred was that he could not crush one nest of pirates for fear of the other coming up behind him, yet he had to prevent raids westwards. He also needed to protect specific locations, which were London and the High Weald. His only choice was to weaken his potential by splitting his army, but keeping each wing closely in contact with the other. Though he could do nothing for the people of Kent, he could use the wooded Wealden landscapes, even up to West Malling and Strood, to launch tip-and-run raids against the enemy. Instead of leaving the initiative to the enemy to come and go as they chose, he was rendering them insecure whenever they moved out of their acquired comfort zone.

Although both the Northern Danes and the Anglians had made promises to Alfred and given hostages, they were now growing restless, so in 893 the royal strategy was to pin down the new arrivals as much as possible in a cat-and-mouse game. Indeed, this tip and run was so effective that the Viking 'forces' now coalesced, with all their plunder and slaves, and started north, over the Thames and into Essex, off which coast a huge fleet had now assembled. In this situation the king had the advantage of local knowledge and, having brought his wings together and shadowed the enemy to Farnham, he deployed his army in force across the front of their column, presumably pouncing as they crossed the Thames. The classic tactic here would be to intercept one part while the other was crossing, or crossed over: divide and conquer. This attack put 'the (joint) force' to flight and secured their plunder and slaves, but some of the Danes escaped and they crossed where there was no ford and so up the Colne to 'an island'. The Hertfordshire Colne joins the Thames near Staines, so we can presume that this was where the royal army now besieged the fugitives on their island refuge.

There are several islands near Staines from which to choose, including Runnymede (1¾ acres) and Church Island (2 acres), Hollyhock and Holm (2½ acres) but I favour Hythe End (4 acres), which is upstream of the others and was, in the past, marshy. Coincidentally it is 'in' Wraysbury, which was once 'Wyrardisbury', which we are told meant 'Wigræd's Fort'. Frustrated no doubt by the marshes, the royal army besieged them for as long as they had food, for this army was the select fyrd and they had only to complete their term of service.[4] Meanwhile, the king had 'raised the shire', so as he brought up this general fyrd they met the select fyrd going home. In spite of this, the Danes stayed put for their 'king' was wounded and they could not move him.

Now the Danish settlers from Northumbria, scenting plunder, dropped down the east coast to meet the Anglian Danes, joined forces, and 100 ships (maybe 3,000 men) went south into the Channel and then west, to besiege Exeter. Another forty ships, meanwhile, went north along the east coast, rounded Rattray Head and Cape Wroth to go down into the Irish Sea, intending to descend on the north coast of Devon. From here they would have had a clear route back to the slave markets of Ireland.

Now King Alfred had no choice but to take the main part of his army westwards in order to secure the Wessex heartlands. Although a diameter or a chord is always shorter than a circumference, it seems that these possibly co-ordinated enemy attacks had taken him by surprise. We must also remember the distances to be covered by messengers and the consequent time lag when responding to such intelligences. Nevertheless, he left some men from the east behind to continue the pursuit of the Colne fugitives and these troops then went to London and joined the city dwellers. Now we will maintain our focus on the Thames and return to Exeter and Alfred later.

It seems possible that Hæsten was ready for Alfred's hurried departure from the Thames for he had already made preparations. He had built a burgh or camp at Benfleet in southern Essex. In spite of much debate by local historians, there is no trace of such an earthwork today, but as South Benfleet has (historically) always included Canvey Island and here the highest, central, ground subsequently became medieval berewicks of Benfleet and Prittlewell, I believe that *this* was Hæsten's real camp and strand. As we have seen, islands within marshes require no earthworks. At this date, Canvey was several associated islands beset by marshes, separated from South Benfleet by Benfleet Creek, maybe a causeway (revealed at low water), with riverside strands at Thorney Bay, Leigh Beck–Benfleet Creek, and possibly at Hole Haven. Here Hæsten left 'property', that is women, children, slaves and some of his fleet, while he went raiding with those of his men who had remained at Milton Regis and Appledore and so were still fresh and available. No doubt he was pleased that his feint and forlorn hope (to use 'the Persian version') had drawn Alfred away to Staines and then obliged him to hurry westwards. The Thames and London were now wide open once again *and* all along the Anglian coast.

Alfred seems to have been a shrewd judge of subordinates as well as an inspiring commander for his London force now made for Benfleet in order to carry the war to the enemy. Intelligences must have been good on either side. This London force was under the command of Alfred's son, Edmund, and his son-in-law, earl Æthelred of Mercia. Once again the royal forces intended to make full use of a wild and wooded topography in order to mount an effective raid on the enemy, fighting fire with fire one might say, as had become their standard response. Woods not only provide opportunities for ambush, they also cover advances, as when 'Birnam Wood to Dunsinane shall come'.

To the north of South Benfleet were Thundersley Woods, Wayburn's Wood and Hadleigh Downs and beyond them Eastwood and Rayleigh Woods on the most prominent points of glacial head in this otherwise very open Hundred. To the west of Benfleet lay Bowers Gifford and Vange, Fobbing and Corringham. Here there was also plenty of marsh and cover with local byeways among terrain that the Danes would probably be very wary to explore, in case of ambush. From the top of the steep Vicarage Hill, looking down on Benfleet itself, there is still an amazing panoramic view of Hole Haven and Canvey Island (now one reclaimed island), even to the distant sight of London. From here the English could easily have surveyed their objective and the enemy's dispositions and probably from woodland cover.

Whatever the precise tactical plan, it must have included both a land attack and English ships attacking the Danish strand on the principal island, in order to prevent their escape. Such an attack would be easiest, quietest, on an ebb tide and, as climate conditions are peculiar to this Thames corridor, there was possibly a dense sea mist as well. Hæsten had apparently taken away many of his ships and men so that the remaining Danish garrison were now overwhelmed. Large numbers of women and children were taken, also a large quantity of treasure, so Canvey (like Torksey) was probably also an artisan hub. Hæsten's own wife and two sons were among those taken. A number of captured ships, some claim as many as eighty, were loaded with the spoils and some taken to London and some to Rochester. Some captured

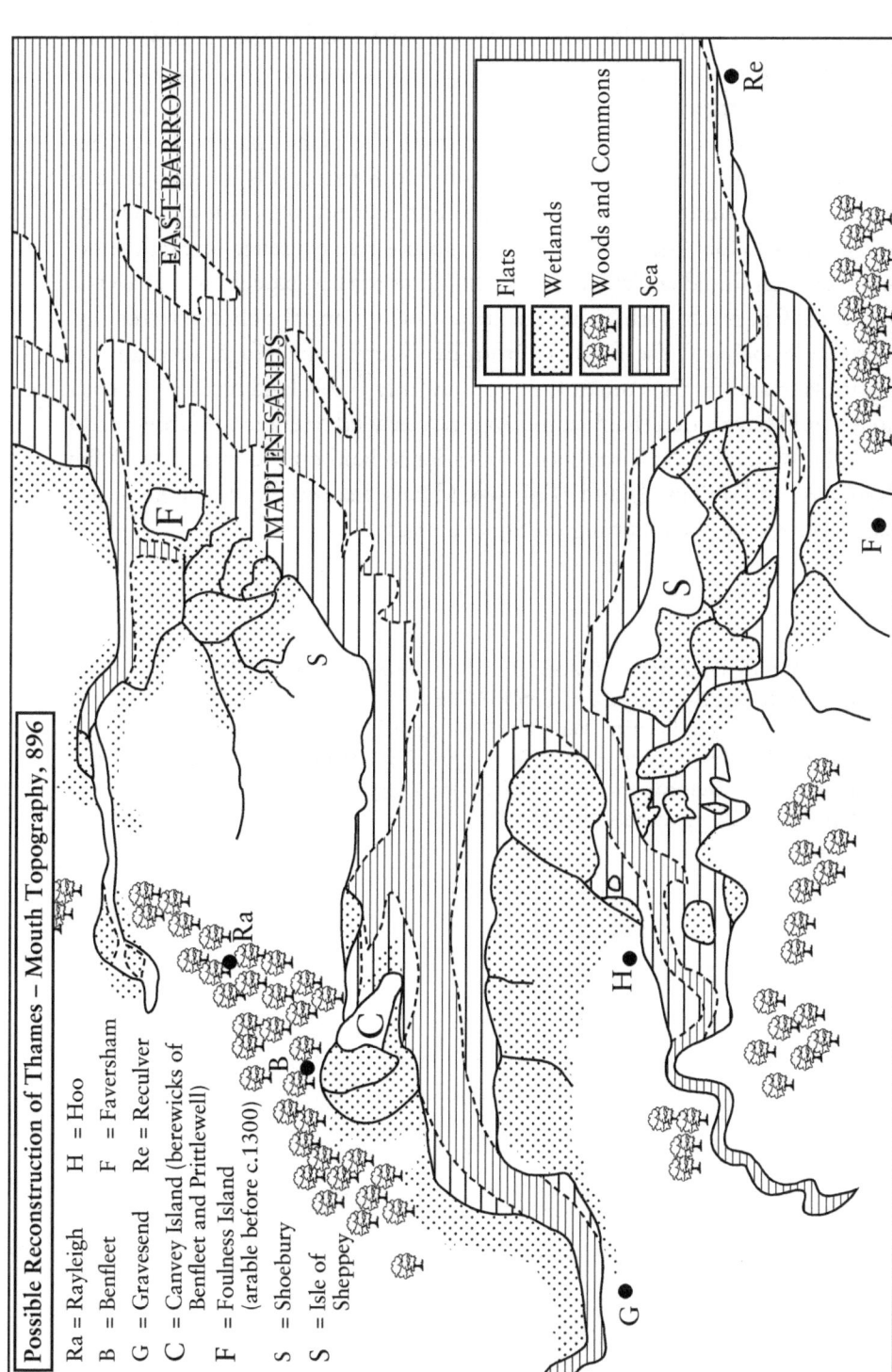

Map 3: Possible Reconstruction of Thames-Mouth Topography, 896.

ships, perhaps those under repair, were broken and burned. A few of the Viking garrison saved themselves by escaping downriver in ships, out into the estuary on the ebb.

Just downriver at 'Shoebury' (we are told), the Danes had built another camp, also with a strand, so, as at Torksey and Repton, this Thames mouth was a typical wintersetl with separate, but related, sites. Despite claims made for both Benfleet and Shoebury, no positive evidence of earthworks has ever been found at either, but we should not really expect more than the natural defences of marsh, water and a clear view along the chosen waterway. Here, at 'Shoebury', the fugitives from Benfleet found refuge, probably on Foulness Island for the core of this was certainly arable land by *c*.1300. A sea mist would have aided their escape and they needed to enter the Crouch and then the Roach by Wallasea Island in order to land on the west side of the dry centre of Foulness Island. This would have made a far less obvious and accessible refuge than landing on Shoeburyness.

Notes

1. D. Woodruff, *The Life and Times of Alfred the Great* (London, 1993).
2. Q.v. Paul Kelly (2019), fig.21 and pp.103–106.
3. Wright (2019), p.106, citing Wright (2014), pp.365–368 and Wright (2017) pp.31–35 and 110–111; also Nick Austin, *Secrets of the Norman Invasion* (1994) for smelting to the north of Bulverhythe and Wilting; also Wright (2019), pp.106–107.
4. Hollister (1962), pp.38 and 85–86.

Chapter Nine

The "Hot Trod"

Meanwhile, Exeter had been besieged, but when the Wessex army arrived, the raiders dispersed and took to their ships; they were not going to fight Alfred! They sailed away eastwards, with both of the remaining 'forces', and next they gathered at 'Shoebury', which (as we have seen) probably included Foulness Island, the largest island in the adjacent marshlands. Here they had access not only to the Thames but to the Roach and the Crouch, even to the Blackwater, and then reinforcements joined them from Anglia and from Northumbria. Nevertheless, they still cannot have been the force that had so boldly set out for Exeter for they now decided on a novel strategy and one that would have been both impossible and unnecessary for a more effective army, they apparently decided to sail up the Thames 'until they reached the Severn'.

Was this really an apparent feint against Wessex, which would have been quite an ambitious plan, or were they now being pursued by a relentless enemy? Were they being hunted out? Surely they knew that to travel overland would be to lose men on the way, on a long upriver slog, desperately pulling for what? Was the Thames' mouth now so dangerous to them that they dared not venture forth to open waters? Were they hoping to be met or were they heading for a rendezvous that was never kept? This last seems an unlikely hope, yet surely they knew that the pursuit, the 'hot trod', would gather momentum behind them and that alerted local forces would try to ambush them as they passed? Attrition was inevitable: though they might be safe on ships when midstream riders and marchers on the banks would be vulnerable and there would be places where hauling, or even portaging, would be necessary. Without maps, how would they know where the Thames was taking them, and why did they think it was possible to join the Severn? Did they possess local knowledge from their time at Chippenham or were they fleeing blind into the unknown? Indeed, did the chronicler who set down their recorded intention actually have *any* knowledge of their intentions or did he just presume them in the light of later events?

This, of course, begs the question, how did they intend to cross from the Thames to the Severn? Why the Severn? Did an English fleet in the Channel now make it too dangerous for them to risk sailing west and around the Lizard, and so to Ireland or to North Devon, or were their remaining ships too small or even lacking in seaworthiness to face such dangerous waters? Was the English fleet now, in fact, superior to that of the raiders? Had they lost too many ships to the English? A river cruise sounds delightful, but it is hardly a bold or even a desirable military strategy, and though this apparently displays a remarkable knowledge of England's inland waterways, it was a desperate policy: to row upriver into the heart of the enemy's territory and towards an army as well as away from one, one from which they had just escaped! The most plausible explanation is perhaps that they initially decided to attack the Wessex heartlands and once they had embarked on the Thames route (avoiding an English fleet watching the Narrows in this way) they found themselves pursued by a strong land force. This would ensure that they could not retrace their steps eastwards; a force pushing them further on and westwards would be economical for English forces, bewildering for the Danes and would gradually but surely wear them down as they pulled against the current. Meanwhile, warning could be sent on ahead and further English troops raised in the western shires.

No doubt part of 'the force' went by ship and part on horse or foot, for the Thames would provide a 'highway'. Maybe, having no hope of taking London and unable to hold on to Kent, they had all decided to return to Mercia? Maybe some yearned to be in Ireland? So, what about the state of the Anglian contingent? If the runners they sent out ever returned, they would have had dismal news to report. The *Chronicle* writer would have observed the result without knowing the strategy, and so he presumed that this was a Danish choice rather than desperate necessity. Could the English have provided the necessary men and replacements and the provisions for their army if this was deliberate pursuit? Well, Wessex and Mercia were no longer disunited, so was this a strategy of alternative objectives now being forced upon the Danes? If it was possible to capture seaworthy vessels on the Severn, the Danes might succeed, if not, then perhaps they hoped to enter Mercia and make for Lindsey and Northumbria and, in a last resort, head for the Wirral and there capture ships to take them to Ireland? Cast it how you will, this was a desperate decision for the enemy to make, one that speaks volumes for English cohesion and competence by land and sea and for Alfred's organisation of men and supplies. Militarily it was a cynical and brutally economical strategy: just keep them moving and Wyrd would do the rest!

Following the Thames to Northmoor would have enabled the Danes to enter the Windrush at Newbridge and so go on to Guiting Power, which route would take them to within 8 miles of Cheltenham. If, instead, they followed it to Winchcombe and the rivers Isbourne and Avon, then Tewkesbury would be accessible, or Evesham, for each place is on the Severn. The River Kennet to the Vale of Pewsey, with a portage along the line of the later Kennet and Avon Canal, would have given a reasonable distance on the level and into the Bristol Avon. During their sojourn at Chippenham, no doubt, they had had an opportunity to reconnoitre the lower reaches of both the Severn and the Avon and maybe they had absorbed some ne'r-do-wells while there who could advise and guide them?

Yes, if they kept them they must have portaged their ships, whichever route they chose, and this in itself tells us that they were now using only the smallest and lightest of craft. One suspects that by now their numbers were much reduced, though obviously still sufficient for the effort involved in hauling several tons of ship and carrying cargo for a considerable distance, with all the necessary pioneering work to clear a track. They could even have abandoned their ships at Hungerford and marched along Ermin Street to Swindon, Cirencester and Gloucester, to capture new vessels on the Severn. On another hand, they could have entered the Churn from the Thames and followed it through the then waterlogged area that is now (after gravel extraction) the Cotswold Water Park, the plain of the Churn, the Coln and the Leach, in order to make Cirencester before taking Ermin Street to Gloucester. Such has been the disturbance of this landscape in recent history that we can now only guess at the 'best' available route.

Long before they reached any portage, sickness and wounds would have taken their toll and with the hatred that the English now felt for them, stragglers would have had no chance of survival. As the 'force' trudged westwards attempting to forage along the banks of the rivers, they would have been vulnerable to opportunistic attacks and ambushes but their own opportunities for retributive action would have been limited. At first, those who were horsed could have undertaken pursuits but for the infantry, marching along the river, it was identical to a convoy: nothing must interfere with the onwards movement. This would surely have limited the escorts' scope. Maximum safety lay in the ships and the ships were the most important objects, that is why I think they kept their ships throughout.

If they were to reach any destination from the Severn they needed ships, and if they were in the middle of a river, then those on the ships would be safe. However, as the rivers narrowed or shoaled it would be impossible to progress under oars, so it would then be necessary to haul the vessels on towropes, rendering those doing the towing vulnerable to attack, especially along wooded banks where archers could lurk. Yet it was essential that when they reached the point of portage, there must still be enough men to accomplish the task *and* for as many vessels as possible, though such an operation would divide the force between watercourses and so leave each end and the portagers themselves vulnerable. They were certainly in a desperate situation.

Somehow they made the Severn, though it can hardly have been with a large 'force' any more. Instead of turning south, they now went north, their situation resembling the conclusion to the First Afghan War, harassed by locals but finally pursued by a main force. Now they certainly needed to keep to the ships and to midstream, slowly and painfully rowing *against* the flow of the Severn, upstream. They were obviously not going to risk the Severn estuary and the English fleet! The English army does appear to have been taken somewhat off guard: no doubt the information about their route was, at first if not altogether, hard to believe? It took time to gather all the thanes east of the Parrett, east and west of Selwood, others staying at burghs, to alert forces north of the Thames and also on the west bank of the Severn, but earldormen Æthelred, Æthelhelm and Æthelnorth all joined the pursuit on the English bank. On the Welsh bank, some of the Welsh then also joined the 'hot trod', for what they could get out of it.

What remained of 'the force' now followed the Severn northwards to Buttington, passing through Shrewsbury, not daring to stop at what would once have been a tempting target. By now foraging must have become difficult, with enemies on either bank to oppose any landings, and the ships were probably deteriorating, for lack of maintenance. Danish ships were lightly built, making the more modest ones quite capable of portaging, but portage as well as constant use would have put a serious strain on them. This was, for example, the experience of the *Bjorgmunknarr* (a far more substantially built, later vessel) when portaged as an experiment over the Mavis Grind, and that was a sturdy merchantman.[1]

At Buttington they gave up and, finding some sort of a burgh or defence, they holed up in the middle of Wales with the dwindling stream heading west into the Welsh mountains. There was now nowhere left to row to! For many weeks the pursuers now besieged them until starvation set in. Finally, the starving garrison went out to meet their besiegers on the east side of the river and predictably, in their condition, the Christians had the victory. Once again there was no wasteful assault on barricades, just the waiting for weakened and desperate men to emerge was sufficient. Ordheh and others of the king's thanes died here but the Danes were slaughtered.

A few of the enemy escaped and fled, probably into Mercia, bearing the news of this failure. The Buttington Oak, which stood here until 2018, was said to be a commemorative planting but no other evidence has been found. More recently Buttington, near Welshpool, has marked the limit of Severn navigation, though (of course) Danish ships had much slighter draughts. It is where the northern end of Offa's Dyke meets the Severn and where it turns back westwards into Wales. The Danes were not seeking to terrorise Mercia, no, they were desperately fleeing from a 'hot trod' and their *sauve qui peut* ended when the river changed direction. It seems that any intelligences they had concerning topography had not told them where the river actually rose.

Had the original intention been to join up with Vikings from Ireland? Well, King Alfred was on the west coast of Devon with the ship force and the forces west of the Parrett were ready and waiting for any such attempted juncture. Once again, faced with widely spaced attacks, he split his forces to deal with them and this was now possible because Wessex and Mercia were acting together, as an English army. He must have felt secure, now that the remaining Danes in Essex were no longer seriously amphibious, in order to withdraw his ship force so far to the west. Clearly the threat to the Thames had been destroyed, at least for the present.

Events now proved him right. There were still Danes in Essex and reinforcements had (you will remember) come from Anglia and Northumbria. Before winter set in, these men secured their remaining ships and also their women and children in Anglia, probably mainly at Thetford, and then they struck out overland. Now they 'went in one stretch, by day and night, till they came to an empty town in the Wirral, which is called Chester'.[2] They obviously feared interception, so they force marched, probably using the Icknield Way and then picking up Watling Street all the way to Shrewsbury. Here, perhaps, they picked up some survivors from the Severn, men they probably hoped might reinforce them. Their story would not have been reassuring.

Having made Chester, they made the burgh secure before news of their arrival had brought the royal army up to face them, but only just in time. No fleet from Ireland came up the Dee to help them and they had little time in which to store food before the besiegers arrived. For two days the royal army seized all the cattle in the neighbourhood, burnt the corn they found or fed it to their horses and killed all the stragglers they encountered. Grimly, the *Anglo-Saxon Chronicle* noted that this was exactly twelve months since the Danes had come to England, over the sea. This was not what they had anticipated when they set out.

Those who survived the winter starvation went, early in 894, from the Wirral into north Wales and there they found some sustenance and plunder. The survivors now hastened eastwards towards Northumbria, probably aiming for York, moving so fast that the army could not overtake them and from there the few made it south, through Lindsey and the Fens or perhaps by ship from the Humber to Anglia. Next they gathered what ships they had left or could take and sailed round Norfolk to north-east Essex and here they seized Mersea Island, a marshy island connected by a tidal causeway, where they now quietly licked their wounds.[3] In all likelihood they were not welcomed by the settled Danes of Anglia, who now had more to fear from English vendettas, so they had been told to 'move on' and this was the best place available.

Raiders on the north coast of Devon, now repulsed by Alfred's ship force, together with a few remnants of the one hundred ships (3,000 men or more) that had been repulsed at Exeter, together turned 'homewards' along the Channel. As they went they ravaged near to Chichester. There may already have been a thriving fish-salting industry here, around Hayling and Thorney Island, and these pirates were now probably short of provisions.[4] Here the townsfolk fought back and 'killed many hundreds' and put them all to flight, even seizing some of their ships. By now this contingent must also have been sadly depleted and in a very bad way.

On Mersea Island the survivors of the Mercian raid spent the summer's end recuperating. It was more a prison than a refuge and local supplies seem to have been sparse, another indication that they were unwelcomed among their countrymen, so they now hit upon another plan. It was, of course, now dangerous for them to stay in one place too long, so just before winter set in, in 894, they again took to the waters. Now, fugitive and fearful, they did the unpredictable: they sailed into the Thames, to the Isle of Dogs, where they took to the Lea and rowed northwards and upriver, for 20 miles to the confluence of the Stort (in my opinion), to Ware, to Roydon or Sawbridgeworth. These were then very marshy and conjoined habitats with no known Roman roads surviving and part also of a densely wooded belt from Enfield to Epping, and so they made their wintersetl at one or the other, using a marsh island once again but, curiously, miles from open waters. Maybe their desperate need was to find timber for ship repairs and adequate food stocks to raid, hoping to be beyond the range of Alfred's forces? If so, it was a vain hope.

Notes

1. 'Borgundnarran', documentary in the series *Secrets of the Ancients* (BBC, 1999).
2. *The Anglo-Saxon Chronicle*.
3. This causeway dates from AD 690, q.v. 'Mersea Island: the Anglo-Saxon Causeway', Crummy, Hillam and Crossan in *Essex Archaeology and History* vol. 14 (1982), pp.77–86.
4. Arthur Wright, 'The Problem of the Peasantry' in *Wiðowinde* 190 (2019), pp.36–37; also Wright (2020), pp.187–189.

Chapter Ten

Mastering the Waters

We have now seen a complete reversal in fortune for 'the heathen horde'. It was thanks to determined and maintained confrontation, flexible tactics and strategy that not only mirrored Danish practice and exploited their weaknesses but one that also combined with a new unity and strengthening of morale. The enemy had come to the point where some wished to settle in the lands apportioned to them, while the more piratical element alternated between desperate attempts at raiding and basic survival. Success in warfare is not all about winning battles, it is, even more so, the attrition of an enemy's means and sapping his will to fight. That is what historians critical of Alfred have forgotten and why the evidence has been distorted (by some) to suggest Danish or 'Viking', superiority, a grave manipulation of the history of this period.

By the summer of 895, the London (and possibly the Hertford) city dwellers and others had had enough of this hornet's nest at Roydon or Sawbridgeworth within striking distance of their trade and provisions and, no doubt, interfering with their hunting grounds. They marched on the Danish camp or burgh, probably striking east from Ermine Street and St Albans, but were put to flight, with the death of four of the king's thanes. When this news reached Alfred, he brought his army up and camped near the city while the harvest was being carried. He also took this opportunity to reconnoitre the River Lea, which the pirates used for their raids, and seeing a suitable spot, ordered burghs to be built on each side of the river. Coincidentally, this would also be the start of the passage season, offering good hawking over wetlands, so the king's time may not have been entirely absorbed with duties!

Seeing this and understanding that their ships were now trapped in the Lea, the hunted Danes sent their women and children north into Anglia (for the Icknield Way was close by) and themselves set out westwards as a diversion, presumably skirting London to the north perhaps to pick up Watling Street (ancient Roman Road), marching until they came to Bridgenorth on the Severn and north of Worcester, where they built a burgh. Meanwhile, while the army rode after the fugitives, the men of London seized the abandoned ships on the Lea, sailing the serviceable ones to London and breaking up the rest. Here we have the proof that many Danish ships had become unserviceable due to neglect and hard usage, leaving the ship men desperate and marooned, unable to take to the high seas.

In the summer of 896, 'the force' dispersed, some to live in Northumbria and some in East Anglia, in their own settlements in what was now the Danelaw, while those without property acquired serviceable ships and sailed away to the Seine. Not that the settled Danes were idle, they still required slaves, both for use and for sale, so those in Northumbria and Anglia raided the south coast of Wessex.

Here we have an interesting comment in the *Chronicle* recording that the Danes used 'ash ships which they had built many years before', a curious choice of timber and also the confirmation that they were old ships by now. Slow-grown ash is relatively light and the wood is straight-grained and easily hand or steam-bent, and some is exceptionally tough. It dries readily and is fairly stable in use but when used outdoors, especially in shipbuilding, it requires adequate protection, not being a durable timber, and it is prone to insect attack (beetle). Here, I think, we have a root cause of Danish misfortunes, the condition of their ships, which though built for inland waterway work, would respond badly to prolonged voyaging, lack of maintenance, hard usage and continual portaging. The only way to protect the vulnerable hull (let alone caulk the strakes) would be with tar, yet abrasion internally by feet, or externally over ground or even rollers, would soon scrape this away and further supplies of Stockholm tar were probably scarce in England, where the necessary pines (from which such tar is derived) did not grow.[1] It had to be imported.

Now we know why they chose Roydon or Sawbridgeworth, for although the predominantly marshy area of the Lea and the Stort would not provide the fertile, deep and well-drained soils, required by ash, the adjacent higher ground *still*, today, presents ash groves. Today we find Lilly's Wood in Ash Valley and there is no reason why this or similar enclaves did not exist in 894. There would also be a variety of other available timbers and maybe birch, from which to make a substitute tar wash. Here they could attempt to repair their disintegrating ships and maybe intercept supplies of (Stockholm) tar bound for London. The ash, of course, was the Norse 'tree of life' and this may have something to do with this Danish shipbuilding tradition, though the ease of bending and lightness of the wood were clearly other considerations.

In response to these new raids, King Alfred ordered his ship force to be sent on patrol and it belonged to a very different shipbuilding tradition. These vessels were 'twice as long as the others, some had sixty oars, some more'.[2] They were swifter and steadier, also higher, so with a raised freeboard that would enable them to tolerate beam seas and rough waters, built neither 'in the Frisian manner nor the Danish' and possibly owing their celerity to sails. I think that the deprecatory references to 'ash ships' indicate that the English tradition was one of oak-building, a more difficult art of construction but far more durable in service. Here we seem to have faster, heavier and more seaworthy sailing craft, certainly effective when ramming the ash ships and, moreover, packed with warriors. Is it any surprise that the Danes seemed no longer to be such masters of the waters?

Still, superior technology is not invariably advantageous. In 896, six enemy ships descended on the Isle of Wight: they seem to have made a strand and camp here because they also raided westwards to the coast of Devon. King Alfred sent out nine ships against them, which found three ships beached, their occupants raiding inland, and three that then stood out to meet them 'at the river's mouth'. The English took two ships but the third escaped, albeit with only five men left, when the deeper draft and heavier English vessels ran aground. My guess is that this was in Southampton Water for the rise and fall of the tide here is notorious and the *Chronicle* says that it now ebbed 'many furlongs from the ships', leaving them stranded.

Now the English were awkwardly aground with three ships on the same side as the pirates and the others aground on the other side of the deep-water channel. So the Danes decided to strike first over the sands and attack the stranded English and Frisian crews: in the ensuing fight sixty-two Englishmen were killed but also 120 Danes. When we consider that there were probably no more than 200 men on all the Danish ships, maybe fewer, this was a serious blow to their motive power. The king's reeve, Lucumon, Athelferth of the king's household and Wulfheard, Æbbe and Æthelhere, all Frisians, died here. The returning tide floated the lighter ash ships first and so they rowed out. Nevertheless, the English and Frisians seem to have carried their pedestrian attack on the sands to the enemy, even maybe utilising the ships they had captured and rendering others useless before the tide turned for these three escaping vessels were badly damaged. Either at Selsey Bill or Beachy Head, probably the former where they would run foul of the Looe Channel, the sea threw two vessels onto the shore and the miserable survivors from their crews were captured. They were led to Winchester, where the king ordered them to be hanged. As for the third ship, with many badly wounded men aboard, they finally made Anglia. The *Chronicle* adds that that summer no fewer than twenty ships, with their crews, perished along the south coast. I think we can presume that they were Danish vessels caught by the English 'navy' or by bad weather.

Although these are called ash ships and, as such, are very different from the true Scandinavian oak constructs that we know more about, we do have a part parallel from much later (*c.*1030). The *Skuldelev 5*, one of several blockships sunk near Roskilde in Denmark, was a mixture of ash, linden (lime) and fir. Fir was not available in England[3] but the other timbers were available here, so the exact form of these earlier Danish vessels was likely to have resembled that of *Skuldelev 5*, now replicated at Roskilde as the *Helga Æsk*. At one time the Kvalsund ship, discovered in 1920, (built of oak but with pine ribs) was thought to be datable to *c.*690, so representing a type of longship much earlier than the Oseberg ship, but very recent work[4] has revised the dating to 780 to 800. This vessel represents the transition between rowing and sailing and has a very low freeboard and mid-section profile of only eight strakes a side. Her complement was probably twenty to thirty men. She was, therefore, more an inshore than a truly pelagic craft and she fits our time frame better, and we may note that our references to Danish ships all seem to be to rowing rather than to sailing vessels, though the Kvalsund ship has been proposed as mounting a mast. Such a vessel, if fitted with a sail using a mast fish, would make for very exciting sailing, as does the replica *Skuldelev 5*.

What we learn from such replications as the *Helga Æsk* is that these low-freeboard vessels were relatively poor sailing ships for the deep sea, even if capable of mounting a sail, for although they could probably manage 11 or 12 knots when under sail in a favourable sea, in any sort of rough weather they would need to strike mast and sail and use oars alone. This would reduce their speed to 3–5 knots at best, leaving them at the mercy of tides and currents: head up into wind and wave would have to be their rowing response in dirty weather. Moreover, these inland or inshore craft relied absolutely on their crew, they were unballasted (other than occupants and supplies) and if they lost many of their crew their speed *and* their stability would be affected. Even when sailing large in good weather, they would need a full crew to man the weather gunwales (just like a sailing dingy) in order to avoid swamping. These were not vessels designed for sea battles, rather they were designed to penetrate inland waterways.

The Graveney boat, dendro-dated to 895–950, was a shallow-draft, flat-bottomed vessel with a 'T' keel (also a feature of the Sutton Hoo ship) but she was certainly an oak-built merchantman. Her cargo has been said to indicate that she was trading with the Rhineland, but given her low freeboard that seems unlikely and a coastal role seems more likely. Association with hops has also led to a good deal of speculation and controversy but, as Martin Cornell has comprehensively discussed, they do not prove a brewing connection at this date.[5]

Another early vessel is the ship found at Grønhaug, Avaldsnes (Rogaland in Norway). This is in the oak tradition, however, and it is also a royal burial dating from 790 to 795.[6] Oak seems to be the preferred Scandinavian timber and this seems in common with our Alfredan English ships, not least because oak was so common in England. Maybe that is why we presume that the Sutton Hoo ship was built in oak? So we come to an interesting and potentially heretical possibility: Bond and Styleger have suggested that ship burial, as opposed to boat burial, was itself introduced into Western Norway *from* Eastern England.[7] What, then, was to prevent aspects of the building of ships in oak also following a route from England to Norway and the Baltic? Could it be that efficient, sailing, sea-going, long-ships were not initially Scandinavian but an *English* original? Certainly the *Skuldelev 5* seems to be a survivor from an earlier Danish tradition of building, persisting into a more sophisticated and later age of deep sea vessels and sailing ships. Our earliest evidence seems to be the Nydam (oak) boat (AD 320 to 360) though a 'pine'-built boat was found with her and then burnt by nineteenth-century soldiers. As this vessel burned so well in spite of being damp, I wonder if it was in reality made of ash?

The *Historiorum adversum Paganos Libri Septem* of Paulus Orosius was translated into Old English by command of King Alfred the Great and there was appended to this a contemporary description (addition) of northern Europe that incorporated accounts by two traders who dealt with the royal court, Ohthere and Wulfstan.[8] The importance of their accounts is that they were practical men, sailors, not clerics gathering hearsay, and their journeys have been checked and verified. They gave the king, their 'hlaford', details of unknown waters and peoples they had seen. From them we can also gather important information about ships and sailing.

Ohthere speaks of coastwise sailing without a compass, keeping in sight of land and landing at night, while Wulfstan sailed continuously day and night. Each averaged 2 to 3 knots, though more was possible depending on wind speed and direction; sailing at night (without charts or compass) the pace would necessarily slacken as it was essential to take regular soundings with a lead when following a shoreline. Of course, these were trading ships and not warships but we should assume that many Danish vessels were of this type. Moreover, the two men might have sailed in ships of different construction, which brings us back to the differences between English ships and the 'ash ships', the first large and with a high freeboard, so seagoing in design, the second smaller and with low freeboard, probably not so much sailed as rowed. English ships, we are told, were not built to anyone else's design but were unique and identifiable.

The Norwegian Gjellestad ship is, at present, presumed to have belonged to the ninth century. She seems to have had an oak keel and, like the Oseberg ship (a 'karve' buried *c.*834), a low freeboard, and so she may also have been an oak ship from the Skagerrack-Kattegat region.[9] The Oseberg replica built in 2012 proved to be a fine sailing ship capable of 10 knots. On the other hand, the Klåstad ship, replicated in 2018 (as the *Saga Farmann*) and possibly datable to *c.*989, was a shallow vessel and trader similar to the *Skuldelev 1* ship dated to 1030 to 1050. *Skuldelev 1* was probably built on the west coast of Norway as she has an oak keel, lime frames and the rest is pine. She was deep and seagoing, capable of carrying perhaps 20 tons of goods, but not a fighting ship nor an easily portaged vessel.

The Slavic waters of the Baltic have yielded oak boats, capable of sailing or rowing, at Ralswiek, number 4 being longer than number 2 but each probably with ten-man crews. Litwin has drawn attention to the differences in boat-building traditions between the Scandinavian and Slavic types of boat section in particular (e.g. Szczecin and Czarnowska 1 boats),[10] so we can begin to understand that regions (as well as individual shipbuilders) had distinctive traditions that would affect aspects and the handling of ships and boats.

Maybe the designation 'ash ship' was only a common or vernacular substitution, a description covering all cheaper and less substantial boats, for if pine was unfamiliar in England and oak the preponderant shipbuilding tradition, then a derogatory reference (implying inferior goods) could have encompassed all other non-English constructions. After all, the use of mixed timbers in some surviving vessels does suggest a lack of preferred timber in some regions, a 'making do' with whatever was available, while ash, pine and lime are all less durable timbers liable to decay and (most important) prone to beetle attack.

An unusual rune poem, which has only survived because it was copied from the Cotton MS Otho (B.x, folio 165a-b) by Humphrey Wanley prior to the disastrous fire of 1731, provides us with a possible sidelight on ships. It is broadly attributed to the eighth to ninth centuries, though Dr Gupta believes it had an earlier, oral pedigree. In it 'ash' (ᚨ) is – 'old and tall: honoured by men;

with its stalwart stem, it stands its ground
though no few foemen fight against it' –

suggesting that it was connected to conflict, though it may be a reference to being cut down and ash was useful for both ships and spears.[11]

Again, the reference to 'oak' (ᚨ) reads:

'on whose acorns, for earth's children,
farrow feed as mast, fares out to sea,
over the gannet's bath; there gulfs and storms
find if faithful – or false to its troth' –

Also of interest in relation to wintersetls is 'lakes' (ᛚ) –

'and waters, on the long voyage
seem of endless ambit; when the oceans surge
and tempests tower at the tossing prow,
that horse-of-the-brine heeds not her bridle' –

telling us that safe harbour and penetration into inland waterways was essential when winter gales made a ship uncontrollable in a seaway.

Notes

1. Oliver Rackham, *The Illustrated History of the Countryside* (1994), p.44; *Anglo-Saxon Chronicles*, p.107.
2. See Savage (ed.), *The Anglo-Saxon Chronicles*, p.107.
3. According to Rackham but see the *Domesday Book*'s entry at Westbury on Severn (f.163) for a fir wood.
4. Nordeide, Bond & Thun, *Journal of Archaeological Science* vol. 29 (Feb 2020).
5. Q.v. Martin Cornell in the 'Zythophile' blog, where he discusses the alternative uses of hops and the lack of evidence for a Kentish brewing tradition using hops at this date.
6. Q.v. Bond & Stylegar, *Viking* (Journal of the Norsk Arkeologisk Selskap) (2009), Grønhaug & Storhaug.
7. Niels Bond & Frans-Arne & Stylegar, 'Between Sutton Hoo and Oseberg – Dendro Chronology and the Origins of the Ship Burial Tradition' in the *Danish Journal of Archaeology* vol. 5 (2016), issue 1–2.
8. *Two Voyagers at the Court of King Alfred*, ed. Niels Lund (York, 1984) an English-language companion to *Ottar og Wulfstan* (Roskilde, 1983).
9. Q.v. Ole Crumlin-Pedersen in *Ottar og Wulfstan* (op. cit., p.32).
10. Q.v. 'Medieval Baltic Ships and Construction Aspects', Jerzy Litwin in *Actes des congrés de la Societé de Archaeologie Médiévale* (1998), pp.90–92.
11. Rahul Gupta, 'The Old English Rune Poem', in *Wiðowinde* 195 (2020), pp.29–31.

Chapter Eleven

A Subtle Strategic Legacy

In AD 899, six nights before All Saints' Day (All Hallows, 26 October), Alfred son of Æthelwulf, died aged 50 or 51. According to his biographer Asser, he had suffered from a medical condition all his life and recently it has been suggested that this was either Crohn's Disease or perhaps haemorrhoids.[1] What he had achieved in such a short time and in such discomfort was and remains remarkable.

One might say that he was not the first Anglo-Saxon king to unite England, but both Ine of Wessex (689–726) and Offa of Mercia (757–796) seem to have been limited to personal ambition and self-aggrandisement, for they faced no overwhelming external threat. True, Alfred acknowledged his own debt to these kings when compiling his book of laws (his *Domboc*) but Alfred's achievement was not only to nullify the threat faced by all kingdoms and regions but to unify them, especially those giants (and rivals) Wessex and Mercia, and to inculcate a spirit of joint response, of unity and of dogged determination. The necessary work and expenditure was not welcomed by all, and especially by his wealthiest subjects, and the demands of military service were, for the age, enormous, but then the threat was colossal. For the majority of his subjects, Alfred's obvious determination to eradicate the curse of the Danes was surely the answer to their personal fears of slavery, murder, rape and arson, fears manifested in their deep-seated hatred of these pirates that had now appeared and persisted.

Of course, he was not 'the father of the Royal Navy', as older histories once declared, for ship forces existed before he commanded special vessels to be constructed, and it is highly doubtful that it was any scholarly knowledge provided by Asser of classical shipbuilding that revolutionised English ship design.[2] The scholastic copying of ancient pictorial texts was certainly not reproduced in the shape of English shipping. No, the technical knowledge required to build ships of this clincher type, especially to work in oak and to mount a mast fish so that a sail could be stepped (you need some sort of keel to which to fix such an appendage), did not arrive overnight from blueprints drawn up by candlelight by a religious bibliophile. Such things require long traditions and careful experiment by practical shipwrights. No one built a Space Shuttle by replicating the appearance of one of Dan Dare's ships, and even today we are relearning the complex relationships between ship design, construction and performance in such vessels. Though the basic differences in design and practice between Danish and English ships, as highlighted by the *Anglo-Saxon Chronicle*, appear to have often gone unnoticed before now and do point to a significant divergence in design, execution and handling, they neither of them replicate Roman shipbuilding.

Neither is there evidence that these Danish invaders brought their 'wives and children' with them. The idea that wretched refugees from destitute lands huddled in flimsy, open boats in order to seek asylum and build a new life is mawkish and sentimental fiction. If they were *that* poverty stricken, then how could they afford a ship, or even a place in one? No, the only 'kinder transports' went the other way to death camps, for a warrior who could return a slave or two, one occupying the bench of a dead companion, would be providing his family homestead with a valuable asset, one to use, abuse or sell. When we are told of 'wives and children' we should rather think of temporary cantonments of slaves and concubines. These pirates only agreed to settle when the hacksilver ran out, largely because 'tribute' (protection money) was drying up and risks were increasing, otherwise theirs was a war of movement with as few ties as possible and plenty of licence.

Alfred was relentless in his pursuit of these brigands and pirates, and as his organisation improved so his response became inflexible; he was determined to rid his kingdom, generally accepted to have comprised a unified England (after he reoccupied London), and to keep the Danes within those territories he had already conceded. Apart from being honourable to his promises, it is doubtful he could have made permanent inroads into the Danelaw anyway, but he also had no intention of being a client king, of paying more 'tributes', or of seeing his peoples arbitrarily enslaved. His own laws, probably codified somewhere around the late 880s, gave 'fair-dealing' provisions, certain legal protections, to English-owned slaves. The primary requirement made of all was loyalty and the unforgiveable crime was treachery to any lord in authority over a person. In the 'Proverbs of Alfred', proverb two links obedience to a lord with honour to God.[3] This last, absolute loyalty, was to be of tremendous importance in the years to come and prove to be a principal component in the final evolution of an English constitutional foundation. For the present, that was still a long way off but here is its genesis.

I see slavery as the dominating influence at this point in our story. The Danes, rather we should say the assorted Scandinavian 'heathen horde', originally came for loot, 'tribute', *and* for slaves. The whole northern European social and economic structure depended on slavery. The Anglo-Saxons made use of both slaves and serfs, the Scandinavian peoples depended absolutely on 'thraldom', that is on slave labour. They were not tied into rigid kingship and, or, any defined hierarchical social structures, so free men increased their social and economic status by working the land with thralls. While loot was always a bonus, it is obvious that eventually, in any such constantly repeated circumstances, the hacksilver and gold will give out; the gilt-edged investment was always in human cargo. Good stark labourers and pretty girls were good for money right across northern Europe, while monks, matrons and the elderly, being unfit for either purpose, were put to the sword, or worse.

When the loot gave out there was still money to be made from people; when resistance became more effective (so the game became more dangerous) and land (and settlement) began to look attractive, then the new, 'lordling', settlers still needed labour and breeding stock if 'the promised land' was to be habitable. Initially the prospect of a land grab, one offering good prospects of slaves and loot, was no doubt attractive to some but after a generation or two the perspective would surely have changed? Danish settlers, fixed to one place, would surely have become vulnerable to raids themselves, to English slavers and revenge attacks, a lawless landscape once the protection of the 'heathen horde' had dispersed. The removal of the peripatetic elements to new hunting grounds would have rendered isolated settlers very vulnerable. Moreover, incoming Vikings, new war bands, would make no distinction between English and Danish settlements, no one was flying national flags or asking for union cards. Anyone in the path of the pirate slavers would have become fair game and surely such pressures themselves would drive Danish settlers into the arms of the English king, the only effective defence against lawlessness.

One might argue that in conceding the Danelaw, Alfred had also promoted English resistance and loosened the demands upon his own treasury, for men will fight for their families and slavers will focus on their primary source of secure revenue, every action having an equal and opposite reaction. As a corollary, the Danish settlers could expect to receive as good as they gave. They were now vulnerable, being tied to their holdings as the English were to theirs. Like it or not, Danish settlers needed the protection of English law. What gave additional direction to this philosophy, this possible policy, was the growing Christian awareness that slavery was contrary to the Will of God, though perhaps not so contrary when it involved 'heathens'!

Christian Anglo-Saxons had no hope of avoiding the torments of Hell when they died, unless they were in holy orders. There was no concept of purgatory, 'refrigarium' or 'resting in the bosom of Abraham'; such doctrines lay far in the future. No mortal is without sin for only Christ was ever the 'one true and perfect life' in history, so after death *all* had to await the dreadful day of judgement in Hell, waiting for 'Domesday', before their souls could be weighed and just some of them released to Paradise. However, certain Holy works were perceived to offer some chance of immediate assumption to Heaven: works such as founding monasteries always 'guaranteed' the rich and powerful a passage to Paradise. We have some evidence from this period, and even before, that the freeing of (Christian) slaves was being seen, in the same light, especially when *manumissio in sacrosanctis ecclesiis*,[4] that is a formal ceremony of freedom conducted in a church and guaranteeing such an act. Such emerging empathy with slaves was guaranteed, as in Georgian England, to become a social influence, especially when it was approved by royal authority.

It seems that Alfred's interest in his *Domboc* was not especially systematic in that laws of Ine of Wessex and Offa of Mercia were mixed with those of Æthelberht of Kent (589–616), and one scholar has suggested that Offa's contribution may have come from the Capitulary of 786, which was presented to him by Papal Legates.[5] For all these monarchs, Alfred included, it was not so much what they did for law as what the law did for them: it invested them with a mystique of wisdom that could only be Divine in origin, and this reinforced the concept of 'God's annointed'. The issuing of a comprehensive (if poorly ordered) set of laws was one way of reinforcing the power and mystery of any individual monarch, no doubt the reason why their preface is based on biblical material, especially on Mosaic Law.

Similarly it has been suggested that the *Anglo-Saxon Chronicle* (now known to us as '*Chronicles*' from its survival in several separate sources) was a compilation designed to promote unification of the Anglo-Saxon kingdoms in the face of the Danish threat.[6] I would suggest a parallel purpose in the consolidation of Alfred's paramount kingship that, after all, had to be maintained for strategic success. Histories are written by victors and although earthly estate is (not) everlasting, as that famous elegy 'the Wanderer' tells us, for 'each of all days ageth and faileth ... (and) all this earth's frame shall stand empty', yet a reputation survives, especially when the vehicle is a literary tradition.[7] Literate kings were aware of this, nor is this necessarily narcissistic, for ideals are transmitted by exemplars. What is surprising and also instructive is that succeeding generations maintained these chronicles, thereby adding not only to the mystique of kingship but to both an emerging national identity and the tradition of record keeping. No such vehicle, no such comprehensive 'history', survives 'over the water' in Europe.

The king (Alfred) was famously devout and God-fearing, his biographer Asser tells us so, founding a monastery at Athelney and a nunnery at Shaftesbury. With the aid of his scholarly advisors, he personally translated four major Latin works: the *Regula Pastoralis* of Gregory the Great, the *De Consolatione Philosophiae* of Boethuis, the *Soliloquia* of St Augustine and the first fifty psalms.⁸ His commissioning of Orosius's history of the world (or seven books against the pagans) and of Bede's ecclesiastical history may well have influenced him to commission the *Chronicle*, for its value as a lasting memorial cannot have been lost on him as a literate monarch. His was an age that believed implicitly that the Almighty's physical aid could be purchased and it was especially important for kings and leaders to acquire such leverage. Divine Will governed the actions of God's 'chosen men', so even expiation of sin was possible if suitable 'emollients' were applied. In this Alfred was uniting the physical and the spiritual worlds, to the end that his peoples and kingdom(s) should obtain the very best possible available defences and that, after all, was the spiritual 'armour' offered by the Church.

Although it is impossible to be specific, it seems that he also extended and regularised the network of burghs. Instead of using them merely as field fortifications, temporary defences, as the Danes normally did, he developed a network connected to 'herepaths' (highways) and some were truly imposing in size. Nor was his purpose simply military: many seem to have served as safe trading centres where markets could be held and, of course, market tariffs raised for the Crown. He, or his heir, also appear to have been responsible for a document known as the Burghal Hidage, which not only lists these defences but provides an elaborate formula for their support that, incidentally, allows us now to calculate their precise sizes and the sustenance required by their garrisons. It tells us (in all) how many hides 'belong' to the men of Wessex, that is how much land is required to support these burghs. So, at 240 acres to the hide, Kent and Sussex contributed 2.9266 million acres, Wessex (proper) 2.9945 million acres, Anglia 0.6240 million acres and Mercia 0.3360 million acres.⁹ The list of places makes it clear that the English heartlands were being protected, with emphasis on defence of the south coast and the eastern (the Danelaw) borders, hence the disproportionately small contributions of Anglia and Mercia, while far away in the west we see a scattering of (what we might now call) 'castles' against the old Damnonian tribal lands, places of only 5 acres or, in the case of Southampton, Lidford and Lyng, less than an acre in size, more like 'towers'.¹⁰ Winchester, capital of historic Wessex, and Wallingford were, by contrast, super-fortresses, respectively they required support from 576,000 acres each!

So, how do we come by these 'areas' or physical sizes of fortresses, burghs and 'castles' simply from the acreages (hides) of 'support' appended? The key is in the colophon to this document, which commences by telling us how many hides are required to maintain an 'acre's breadth of wall' and then it says that if a hide is represented by one man, then every pole of wall can be manned by four men, and there follows a ready reckoner by which to calculate the hides required for any length of wall, from twenty poles to 12 furlongs in length. Well, a furlong is 220 yards, which is the *length* of an acre (of 220 × 22 yards), while a rod or pole or perch is 5½ yards. Thus the calculation is easy: each man represents 1.375 yards of wall and he covers a field of fire outwards of 1 furlong, or 220 yards, a 'bowshot'.[11]

So we have sixteen men covering a linear perimeter of 22 yards 'anes æcres bræde', with a field of fire an acre (220 yards) beyond the perimeter. So sixteen men = one acre's breadth, simple. So our Winchester super-fortress had 'belonging to it' 2,400 hides = 576,000 acres, multiplied by 1.375 = 3,300 yards of nominal perimeter; hypothetically this would give a square of 825 yards each way = 140½ acres. A site of this size with a garrison of 2,400 fighting men, making some allowance for roadways and administrative structures, would give us something like a 50ft square for each man, enough for a dwelling. According to Loyn, the traced and excavated perimeter of this earthwork comes to 3,280 yards rather than 3,300 yards.[12]

Of course, burghs did not come as a standard plan or standard layout. Bath, at 1,000 hides, was 24½ acres (internally) and archaeology has estimated 23½ acres. In this burgh every man would, theoretically have 32½ft each way. Wareham, at 1,600 men, was 62½ acres, maybe less, and its perimeter of 2,200 yards agrees with Professor Loyn's 2,180 yards. Lyng had only 100 men on a quarter of an acre, a mere 10 ×10ft per man, very much a 'castle' rather than a potential township. Of course, we cannot make the exact tactical view we would wish to have, so entrances (or even towers) may have existed. The 3-acre Pilton Camp, with its nominal circumference of 1,485ft, may today be measured at 1,520ft and it probably had water obstacles in place in the past, so slightly abbreviating the actual vallum required.

Portchester is a fascinating example for this place did *not* involve earthworks – it was an intact Roman fortress and it still stands today. In Alfred's day this stone and brick monster would have been impregnable and it is allocated a mere 500 hides. Let us draw closer. The Roman fortress is 700ft along each face, 600 if we subtract the internal 'towers' (once artillery platforms). The calculable area covered is 11 acres but the internal space is only 8 acres, so let us look at 8. Now, according to our Burghal Hidage formula there would be 515.625ft along each face, making only 6 acres in area. However, the church, which still stands, was there in Saxon times and if we subtract the church site we reduce the internal area to 6½ acres. If the presence of the church reduced the garrison, then the high masonry walls more than compensated for the lack of men. It was a minster church with a religious community safely planted within an impregnable fortress. The internal allocation for each soldier would be something between 23 and 31ft (each way), depending on the convents' actual area and the internal roadways involved.

It is doubtful if these burghs were kept fully occupied year after year, forever on 'standby', but their presence, their garrisons and their 'herepaths' help us to understand how King Alfred could so rapidly and effectively respond to Viking incursions. We can also understand why raiders now tried to avoid obvious routes like the old Roman roads, seeking instead byways and minor waterways where there were no garrisons to intercept them. They were also a legacy to pass on to succeeding generations, as was the comprehensive organisation of all kingdoms (combined) for war, but everything depended on the maintenance of such bulwarks and organisation. And some burghs survived for remarkable periods of time, though changing in aspect as the years went by.

Take for example, Winchester, as recorded in the *Winchester Domesday* of *c.*1110 ('survey I') and *c.*1148 ('survey II'), which by the twelfth century had been sub-divided many times over, due to 'landgable' or 'burgage tenure'. This was a low, fixed, perpetual money rent that once, presumably, provided for the accommodation of the garrison but then was transferred to burghers, who could sub-divide and rent out their plots at will. As an administrative centre to rival London, it offered considerable opportunities for trading, secure trading, and the holders of these plots could assign, devise and even tallage their sub-tenants as they saw fit, being (in a city) part of the money economy.[13] If each man (see above) of the 2,400-strong garrison occupied something like a 50ft square, then if we convert each to a 'landlord' we have an indication of how Alfred organised the sustenance and maintenance of his extensive network of burghs and garrisons. We also have a suggestion as to how these burghs later became such densely packed aggregations of tenures.

Under King Alfred it became necessary not only to brigade together the armies of separate kingdoms but also to reorganise their service obligations, so that at any one time a standing force existed while reserve forces were, so to speak, 'at rest'. To accomplish the provision of these contingents when in the field (or in camp, in burgh) it was essential to gather together the former *feorms* of food rents owed by freeholders of the several kingdoms into some sort of commissariat system, presumably with local obligations met by local landholders as contingents passed through their territories. But note, such an imposition on the pre-existing arrangements of local self-sufficiency would, in practice, create a form of centralised military and supply structure, one authorised by the controlling authority of kingship. In this, I suggest, we see the roots of the later 'geld' system, where feorms were commuted to specie payments assessed pro rata according to land-owning capacity and privilege. The weakness of such a development lay in the temptation to the centralised monarchy when immediate emergencies passed: it would then leave a king open to placing continued imposts (initially in kind or as services) upon his freeholding subjects, the origins of 'unjust' or exploitative taxation. The creation of a centralised system of authority automatically allows the centralised power to justify all demands as part of a systematic defence structure.

Battles are the catalysts of change but they do not, of themselves, win wars. It is painstaking planning and the organisation of all forms of infrastructure and resource that achieve ultimate victory. There is an obvious temptation to romanticise King Alfred but I think the jury is still out on the question of whether he was a benevolent despot. His achievements came from a ruthless determination to maintain his lands and peoples, and to that, or those, ends everything else was subordinated. Drawing the royal and noble households of several kingdoms together cannot have been achieved by argument alone and the enemy were still 'at the gates' and intent on breaking and entering. Even giving away part of the island, that is giving it to the Danelaw, did not resolve the problem, it simply made it manageable. Yet though he superficially 'gave it away', it was to become, in my opinion, perhaps his subtlest and most astute strategic decision, as we shall see in due course. The long-term effects were to draw the old kingdoms even tighter together, though the intention to do so is, of course, impossible to prove. To my mind King Alfred deliberately melded together strategic genius and political structure when he did this and the result became a unique legacy. When he died, King Alfred needed an equally energetic successor who would accept his mantle in its entirety – but he had left him and also his successors a secure foundation.

Notes

1. Craig, G. 'Alfred the Great, a Diagnosis', *Journal of the Royal Society of Medicine* 84(5) pp.303–305; Jackson, F., Letter to the Editor, ibid., 85(1) (1992).
2. Q.v. Edwin & Joyce Gifford, 'Alfred's New Longships' in Timothy Reuter (ed.) *Alfred the Great (Studies in Early Medieval Britain)*, pp.281–289.
3. Q.v. Lund, *The Proverbs of Alfred* (1942 & 1955) 2 volumes. Also *An Introduction to Early English Law*, Bill Griffiths (1995) note to p.43.
4. Q.v. Wihtred of Kent's Legal Code of 695.
5. Patrick Wormald, *The Making of English Law: King Alfred to the Twelfth Century* (1999 & 2001), p.528.
6. Q.v. Joanne Parker, *England's Darling* (Manchester UV, 2007).
7. Michael Alexander's translation in *The Earliest English Poems* (Penguin, 1977).
8. Q.v. B.A.E. Yorke in Lapidge (Blackwell), pp.27–8.
9. Wright (2014), pp.122–124; Arthur Wright, *Raising the Dead* (2021).
10. A 'castle' does not need to be more than a ringwork, indeed many 'Norman castles' were just that', see Wright (2019) p.41 and (2020), pp.49–51.
11. Q.v. Wright (2021).
12. Henry Loyn, *Anglo-Saxon England and the Norman Conquest* (1962), pp.135–6.
13. Q.v. Wright (2014), pp.286–9; based on Barlow, Biddle, von Feilitzen and Keene, *Winchester Studies 1, Winchester in the Early Middle Ages, an Edition and Discussion of the Winton Domesday* (OUP, 1976).

Chapter Twelve

Inheriting Both Sword and Strategies

Alfred was succeeded by his son Edward, the king we know as Edward the Elder. His cousin, Æthelwold, perhaps understandably angry that he did not succeed by his father's right, seized the manors at Wimbourne and Christchurch and also abducted a nun, or at least took her against the bishop's command and without the king's leave. In an inconspicuous start to the reign, Edward then rode with his army to Badbury Rings. Æthelwold decided to barricade his manor of Wimborne and make defiance, but he then stole away leaving his men to the king's mercy and his woman behind.

He next joined 'the force' in Northumbria and in 902 sailed to Essex with all the ships he could gather and 'lured the East Anglian force into breaking the peace'.[1] 'The force' from Anglia then marched on Mercia in 903, following the Thames and then the Isis, then it crossed the Thames (Isis) and, presumably following the River Ray, raided the area around Braydon. At this time there was probably still the great Braydon Forest, which we know had, in the seventh century, covered some 7,000 acres between Swindon and Chippenham. Not only was this near to the former Danish stronghold, therefore, it also offered woodland and moorland cover for raiding parties, a change of tactics for 'the force'. I suspect that as well as ships they had horses, to facilitate their raiding. Then they returned 'homeward', that is to Anglia, no doubt delighted with the guidance offered by the renegade Æthelwold.

King Edward gathered his army and set off on a 'hot trod' after them, determined to teach them a lesson. In retaliation he ravaged all the land between 'the (Devil's) Dyke and Fleam Dyke and the Ouse', in fact everything up to the northern fens.[2] Now one Devil's Dyke is located on the South Downs near to Brighton, in Wessex territory, so I believe this entry actually refers to the Devil's Dyke or Devil's Ditch (a post-medieval attribution) from Newmarket to Reach.[3] Edward was probably marching along the Icknield Way, going east by north from London, and my guess is that the Isle of Ely was possibly the Dane's destination for here, deep inside the Wash (a vast inland waterway leading to the North Sea) there was a port at Haddenham, Hill Row, and it would have made an ideal location for a slave market.[4] The fact that the Danes had not attempted to take any major towns or markets during their raid suggests that their primary purpose had indeed been slaving, snatching able-bodied peasantry from defenceless villages. Whether Edward penetrated beyond 'the northern fens' we are not told, but he does not seem to have attempted to attack Thetford, so he probably expected resistance to gather there and to respond to his incursion.

Being apprehensive of a counter-attack when he had such extended lines of communication was, in all likelihood, the reason for his instruction that the English withdrawal should be comprehensive: that all divisions of his army should retire together. However, the Kentish men refused to leave, though he sent back *seven* orders as he retired, telling them to fall back. Now, in response, 'the force' of East Anglia fell upon the Kentish contingent and ealdormen Sigulf and Sigelm, Eadwold the king's thane, abbot Cenulf and many others were slain. The Danes also lost heavily, including Eohric their King, Ætheling Æthelwold (the cause of all the strife) and Byrtsige son of Ætheling Beornoth, with many others. There was great slaughter on all sides and the Danes lost the most, but they held the field.

The *Chronicle* then goes on to say that the men of Kent next fought an engagement at Holme, just south of Peterborough, but we cannot be certain that these two engagements were not one and the same. It seems unlikely that the men of Kent would venture so far yet again and for no known purpose. Now Holme is on the old course of the Nene and close to Whittlesley Mere, therefore on the ancient route from Ely to Peterborough. Therefore, I suggest, the purpose of Edward's excursion to Anglia was to free the captives and having done this, probably at Ely, he ordered a retirement, 'mission accomplished'. The men of Kent, however, keen for vengeance, rowed and marched along the Nene. The likely outcome is that at Holme they met Danes from Lindsey, while behind them Danes from Thetford, emboldened by the king's withdrawal, marched westwards and so the Kentish contingent was trapped and suffered for their indiscipline. Yet overall the campaign had been a victory for Edward and his main force, resulting in the freeing of many captives.

The direct line of Kentish retreat would now have been the old Roman Road going south from Peterborough to St Albans and then to London, and maybe it was during this retreat that the Kentish men lost ealdorman Æthelwulf, abbot Virgilus and the mass priest Grimbold. After this we may suspect other minor skirmishes but we are told nothing more until 906, when 'peace was fastened' at Tiddingford, both with the Anglians and the Northumbrians.

However in 909, presumably in response to further raiding, King Edward sent the Wessex and Mercian armies together into the north, presumably into what was then an enlarged Northumbria including Yorkshire, where they ravaged men and cattle and killed many Danes in the space of five weeks. He was now on the initiative and pushing northwards, and in August 910, just for good measure, he seems to have caught them out raiding again and gained a resounding victory over the Danes at Tettenhall (Wolverhampton). They had heard that King Edward was in Kent with 100 ships and, perhaps supposing that his entire force was the 3,000 men or so in them, the Northumbrians thought themselves safe to re-invade Mercia. Gathering together both the Wessex and Mercian armies, King Edward overtook them and caught them off guard as they retired. He put them to flight, killing a large number including King Healfden, eorls Ohter and Scurfa and the holds Athulf, Benesing and Anlaf the Swart.

'A great force' also came from Brittany and ravaged on the Severn, but (it is said) most of them died. Æthelflæd, lady of Mercia and Alfred's daughter, built a burgh at 'Bromesbyrig'.

In the following year, 911, Æthelred of the Mercians died and so King Edward received London and Oxford, with all the lands he had governed. Now began a major burgh-building programme, to add to those already in commission. So Lady Æthelflæd built one at 'Scergeat', in 912, and another at Bridgnorth, which would cover the Shropshire borderlands. King Edward, meanwhile, ordered one built to the north of Hertford, which covered the rivers Maran, Beane and Lea, and in summer he went to Maldon (on the Blackwater), probably already important for the export of cloth,[5] and ordered a burgh there, though it may not actually have been completed? Probably for the same strategic and economic reason and to cover the river routes and the London road, he ordered another to be built to the north-west of Maldon at Witham. At the same time, a second burgh was built at Hertford on the south side of the Lea (probably Hertfordingbury). With the king now in command of the waterways both to the east and to the west of their shire, many of the Danish-dominated inhabitants submitted to him instead. In this way he secured the southern borders of the Anglian Danelaw.

In 913, Lady Æthelfled built a burgh at Tamworth early in the summer and then another at Stafford. Now the northern borders of Mercia were protected from the Danes. The following year another was built at 'Eadersbyrig', Eddisbury, an Iron Age hill fort south-west of Northwich, overlooking the Cheshire Plain and Delamore Forest and which would, alike, cover the Mersey (against Irish slavers) *and* the Welsh border. Then she built one at Warwick, which would cover Watling Street running from Chester to Lichfield, Leicester and London; each end was therefore in the Danelaw but the burghs protected English interests in the centre and denied its use to the Danes. Danish raiding routes were being systematically blocked.

After Easter 'the force' rode out from Northampton and Leicester, breaking the truce, and killed many men at Hook Norton, south-west of Banbury, and thereabouts, thereby bypassing Warwick to the south and travelling by land. Yet when the inhabitants awoke to their peril they seem to have ambushed the raiders as they made for Luton, perhaps heading for the Wash. We are told that not only did they put the Danes to flight, they rescued all whom the Danes had captured as well as the horses and a great part of their weapons, which sounds as though they were driving a slave gang to Haddenham (Ely) for export. 'The force' had obviously covered a considerable distance in this raid and it had taken time to gather an opposing army, but because no one made the mistake of acting alone and prematurely, the Danes were well and truly bested and their captives released.

Though the Danelaw had been given a bloody nose, the Danes over the water, in Brittany, had ambitions and needs of their own and planned a separate expedition. In 914, a 'great force' of ships under earls Ohter and Hraold again rounded the Lizard to enter the Severn and then set about slaving along the Welsh coast, entering the Black Mountains and also south-west Herefordshire, formerly the kingdom of Ceolwulf and now, through his alliance with Alfred, probably a Wessex territory. They captured bishop Gyfeiliog here and carried him off but King Edward ransomed him for 40 pounds, wisely staying his hand (it seems) until the bishop had been returned. Then, when the raiders moved inland and left the river, the men of Hereford and Gloucester struck, put them to flight, killed eorl Hraold and Ohter's brother and drove the survivors into a trap where they could besiege and starve them. This sounds as though they were trapped on the river, perhaps at somewhere like Symond's Yat where it could be blocked, by felling trees or by ships, and with both banks patrolled by Englishmen. Once again the Danes had made the mistake of marching inland, even though using a waterway, so they now gave hostages and made promise to sail away if they were allowed to pass.

The king did not trust their promises and along the south bank of the Severn, from the mouth of the Avon (near Bristol) to west of the Cornish border, he set patrols to watch for them. Sure enough, they next attempted raids to the east of Watchet (Minehead, 'Mynydd') and Porlock, both on the north coast of Exmoor and both raids at night. What could they hope to gain here in such an apparently impoverished landscape? Well the Brendon Hills have been mined since at least Roman times for iron and copper (and associated gold) so the obvious reason for the raids would be to capture good, strong labourers or even metals. Danes had been here in 836, almost certainly for the same reason. This time, on both occasions, the only Danes to escape were the few who managed to swim to their ships standing offshore, the rest were slaughtered.

The ships then removed themselves to Steepholme Island, a limestone island in the Severn estuary well offshore and with only limited beaching on which to strand their vessels, for 'the force' was now too depleted to risk the Wessex shore again. Here they remained, living off seabirds and fish until these ran out and men began to starve. Having no hope of landing on the Wessex shore in the autumn, they finally sailed for Dyfed and then for Ireland, presumably with some sort of Welsh cargo to sell.

Notes

1. Anne Savage (ed.), *The Anglo-Saxon Chronicles*, p.112.
2. Ibid.
3. For a discussion of the Fleam Dyke, Devil's Ditch, Icknield Way and Wool/Worsted Street see T. Malim (et al) 'New Evidence on the Cambridgeshire Dykes and Worsted Street Roman Road' in *Proceedings of the Cambridgeshire Antiquarian Society* vol. 85 (1997), pp.27–122.
4. Q.v. Wright (2020), p.53.
5. Q.v. Wright (2014), pp.373–380, also (2020), pp.175–177. It certainly was a thriving industry in 1066–86 and had been in Roman times and also (apparently) in Offa's reign, so it seems reasonable to presume continuity.

Chapter Thirteen

Unity of Purpose

Now King Edward was free to turn his attention elsewhere, so before Martinmass (10–11 November) 914, he took his army to Buckingham and built burghs on either side of the river Ouse, so blocking the route Danes could take from Bedford and St Neots' westwards into Mercia. Seeing this, eorl Thurcytel and other men of influence agreed to accept Edward as their lord and in this way he pacified Bedford and parts of Northamptonshire. Consequently, the following year, King Edward went to Bedford in November and took command of the town, ordering a burgh to be built on the south side of the Ouse.

Nevertheless, in 916 there was trouble on the Welsh border when abbot Ecgbriht 'the blameless' was ambushed and killed, together with his escort, before midsummer. Immediately, Æthelflæd sent troops into Wales and they stormed 'Brecenan mere' (Brecon-mere) and captured thirty-four wives, one of whom was the king's own wife! As this place is styled 'mere' it seems certain that this Mercian raid targeted the royal 'crannog', an artificial island on the north side of Llangorse Lake, which is a large body of water between the Black Mountains and the Brecon Beacons. Such a raid required tremendous intelligence work and local knowledge, and the fact that it was mounted within three nights of the abbot's murder puts this episode on a par with an SAS raid. The capture of these women would have been a tremendous prestige blow to the king of Brecknock (for kings cannot afford to 'lose face'), and it also tells us of the quality of some contingents of the Wessex–Mercian army.

Meanwhile, Edward returned to Maldon to witness the completion of the burgh he had founded in 912. Then he allowed eorl Thurcytel to go over to Frankland with whatever men would serve with him. If this sounds strange, well, better to export England's troubles than to increase them through moral scruples, as a pragmatist might say. Next year, in 917, the king ordered burghs at Towcester and 'Wigingamere' (Wigginton, by Hook Norton) to be occupied and strengthened, so covering his northern border against raids from Northampton and simultaneously covering the rivers Tove and Swere. Clearly he expected renewed activity and conflict, and in this he was not disappointed.

That same summer, 'the force' in Northampton, in Leicester and beyond, 'broke the peace' by descending on Towcester. The occupiers held their burgh and when a relief column arrived the Danes retreated, but not for long. Raiding by night, they seized both men and cattle between Bernwood Forest and Aylesbury, that is from just north-east of Oxford and eastwards into the Chilterns, a heavily wooded area. In later centuries this area became famous for its woodland 'bodgers' and workers, so in 917 it may already have carried a population of 'forestry workers' as well as having woodland intercommonings (grazing) for cattle. Once again, the obvious assets were captives and provisions, 'livestock' with which to work the Danelaw holdings.

Simultaneously, another force from Huntingdon and East Anglia took the field, leaving their burgh at Huntingdon but building another, stronger burgh at Tempsford, which was nearer to Bedford and well south of Huntingdon and which gave them command of the Ouse. Each side was now playing a game of chess based on fortifications. Next they moved on Bedford, but the garrisons there sallied forth and put the Danes to flight. Now the Anglian and the Mercian Danes combined and surrounded 'Wigingamere'. They rustled the cattle outside but they could not win the burgh itself and so they retired, once again before relief could arrive and trap them between two fires.

Now the Mercian English became enraged and all the nearest garrisons (and others) combined to make a determined attack on Tempsford. After besieging the place, they took it, killed the Danish 'king' and also eorls Toglos and Manna, Manna's son and his brother, so capturing the place and many of its garrison. The fate of these captives is not recorded. As autumn approached, the men of Kent, Surrey and Essex also combined and marched north to Colchester, still a walled Roman town and on the edge of the Danelaw, besieged and took it and killed all within who could not flee over the walls.

Intent on revenge, the Danes of Anglia now recruited Vikings, warriors from other parts of Scandinavia, mercenary 'ship men', to help them. This force descended on Maldon, but the town was stoutly defended until a relief column arrived, when the defenders and the relievers together pursued the fleeing Danes and ship men, killing many hundreds. In the same autumn, King Edward took his West Saxon army to Passenham, north-east of Buckingham, and there covered the Ouse route and the Tove, while Towcester burgh was reinforced with a stone wall. Seeing this renewed activity, the Danes of Northampton, under eorl Thurferth, even those as far away as the Welland (Market Harborough), were dismayed and submitted to King Edward. Now the West Saxon levy 'in the field' returned home and their replacements took over, occupying and rebuilding the burgh at

Huntingdon. The Danelaw frontier was gradually but surely being pushed northwards as Wessex–Mercia increased its hold over the Danish settlers, bringing them under royal control and law, so the people around Huntingdon now submitted as well.

The year 917 had been a whirlwind one, but yet, even before Martinmass, the king marched his troops south-east to Colchester, probably using the Iron Age road known as Wool Street from Cambridge to Colchester,[1] and there he repaired and restored the burgh. We have already seen that men from Essex had been part of the besieging force here, earlier in the year, and now those inhabitants who had been under Danish rule, and also men from Anglia, submitted themselves to Edward. The 'force' at Cambridge then chose him as its lord and protector, so that many men now promised to keep the peace on both land and sea.

Meanwhile, the Lady Æthelflæd had taken Derby in the summer, though not without losses. In the following year, 918, she took Leicester peacefully and the greater part of 'the force' that was there accepted her overlordship. Then an embassy came from York with pledges and oaths but, before midsummer, Æthelflæd died at Tamworth and her body was taken to Colchester for burial. It is said to be in St Peter's Church on North Hill and was probably brought there by the king and in order to offer secure interment, for he rode to Tamworth on the news of her death. He had actually been at Stamford when the news had come to him, building a burgh on the south side of the River Welland, so that all the peoples of these northern boroughs would in turn submit to him.

After accepting the acclaim of the Mercians, he also received assurances from the Welsh Kings, Hywel, Clydog and Idwal. He occupied and restored the burgh at Nottingham and garrisoned it with both English *and* Danes, as *all* the peoples of Mercia had now submitted to him. In 919, he advanced to Thelwall (Warrington) and ordered another burgh to be built, and also ordered a Mercian force to go to Manchester, then part of Northumbria, in order to repair and garrison its burgh. The following year, he took troops to Nottingham to build a burgh on the south side of the Trent with a bridge between the two burghs, then he went to Bakewell, in the Peaks, and ordered yet another burgh. The Northumbrian Scots, the Strathclyde Welsh, English, Danes and Norse inhabitants, all swore him as lord and in 921 he built a burgh at 'Cledemutha' (Ruddlan).[2]

The success of Edward and of Alfred before him had hung to a considerable degree on the use of burghs or forts (though some had already been in existence), thereby forming a foundation on which these two English kings could build. Some authorities have claimed that the forts built by the Danes have survived as towns rather better than the English ones, but I

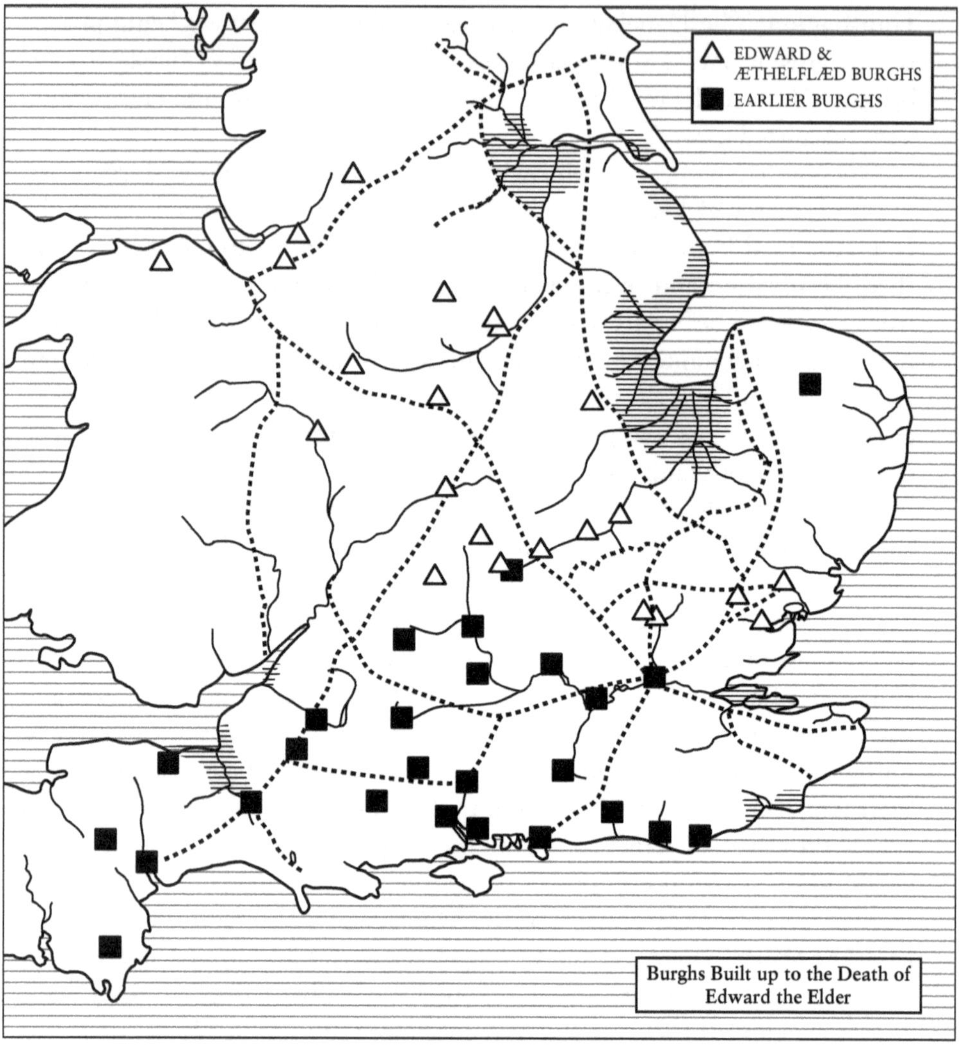

Map 4: Burghs Built up to the Death of Edward the Elder.

cannot agree.³ I think the evidence is conclusively otherwise and that such an assertion is difficult to prove for indeed many of the places they chose had earlier, pre-Danish roots and many places changed hands at regular intervals. Moreover, it ignores the obvious success of places such as Winchester, Oxford and Colchester, while the example given at Stamford fails to consider the occupation of *both* banks of the river ordered by Edward the Elder. The implication that only the Danish burghs later became 'economic centres of the country', places that then helped to develop road networks, itself ignores pre-existing and sometimes ancient communications networks, including possible earlier commercial foci. Sometimes it is just too easy (or even fashionable) to attribute 'progress' to an influx of Scandinavians, who

> **Map 4: Burghs Built up to the Death of Edward the Elder.**
> We can see particular emphasis laid on the control of road and river routes and that Edward's and Æthelflæd's burghs were designed to push the Danelaw border regularly eastwards.

were not settlers, and in the process deny due credit to English kings and institutions, as we have seen with King Alfred's campaigns.

This mythology of the ethnically 'superior' Vikings is compounded by the continued repetition of place name evidence and the linking of these places to chance archaeological discoveries. Hybrid artefacts and influences spreading northwards from Jorvic do not *prove* a saturation of the landscape by incomers, only that there were some seigneurial steadings. Evidence of weaving at such isolated places only tells us that largely peripatetic warriors had slaves to produce textiles. The introduction of superior potting in the tenth century does not *have* to rely on Viking know-how, much less does it distinguish an industrial revolution. Neither pottery nor the reuse of scrap metal kick-start a major economic improvement, for had it not been for the wealth of England in the first place 'the great heathen army' would never have invaded. They did not come to instruct but to plunder. Centres such as Stamford, Thetford, Lincoln and Torksey made pottery because they had no local wood tradition, no turning or coopering available in woodland-sparse landscapes. Moreover, their pottery tradition came from France and not from Scandinavia. Neither were they near to metal mining areas.

Place name scholars have placed particular emphasis on the '-by' element in place names (pronounced 'bee') as proof positive of Scandinavian occupation renaming landscapes, though why they should have done this has never been explained. Ken Buckingham has pointed out that such elements are most evidenced in Lincolnshire (though spreading out elsewhere) but otherwise are *only* predominant in Uppsala Laen (Sweden) and Ostjaelland (Denmark), and do not occur in Normandy, Ireland or Iceland, being sparse even in Finland, all of them Viking colonies. There is little enough chronicled Viking activity in Lincolnshire and few such linguistic elements to be found in Viking Anglia. The lack of such elements in Northumberland, yet their sporadic occurrence in Durham, would seem to mirror the old division between Bernicia and Deira, which by the Viking period had become one, as Northumbria.[4]

Indeed, a recent study of the genetic structure of the British population concluded that there was 'no clear genetic evidence of the Danish Viking occupation and control of a large part of England ... suggesting relatively limited import of DNA from Danish Vikings'.[5] Margaryn concluded that: 'Viking Age Danish-like ancestry in the British Isles cannot be distinguished from that of the Angles and Saxons.'[6]

This caused Buckingham to observe that Scandinavian descendants therefore existed in England *prior* to the Viking Age and that the 'bee' names of coastal Cheshire and south Lancashire are very unlikely to have been provided by colonisers from Ireland, where such names are *not* found! As the DNA evidence suggests that both Saxon and Danish groups arrived in England in different areas, are we looking at Danish Angles rather than Danish Vikings? If the Angles came from Denmark, then (as he puts it) looking for later arrivals would be 'like looking for white paint on a white canvas'.[7] Such an explanation certainly helps us to understand how those pirates who now chose to settle could so easily influence the residual populations of the Danelaw they chose to inhabit.

Edward the Elder died at Farndon (Newark) in July 924, apparently soon after supressing a Welsh and Mercian revolt, and his son Ælfweard died sixteen days after him at Oxford. The sudden deaths of both these men suggests either a contagion or battle traumas, but the *Chronicle* is silent on this matter. Both were buried at Winchester, the ancient capital of Wessex. Now Æthelstan of Wessex was chosen king amid some political infighting and delay, but finally with Mercian support, so supplanting his brother, Eadwine. It was perhaps a dubious beginning to a glorious reign and Æthelstan gave his sister as wife to King Sihtric of Northumbria in 926, in order to cement the alliance made by his father. Then, when Sihtric died in the following year, he inherited the Kingdom of Northumbria, so it had been an astute move. Now all the kings of England came under his rule and gave pledges and oaths at Eamont Bridge (near Penrith). A dynasty of conquerors had now and finally created an England, a unified England and an England sworn to Christianity. The problem was now to maintain them both and in 934 Æthelstan seems to have dealt with a Viking force at York, which invasion probably spurred King Constantine II of Scotland to march on Northumbria, so breaking his treaty oaths. In this way the scene was now set for a famous reputation and also for a very famous, but tantalisingly enigmatic, battle.

Notes

1. O. Rackham's *Illustrated History ...*, pp.120–121.
2. Q.v. *Medieval Archaeology* 31 article by J. Manley, K. Brassil, S. Browne, P. Courtney, E. Healey, P. Rowley-Conwy, pp.13–46 (online 18.5.2016) excavated 1979–80.
3. Christopher Taylor, *Roads and Tracks of Britain* (1979), p.97.

4. Ken Buckingham 'The Mystery of the 'Bees' in *Wiðowinde* 198 (2021), pp.17–24.
5. S. Leslie, B. Winney, G. Hellenthal et al, 'The Fine-Scale Genetic Structure of the British Population', *Nature* 519 (2015), pp.309–314.
6. A. Margaryan, D.J. Lawson, M. Sikara et al, 'Population Genomics of the Viking World' *Nature* 585 (2020), pp.390–396.
7. Buckingham, 'The Origins of Danish Settlement in England' in *Wiðowinde* 194 (2020), pp.24–29.

Chapter Fourteen

Problems of Integration

Ultimately success had come from momentum. Alfred had created the will to fight and the machinery that made opposition to the Danish hordes possible, he had then converted that will and opposition to the offensive and to relentless pursuit of his enemies. The morale that this generated both sustained his troops and dismayed his enemies, and this, in turn, gave an aura of divine intervention that fed the psychological mindset on either side. For the Anglo-Saxons it was a further pre-condition that reconciliation with any enemy would include their proselytization and their adherence to laws framed within a Christian idiom, which would make ultimate unity, or at least fusion of ethnicities, inevitable, whatever the temporary disappointments on the way.

Yet this faith involved more than lip service or a belief in magical powers, it required that the enemy should become absorbed into the developing consciousness of the English kingdom and especially their changing attitude to slavery, or thraldom. As we have seen, the underlying motivation of the Danes had been the slave trade, both domestic and international, and this, in turn, had generated a predictable and opposite reaction in the English. Yes, the English also believed in slavery *but* as a condition resulting from criminal actions or economic misfortunes, but *not* the haphazard and arbitrary will of lawless 'heathens' driven by profit and ideas of racial superiority.

It seems to have been this more than anything else that drove the English to fight back. The Danes were *not* seeking land, but it did become the substitute when hacksilver ran out. Ransoms were sometimes sought, for important captives or even for holy books, but the *Chronicle* makes a point of telling us of captives being rescued and most of the places the Danes latterly attacked offered little prospect of loot.[1] We should also note that whilst some of the Alfredan burghs, according to the Burghal Hidage, were modest outposts – what later ages would call 'castles' – the larger ones made generous internal allowance of space. Was this individual space for warriors alone? I think not. No, rather I think it was allowance for refugees, potential captives (slaves) that dictated this generosity. That these burghs also probably served as commercial centres, encouraging local commerce and markets, should not detract from their ability, in need, to shelter refugees from their surrounding farmsteads and vills.

Burghs were the essential nails that held the strategic landscape together as well as providing tactical refuges. They also protected and encouraged developing local economies and became centres for regional mints. Given the limited technical knowledge of the age, a well-defended burgh was a sure defence against surprise attack and we have no references to prolonged sieges. Neither side was equipped to stay in the field indefinitely and no doubt refugees took in all the provisions they could either drive or carry, leaving attackers without sustenance. In addition, if a relief column appeared, attackers would be caught between 'the hammer and the anvil'. We have seen references to this. Unlike the later Norman 'castles', these burghs were not usually sally ports for mobile field units or refuges for the rich but communal refuges and, as such, required large bodies of men to man their walls. In doing this, in concentrating rather than scattering local populations in the face of a threat, the burghs provided themselves with garrisons but also with the will to resist.

Though the elite troops on either side could afford to 'defend their men with walls' (armour), there were very many who could not afford armour, so 'defending the walls with men', that is providing cover for such unarmoured levies behind a palisade, was a very secure and reassuring, as well as an essential, policy. Walls offer the unarmoured man considerable personal defence. It was therefore in the interests of the English to maximise the number of free men, men qualified to bear arms, another incentive to manumission. Consequently, there were both prospective (religious) and immediately practical considerations at work to reduce the slave populations in Wessex and Mercia, though the culture of the Danelaw relied absolutely on thraldom. For Danes, and for Scandinavians (proper), their hope of attracting further and local recruits in England would depend on demonstrating continued success, such men being ne'r-do-wells, brigands and 'wolf's heads', renegades from English societies and culture. Danish reversals would discourage such recruitment by the Danelaw.

Hatred of the Danes certainly ran deep, for even after the Danelaw had, nominally, come under English kings, the epithet used to describe the hated enemy continued to be 'Danes' rather than 'Vikings'. So we discover a number of traditions linking the flaying alive of Danes to the coverings found on some church doors, though one suspects that these were and are apocryphal. Rochester had such a door covered in human skin, for Pepys saw it in 1661, so did Westminster Abbey, East Thurrock, Copford and Hadstock churches. Well now, Copford church was not founded until *c.*1130 and while Hadstock has been claimed as Cnut's minster, founded *c.*1020, the door in question has been dendro-dated a little later, to between 1040 and 1070 (possibly 1034–42).² Although skin fragments from this door were once ascribed to a 'blond man' by a pathologist, modern archaeological opinion favours cow hide. In all these cases, the iron strapwork was nailed on over the hide, so firmly restricting dating to the date of the door's manufacture. Nevertheless, such traditions, which persisted for centuries to come, were wish fulfilments eloquently declaring popular feeling against the Danes and all who aided them, a useful polarisation and one that religious chroniclers were not slow to develop for their own purposes.

So the problem for Edward's successors was five-fold. In the first place, not only had peace to be maintained, between England and the Danelaw, but the wounds of old hatreds and vendettas had to have time to heal. There were also cultural (ethnic) differences as basic as different ways of measuring land – the English in 'hides', the Danes in 'carucates' – but particularly there were differences in legal systems, yet it was now essential that English penal laws should run in common over all territories. Christianisation certainly helped in this respect, and although not susceptible to syncretism, it does seem that the Anglo-Saxon Church was to some degree tolerant of older practices and beliefs when once they had been absorbed into Christian personifications and practices, so it was just as well that the older Germanic (Saxon) gods were so similar to the Scandinavian pantheon. It was also essential to maintain the machinery of state, as we might begin to term it, which provided the sinews of war: men, money and munitions. In addition to all this, the king had to be alive to those envious and rapacious eyes watching from Ireland, Scotland, Wales and Scandinavia, watching for an opportunity.

Although we have no certain knowledge of Edward, Alfred had been manifestly well educated for a king in his age. Not only did he make his own translations and collect and publish a comprehensive collection of laws, he perfectly understood that 'it is not what kings do for laws, but what laws do for kings'.³

> *'Ac wel me wot vor to conne boþe wel it is*
> *Vor þe more þat a man can, þe more wurþe he is.*'⁴

So not only did a knowledge of legal wisdom confirm Divine bestowal of kingship, through apparent Divine revelation, the pursuits of knowledge and learning also, in the eyes of the world, increased the worthiness of any man wielding power in England. The encouragement of such a perception was very much in the interests of the Church, an interesting fusion of practical polities.

In addition to his personal scholarship, Alfred seems to have created what later ages would describe as a chancery and exchequer, and scholars describe this as the Winchester School, but then proceed to dismiss it as less important than the monastery-based, monastic schools because it did not turn out religious works.[5] Nevertheless, the records of state (as we might term them) were kept somewhere and Winchester had them at a later date, it also had the skills required to collate surveys and financial information.[6] I suggest that *this* was the Winchester School, for monastic schools evidence no such practical expertise. Somewhere those foundations of vernacular expertise were laid that finally culminated in the unique Domesday Survey(s), and if not at the Old Palace in Winchester, then from whence did such accomplishment arise? Not from any monastic school or house, that is certain, or Domesday could never have been compiled for in 1086 it relied absolutely on older English records *and* English units. *Domesday Book* was not a 'French' creation.[7]

It has been proposed that Edward the Elder rather than Alfred commissioned documents such as the (rare survival) Burghal Hidage and possibly the Tribal Hidage. If he did, one still needs to acknowledge that the information that the latter contains, concerning tribal lands that existed long before the creation of Mercia, let alone Wessex, was kept somewhere until this date or it would have been lost by *c*.900. I have proposed, elsewhere, that the final Tribal Hidage document is, in fact, a conflation of three documents, the first of which certainly was *not* remotely connected even to Alfred's period. As to the Burghal Hidage, we should note that its list does not include many burghs known to have been built by Edward and so I, for one, suggest that it is Alfredan in origin.

What we have always overlooked, of course, is that which we could not see, the intangible achievement, or achievements, which even contemporaries could not recognise because it, or they, did not figure in their contemporary solidarities: such things are barely recognised even today. No body of peoples, no kingdom, can be successfully unified in defence without an adequate social and economic structure and this combination (for they always go in tandem, the one giving support to any weakness in the other) is the most difficult element of all to evidence, especially with so little surviving (let alone reliable) documentary material. Nevertheless, the necessary infrastructure and organisation must have been there for Alfred to have been able to forge such a successful war machine, and one that he could also hand on to his successor. The determination to resist slavery in particular, also the motivating of the rich and powerful, the organisation of taxes and currency (and the support of industry, including munitions), the establishment of defence works and standing forces; all these things would contribute and so, when success subsequently attends the defenders, morale and confidence in such measures are thereby reinforced throughout society.

And here we need to say something of the 'fyrd' system, the ancient obligation of all 'free' Anglo-Saxon men to defend *pro aris et focis*, for homestead and hearth. Writers such as Warren-Hollister have detailed the obligations of the 'great' (general) and the 'select' fyrds, the latter (of course) including the 'hearth companions' or bodyguard of 'hearth troops' of each major landholder.[8] The greater fyrd of all freemen and burghers, he has explained, was only obliged to serve for local defence, being legally able to return to their homes by nightfall and, if not, then entitled to be paid for their service. Yet we must also acknowledge that this greater fyrd included men of relatively lowly status, for someone had to labour building the burghs, and may it be that for this purpose the 'free' qualification might now have been extended? The select fyrd, on the other hand, had a tenurial obligation in addition to honour (and were subject to a much larger fine for defaulting) consequent upon a landholding qualification to serve as required. Whether this qualification centred on a five-hide unit (1,200 acres) or more I leave to scholastic debate, suffice it to say that these were the wealthier freemen and so the better armed. It is difficult to imagine these men digging ditches and ramparts and erecting palisades.

However, whatever the earlier nature of these obligations, it is inconceivable that outside the 'gentlemanly' world of internecine kingdom warfare, in the real and harsh world of destruction and slavery now pertaining, men of all degrees would not naturally defend their own *and* seek the support of others so to do. Provided they were led and fed, this new and *real* threat to society would see the great fyrd, the mass of men, prepared to take steps to eradicate the menace of invasion. To suggest that they would only fight if adequately rewarded and otherwise sit at home is another example of transposing the present onto the past. In Alfred's England there was no refuge, no state security, nowhere to run and hide: self-help supervened when there was no escape and self-help relied on joint action. Alfred's achievement was to lead and feed these men who had such fears, difficult in practical application but, when successful, ensuring mutual support.

So we begin to perceive that Alfred created a unique society, one fit for current purpose and different from the antique Anglo-Saxon model, one finally able to cope with contemporary demands, yet the maintenance of success depended on two things in particular, on continuity by a successor and on the enemy's continued adherence to a known paradigm, or set of operations. Alfred had successfully applied the Danish strategic paradigm to his own operations but a real advantage here was the local knowledge that English forces could bring to this model and their landscapes, whilst the Danes could only strike blindly from their bases in search of loot and slaves. We will see that with time Viking forces became better informed in this respect and so this English advantage accordingly diminished. The Alfredan defence machinery was finely tuned to a threat of known dimensions and manifestations, but it was not necessarily of universal application. It was certainly applicable to recent history but it was not necessarily a prospective strategy if a successful enemy could thereby encourage local recruits possessing local knowledge. We will come to this in due course. It is also rare for any succession to follow all the attributes and virtues of its predecessor, including the fiscal competence necessary to support such a complex combination of social and economic factors, but Edward at least seems to have built on his father's achievements.

In fact, Edward's overall strategy may itself have been more subtle than the *Chronicle* suggests, as Doctor Ryan has observed.[9] He seems to have had a military vision that saw beyond the simple proliferation of burghs and the absorption of their hinterlands. Ryan notes evidence of peace agreements in the law codes and, interestingly, evidence from Æthelstan's reign that Edward had even encouraged English thegns to purchase lands in Danelaw districts, an attempt at integration observed by Stenton and which surely led to a dilution of Danish laws and attitudes when the separate ethnographies were obliged to co-operate in everyday and rural matters. Victories such as Tettenhall, of course, would reinforce attitudinal changes but it is interesting to reflect that subtlety as well as force may have played a part, in due course, in the ultimate *modus vivendi* that followed.

Notes

1. For 'ransomed books' see the *Codex Aureus* (Stockholm/Canterbury).
2. *Saffron Walden Historical Journal* Nos 6 (2003) and 9 (2005), see saffronwaldenhistory@gmail.com.
3. Patrick Wormald 'Lex Scripta and Verbum Regis – Legislation and German Kingship from Euric to Cnut' in Sawyer and Woods, *Early Medieval Kingship* (1977), p.115.
4. Lines 7337–47, *Chronicle of Robert of Gloucester*, B.M. Cottonian ms. A xi, source *The Languages of England*, ed. W.A. Wright (1887).
5. M. Lapidge, 'Schools' in Lapidge et al. (eds) (1999 & 2001), pp.407–9; also Sean Miller, *Æthelstan*, p.16.
6. Q.v. Wright (2014), pp.113–31 & 346–7; Wright (2017), pp.162–4 & 175–6, also pp.87–103; also Wright 'English Surveyors and Surveys, the Extents of Norfolk in Domesday Book', *Wiðowinde* 176 (2015), pp.37–40; also Wright (2021).
7. Q.v. Wright (2014), pp.117–121: also Wright, *Raising the Dead* (2021).
8. Hollister, pp.25–31 in particular.
9. Higham and Ryan, op. cit. (2013 and 2015), pp.299–300. See also F.M. Stenton, *The Latin Charters of the Anglo-Saxon Period* (Oxford, 1955), p.30.

Chapter Fifteen

So to a Famous Victory

In 934, King Æthelstan invaded Scotland with both land and sea forces and, in revenge in 937, Norsemen from Ireland, under Olaf or Anlaf, and Scots under King Constantine seem to have decided to take him on in the north. At an unidentified place called 'Brunaburgh' 'King Athelstan, the lord of warriors, patron of heroes, and his brother too, Prince (Æthling) Edmund, won themselves eternal glory' leading a combined Mercian and West Saxon army.[1] 'The Scottish soldiers and the pirate host ("scipflotan") were doomed to perish.' What actually happened in 937 is largely a matter for conjecture and has (consequently) been debated extensively: the 'A' version of the *Chronicle* is sketchy on the important details. This is my interpretation of events.

King Constantine of Scotland made alliance with King Owain of Strathclyde to attack Northumbria and they passed this information to Olaf Guthfrithson in Ireland. The idea that they were in agreement to make one of them 'king of England' is a modern anachronism; most likely they anticipated rich pickings for all and they all intended to take slaves and extort tribute while the Scots and Strathclyde men would also gain territory to add to their kingdoms. So, by combining attacks they hoped to destroy the 'ever-victorious' joint Mercian and Wessex army once and for all. It had now, after all, become an impediment to everyone else's wealth generation and recreation.

Let us now follow this scenario. The northern, or 'Scots', force entered Northumbria and so King Æthelstan marched north to meet them. Meanwhile, Olaf's Vikings possibly landed from the Mersey, in the opinion of some historians, marching overland from west to east in order to take the English from the rear, so having Mercia at their mercy as they passed through eastwards to York. If this was their route then they did not need to join the Scottish alliance in order to strike southwards whilst the English army was pinned down to the east, so it seems unlikely. Moreover, if they had followed this route they would have needed to eliminate three Edwardian burghs covering the old Roman road and clearly designed to impede such expeditions from the Wirral before joining Ermine Street just outside York. On the other hand, and this is the landing I favour, they possibly sailed around Scotland to reach the Humber and, after landing, made the mistake of joining the Scots forces marching southwards overland along Ermine Street. Either way, the place named as 'Dingesmere' was most probably part of the Humber, or the adjacent marshy plain of the Went and the Aire that leads into the Humber and where Ermine Street anciently detoured to pass through the Roman fort of Danum, so avoiding a major river crossing.

Given intelligence of these incursions, Æthelstan now fell back and chose a location described as 'ymbe Brunaburg', that is *near to Brunaburg*. Opinion favours Barnsdale and I agree: a wild, part-wooded, part-waterlogged area, later termed 'forest', the site of 'Robin Hood's Well' today, maybe with the village of Hampole as its focus. Here, covered by the Barnsdale and Hatfield 'forests', we are just north of Doncaster and my assessment is that 'Brunaburgh' was Doncaster itself, with its ('Danum', possibly now 'Brun-danburgh'?) Roman fort, a location where an army could gather and camp whilst being supplied from its hinterland to the south. Northwest of Doncaster runs Roman Ridge, which is an elevated section of the Ermine Street detour, the most likely route southwards for the invaders and running through the 'forested' area, that is through an exposed (elevated) yet confining passage with dangerous topography.

To the west of Doncaster, it is supposed from Sheffield to Mexborough, in the past, ran and runs the Roman Rig, which also goes by the name of the Devil's Bank and the Dane's Bank, a useful earthwork obstacle and defence at that time covering Æthelstan's lines of communication and supply against any attack from the west. Where it ends the 'forests' formerly began and Ermine Street (Roman Ridge) intruded, so compelling an attacker from the north to choose this unfriendly approach. Meanwhile, to the north and north-east of Doncaster, there were (then) extensive wetlands where the 'forests' ended, now known as the Humber Peatlands, the highly convoluted course of the old River Idle thar wound around and doubled back among fens and the Goole and Thorne Moors, also the Don itself. These were very difficult wastelands to traverse without local knowledge and without an amphibious force and, even then, still wide open to guerrilla attacks. They also offered a poor prospect for any local supply of a large force, being sparsely populated.

Where this waste ended the Isle of Axholme began, a vast marshy, fenny stretch of eyots around one larger island (later to become, itself, a famous battle site), which at this date probably covered the 120,000 acres accorded it in 1066.[2] Once again, this was an impassable region and one tailing dismally into the Lincolnshire fens on the south side of the Humber estuary. Nevertheless, this begs the question, why did the Vikings take to the roads and join the Scots, abandoning their ancient reliance on ship transport and river routes? In the past they had entered the Trent from the Humber to penetrate down to Torksey and even to Gainsborough and Repton, so surely they knew this river very well? Or did they? As they were Irish Vikings they may not have known the old Danish routes so thoroughly and so perhaps they lacked confidence. Then there was Æthelstan's army to the west to consider and maybe other forces at Gainsborough; were they afraid of an attack from this quarter and felt they would be safer as part of a large army? Surely, had they entered the Trent, in order to bypass Doncaster, an English fleet entering the Humber could have trapped them: much safer to land the main Viking force near to the mouth of the Aire and then retire the fleet to the Humber estuary, where they would have sea room if attacked. After all, they would only retain skeleton crews.

However we analyse it, the decision to form a joint army on the basis that *les gros battalions sont toujours raison* (as it was later expressed) and so to abandon mobility and surprise, was not a wise one, much less was it imaginative. Yet it emphasises for us the important role played by the ancient roads: armies just did not embark on cross-country rambles! That is why the Scots came south along Ermine Street. Æthelstan had chosen his site well and chosen the tried and tested Alfredan model of burgh and marsh with wildland, a place both a fastness and yet an ideal base from which to strike at any enemy operating or passing nearby. Even if the enemy now made winter quarters at York, they would still be harassed and probably hard-pressed for supplies, and if they went past much further to the west, then he could cut their line of retreat to their ships and to the north part of Ermine Street, isolating them in unknown territory.

All that was left was for the Scots and Vikings to make a frontal attack on the gap between Mexborough and Barnsdale Bar, that is somewhere between the Dearne and the Went rivers, probably along Ermine Street (Roman Ridge), and it would still be dangerous topography of the English' choosing. An overwhelming attack by the joint (enemy) forces might (they might have supposed) force the English into the open. The Vikings knew these English strategies from past experience, whilst the Scots had probably traversed fairly empty country for a long way with their large forces, anticipating better supplies once over the Humber, so both contingents were now at a disadvantage in every way. They could not afford to hesitate.

The date of the battle has been placed in October (which would be the best time for an army to forage) and we know from the lay or poem that it commenced at daybreak, which sounds as if the English were ready and in position, waiting for their enemies to advance. Although much of the poem is formulaic, we are told that throughout the long passing of the day, West Saxons pressed on in troops *behind* their enemies, having broken their shield wall. They hewed the fleeing host *from behind*, suggesting a battlefield success around the middle of the day and, moreover, that it was so decisive that both Scots and Vikings fled with the English in 'hot trod', despatching all they could for as long as they had the strength. It suggests to me that the English had either occupied a good defensive position, exhausted their desperate foes and then counter-attacked, or that maybe they ambushed them strung out along the road; also that their then fugitive foes had difficulty negotiating their escape routes in a strange wilderness.

Many were slain by spears, which sounds as though they were despatched when down, and others were shot down. So thorough was the slaughter that 'five young kings lay dead upon the battlefield, by swords sent to their final sleep': the customary coup de grâce being to cut off a fallen opponent's head. 'Likewise seven of Anlaf's eorls and countless of his host, both Scots and seamen.'[3] Anlaf/Olaf fled, starving and with every hand against his wretched refugees, which sounds like a lengthy pursuit, and somehow regained his ship, though with only a small, blood-spattered and gory ('dreory') retinue, so back to Dublin 'with shameful hearts'. Constantine also fled, leaving his son dead upon the field with other friends and kinsmen. *'Ne weorð wæl mare, on þis ëiglande, æfre gieta, folces gyfylled, beforan, þissum'* – 'nor has there on this island been ever yet a greater number slain.' I think we may account this as a total victory and also a signal one.

My own suspicion is that the Vikings had entered from the Humber, though most historians claim a Wirral landing. Due to the, then, almost impossible territory to the south of the Humber, navigable and traversable only with local knowledge, they then decided to rendezvous on land with the approaching northern forces by landing on the north side of the Humber to pick up the Ermine Street direct route over the soggy (but not impassable) Holme–Spalding moors. Arriving at Market Weighton, they could then take the west-sou'-west old (Roman) road to Castleford, crossing the Derwent and the Ouse and so meeting the Scots at Ermine Street (detour) just north of Barnsdale Forest and the Roman Ridge. By 1086, there were two ferries here, one at Ferriby (for Ermine Street) and another at Barton-upon-Humber, so 'terra firma' was certainly available at these places on the north bank of the Humber.

This overland approach was a mistake, one mirroring the events of 893–4, for the 'ship men' always functioned best when immediately able to retreat to their ships and worst when they elected to travel overland and over unknown territory. In a world devoid of maps it was impossible to move without local knowledge and the best prospect was, therefore, to follow an established 'herepath', such as Ermine Street, in order to advance with any certainty at the head of a marauding force, unless one was following and could follow

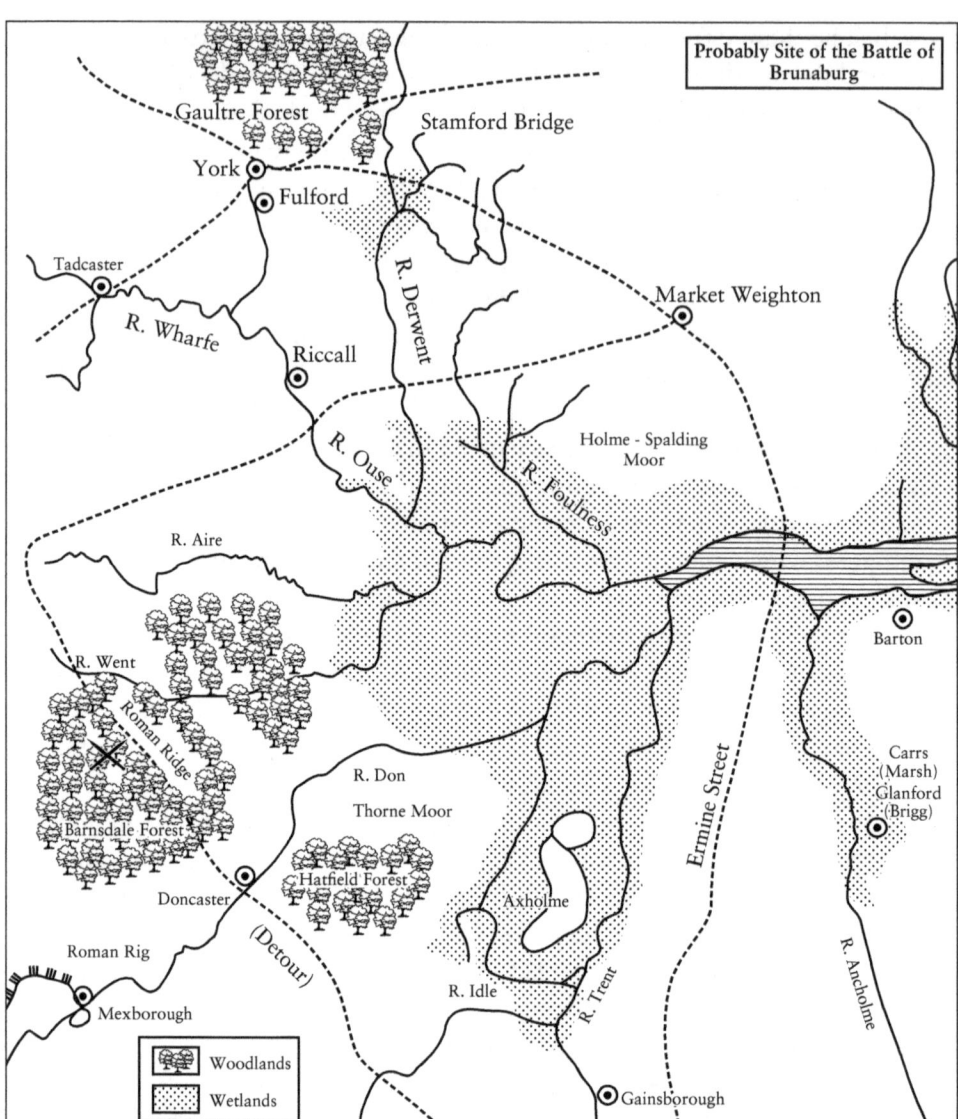

Map 5: Probable Site of the Battle of Brunaburg.

the course of a river. In this case, the now deep-seated hatred of Scots and of Vikings, even (no doubt) hatred shared by some apprehensive Danelaw settlers, would ensure that no local co-operation was available. Frightfulness is its own worst enemy for it creates refugees rather than collaborators. Historians who propose an ethnic bond between all Scandinavian races at this date are imposing a modern and an idealised fantasy onto the past.

The place name 'Dingesmere' is itself a suggestive inclusion. It has been suggested that it could be interpreted as 'Dung-mere' and this would equate with 'Foul-ness', the River Foulness's valley of ancient wetlands south-

> **Map 5: Probable Site of the Battle of Brunaburg.**
> Note that the topography would oblige a joint army coming from the north along the Ermine Street detour to follow the Roman Ridge through Barnsdale Forest with no real possibility of deviating to either flank. Following Ermine Street proper over the Humber would have required ferrying and leaving the army in two halves, always a dangerous expedient, especially in wetlands, so the detour is the likely choice.

west of what is now Market Weighton. It is not improbable that refugees fleeing along the River Went and attempting to escape northwards or to the Humber could then have been driven east, seeking to retrace their route on the old (Roman) road but fearing to follow an obvious course all the way, so they fell into the trap of following the Foulness. Strangers would not know that this river valley (passing north of modern Goole and down to the Humber) only delivered them into the marshy wastes of the Aire, Went and Ouse confluence, with marshlands on the north and south banks even *if* they reached the Humber. Not a place to be at a wet time of year: caught like 'rats in a trap'! Other and Viking refugees may have attempted to travel even further east and to traverse the confluence of the Don and the Trent north of the Isle of Axholme and then the River Ancholme, in order to arrive at Barton-upon-Humber and Castledyke. Perhaps this is where Anlaf/Olaf made his escape back to his ship after a desperate trek? Could Read's Island (formerly Hessle Sand) perhaps, have provided a convenient strand for his fleet when they arrived in the Humber?

The aspect of north Lincolnshire, along the south bank of the Humber estuary, was also exceedingly marshy and fenny, even by 1086, making it unattractive to land operations. Of this strip of land in 1086, perhaps less than one-third of it was farmed in any way and most of the marshy wilderness went unrecorded. In the tenth century it may have been even less attractive. Similarly, facing it, the southern parts of the opposite Yorkshire wapentakes in 1086 were also largely fenny wastes, apart from the North Ferriby foothold where Ermine Street continued north-westwards. Hessle Wapentake had only 22 per cent arable land over six of her southern estates, the majority being at one place, Kirk Ella. To the east of Hessle Wapentake, Weldon Wapentake only managed 12 per cent; the estates of Elloughton and Brantingham, which covered the southern Foulness ('Dingsmere') valley and mire, ploughed only 20 and 9 per cent respectively, whilst Welton, Wouldby and Ellerker ploughed nothing at all in 4,305 acres of terrain! These were desperate wastes to enter for all but the most experienced of local marsh men, perilous in the extreme to strangers.

I hope this strategic overview may have provided readers with some more tangible flesh for the sparse tactical details that survive. The landscape has had to be (of necessity) somewhat tentatively reconstructed, given the immense changes made to both the topography and the economy of this area from the seventeenth century onwards. River capture and drainage have materially altered the landscapes on either side of the Humber but by combining various sources and, in particular, Professor Sheppard's detailed study with old maps I hope I have provided a reasonable overview.[4]

As is so often the case, the rich and powerful, deeming themselves immune to normal sanctions, may prove themselves fickle when it comes to loyalty. Such a man, it seems, was Wulfstan, Archbishop of York, presumably appointed under Æthelstan in 931 and for the next four years a party to the attestations of his royal charters.[4] Then for a space he seems to have left court, leading to the suspicion that he was implicated in this northern campaign against the king, possibly also receiving Olaf Guthfrithson at York when he returned in 939. Of course, the English Church was, by now, on its knees and pragmatism might have appeared more attractive than martyrdom or, at best, to being homeless and penniless. His treachery will figure in our tale of conflict from now on.

In October 940, King Æthelstan passed away and the ætheling Edmund, 18 years old, succeeded him. The Northumbrians immediately proved false to their pledges and chose Olaf as their king, sanctioned (as I have said) by Wulfstan. The *Chronicle*, in its encomium to Edmund, says that even the settled Danes had long been under the Norseman's rule, forced and in chains, in heathen slavery, but that Edmund now released the 'five boroughs' and extended his power to the Whitwell Gap, that is to the area of Sheffield and the River Humber. But the old king was now dead and as Olaf now had his local guides he yearned for revenge.

Notes

1. Lay of the Battle of Brunaburgh, q.v. Richard Hamer, *A Choice of Anglo-Saxon Verse*, pp.41–47 (after Campbell, 1938), (1970 & 1990); see also Rahul Gupta, 'The Battle of Brunanburgh' in *Wiðowinde* 193 (2020), pp.35–37.
2. Wright (2020), p.34 and note 13 thereto.
3. Hamer (after Campbell).
4. June A. Sheppard, *The Draining of the Marshlands of South Holderness and the Vale of York* (East Yorkshire Local History Society, 1966).
5. Simon Keynes in Lapidge et al. pp.492–3.

Chapter Sixteen

Revenge is Sweet

With his new population Olaf Guthfrithson had acquired local and even non-local guides. He also had a tame archbishop, a man who could remind the reticent that (according to the laws of Alfred) they owed duty and allegiance to whoever was king of Northumbria. Nevertheless, having received such a bloody nose in 937 he was in no hurry to make another mistake and it was not until 941 or 943 that he made his next move.[1]

Some historians always want to implant the present onto the past, it makes things easier to explain by providing now familiar concepts that are, nevertheless, anachronisms because they did not exist at the time. So we find 'nationalism' and 'national identity' propounded again and again, which then leads such writers to conclude that everyone wanted to be 'King of England', king of 'the nation'. Such ideas are fantasies, devoid of either logic or historical evidence. Olaf's move, when it came, was not aimed at Winchester or London, the seats of English kingship, but at Tamworth, seat of the Mercian kings. In this he was presumably (for no one can know for sure) intending to push his kingdom's borders south and west, so linking the Humber to the lands beyond the Mersea estuary, thus securing not only territory and thralls (slaves) but also secure export routes to the two most lucrative slave markets, Dublin (Ireland) and Scandinavia in general, markets to both the west and to the north-east.

What needs to be understood is that Northumbria was not just modern Northumberland but, instead, a much larger territory, 'Norþan-hymbra', that is 'north of the Humber'. It had been formed by the union of two earlier kingdoms, Deira and Bernicia, and at its maximum extent the new, joint, kingdom stretched from the Peak District across to the Mersey on the west and to the Humber on the east. To the north it even reached the Firth of Forth, though with what consistency or permanence is uncertain. The Danelaw division of England had reached up to cover Yorkshire by this time, with the Danish Kingdom of York (Northumbria) roughly covering the ancient area of Deira, and Northumbria (Durham and Bamburgh) to the north beginning to operate as a separate kingdom. If so this may have obstructed the Danes and prevented access to the slave-rich Pictish northlands and Strathclyde. By driving south from the Peak District to destroy Tamworth, Olaf was no doubt hoping to open up a route westwards to Shrewsbury and beyond, thus securing the lands south of the Mersey and opening up Wales to exploitation.

He stormed Tamworth and gained much booty and many captives, and in order to do this he had needed knowledge not only of roads but of the Trent–Tame route. King Edmund immediately responded and presumably cut the Danes' retreat along the Trent, either that or Olaf arrogantly sought to consolidate his occupation. Either way, he and archbishop Wulfstan were then forced by Edmund's response to quickly seek an alternative route to Leicester but found themselves unable to make a rapid escape. From here, instead of standing to fight, they escaped at night, presumably losing some of their force on the way to Edmund's men and maybe still finding themselves in a tight spot, for Olaf then sued for peace and friendship. Edmund made this conditional on baptism, sealed with the customary gifts, in 943.[2] The border was now set at Watling Street. Olaf Guthfrithson then retired homewards to undertake a raid on northern Northumbria (Durham) by way of consolation, a territory as independently minded then as it was to remain for centuries to come. Perhaps he was slaving for there was little else to gain in this kingdom. The position of the archbishop seems then to have become equivocal: if he did not object to taking non-Christian slaves may he have had no objection to Olaf seeking them in Scotland? Here, somewhere on the borders, Olaf Guthfrithson met his death and so was succeeded by Olaf Sihtricson as nominal king of the Northumbrian territories. I think that at this point we are probably witnessing the final division of Northumbria into two new kingdoms, one comprising Durham and Bamburgh to the north and another comprising Danish York to the south, which we know occurred in the middle of this century.

Now that Northumbria had come under Olaf Sihtricson and Rægnald Guthfrithson, archbishop Wulfstan defected to Edmund.[3] Meanwhile, Edmund regained the Five Boroughs and also ended a Welsh revolt on his western border, leaving him free to drive northwards on York, accompanied now by the pragmatic Wulfstan, who was looking after his own interests. Having driven Olaf and Rægnald out of Northumbria in 945, Edmund continued into the Strathclyde territory of Cumberland, which he then ceded to King Malcolm of Scotland on condition that he should in future support him both on land and on sea. Sadly, in 946, whilst attempting to end a brawl at Pucklechurch, near Bristol, King Edmund was fatally stabbed and died in May. His brother, the æthling Eadred, succeeded him and the Scots, the Northumbrians and archbishop Wulfstan all swore him oaths and pledges, but such words (as we have so often seen) are easy. In 947, the

Northumbrians took Eric Bloodaxe, who had been driven out of Norway, to be their king and obviously they had no intention of living in peace with Mercia or of keeping their oaths. Once again there came terror and rapine from the north.

Notes

1. The *Chronicle* says 943, but this seems too late, Sean Miller in Lapidge (et al), p.159 says 940, which seems too soon.
2. Miller gives this as 941.
3. Keynes in Lapidge (et al).

Chapter Seventeen

Confusion

In 948, King Eadred marched into Northumbria with fire and sword and in this ravaging Ripon minster was burnt down. Leaving a garrison at Castleford, to cover the crossing of the River Aire, Eadred retired southwards and then 'the force' at York retaliated by overwhelming and slaughtering this isolated garrison. Then was the king wroth and swore he would destroy Northumbria entirely, so the Northumbrians quickly cast off Eric and swore once again to be loyal to King Eadred.

Faithful only to their reputation for bellicosity and perfidy, the Northumbrians next invited Olaf Sihtricson to be their king, probably in 951, and probably having intelligences before him telling of the archbishop's collusion in this, King Eadred ordered Wulfstan to be brought to him at the burgh of 'Iudanbyrig' in 952. Meanwhile, at Thetford (in Anglia) abbot Eadhelm had been killed, so the king ordered many executions in reprisal. The Danelaw was still far from settled. In the north Olaf was deposed and Eric Bloodaxe reinstated, only to be, once again, himself expelled in 954. Yet again the Northumbrians swore faith with King Eadred. In November 955, he died at Frome, on the east of Salisbury Plain, and was succeeded by Eadwig, King Edmund's son.

The problem with the Danelaw seems to have been one of integration. Incoming Danish settlers seem to have brought their own language, customs, measurements, religion and social structure along with them but these were often in conflict with the already established English society with whom they mingled. If we discount the established Victorian idea that tens of thousands of settlers now took over entire shires and landscapes and instead accept such evidence as we have to hand of integration, we see that English and Danes were generally living side by side and we can understand that feuds and vendettas would occur. It seems that in shires that had once been sub-divided into (English) 'hundreds' we see a superimposition of (Scandinavian) 'wapentakes'; in that which had apportioned land by 'hides' we then see the more or less exclusive use of 'carucates' – the first a comprehensive land measurement, the second a measurement of arable land only.[1] Nevertheless, a century later we still encounter, in *Domesday Book*, residual 'hundred' headings in 'wapentake' shires, attesting the residue of this confusion. Moreover, in such shires we find place names reflecting both Danish and English elements. Nothing was clear cut in the Danelaw.

I think we should envisage these Danelaw Danish settlements (at first) as enclaves, but then gradually merging and sometimes being absorbed into the older English traditions. Requiring Danish settlers to convert to Christianity was a major demand, but one commonly made of Danish leaders by English kings when demanding truces and accords. Another anomaly was that English thralls (slaves), who represented the lowest levels of Danish (Danelaw) society, were ethnically represented by a king whom Danes must now obey. We can only guess at the legal problems that might have arisen from this conflict of authority: English slaves had rights!

The fluctuating nature of the Danelaw borders did not help, so we see as late as *Domesday Book* that a large belt of the east Midlands used both 'hides' and 'carucates' intermixed, reflecting the old 'Five Boroughs' see-saw of power and administrations. Is it, then, any wonder that regions like Northumbria (including York) and Anglia found it difficult to settle under a single English kingship, found it difficult to decide where power might lie and, seemingly, so ready to switch allegiance at times? Modern politics provide us with similar patterns of polarisation.

King Eadwig was an enigmatic figure whose reign is marked in the *Chronicle* by an entry saying that archbishop Oda of Canterbury separated Eadwig and Ælfgyfu on the grounds of consanguinity! Yet, as Edward the Elder's widow and mother of Eadred, Ælfgyfu was involved in the power struggle between her grandsons, Eadwig and Edgar, and Eadwig went on to deprive her of all her lands. In 957, it seems that Edgar became de facto rule of Mercia north of the Thames, though Eadwig retained the title of 'rex Anglorum', a regrettable and curious attempt to return to older polities. Eadwig died in October 959 and was succeeded by his brother, styled by some 'the peacemaker' and, apart from a bloody event on Thanet in 969, his reign remained peaceful.[2] It has been suggested that strong and brutal military power now created this peace, though I would also include the proven military record of Wessex–Mercia established by Alfred and maintained by his successors.[2] One further point remains, though it was apparently criticised in the *Chronicle*, that his law code established the separate legal status of the Danelaw and no doubt this greatly assisted the maintenance of law and order. At least the inhabitants now knew where they stood, even if the Church objected to such attempts at harmonisation and concessions to heathens.

Though we do not know when various surveys and records were made, we do know that a comprehensive archive had accumulated, presumably at Winchester, which not only included the Tribal Hidage, apparently with two 'updates' to its original survey, but also the Burghal Hidage.[3] There also appear to have been other surveys or records, documents or muniments that helped form the basis of the Domesday records a century later. It is not altogether unlikely that the difference between carucated and hidated areas was already being noted and recorded, and those comprehensive surveys, known as 'extents' in East Anglia, were almost certainly in existence by the end of this tenth century, perhaps as an attempt to redefine jurisdictions.[4] Such records, though not part of any recognised battle, would have some value to a commander seeking an overview of a theatre of operations, and they certainly helped kings consolidate their social, economic and topographic ambitions.

One other contemporary observation should be noted, the *Chronicle*'s attribution that reads, 'one misdeed he did, though too often', which was that he 'loved alien customs and heathen practises and brought them too much into this land, he invited foreigners and attracted harmful people', which sounds as though Edgar's toleration of the new Danelaw settlers and attempts at harmonisation were not appreciated by the writer, a clerk who undoubtedly reflected the Church's official position.[5] It might also indicate that the king made use of mercenaries to bolster his select fyrd, tolerating their 'heathen practices' for the good of his realm and, who knows, maybe he recruited Danes, so integrating this ethnic group within his kingdom? We think that the 'D' version of the *Chronicle* for this period was written up by Wulfstan the Homilist, *c.*1000, and it does appear to confirm such a suspicion.[6] No doubt many Englishmen shared Wulfstan's apparent xenophobia, just as they accepted that the Church was the arbiter of Divine will and so had a right to make such pronouncements.

Perhaps the most famous (or infamous) of Wulfstan's writings was his defeatist panegyric designed to excuse the failure of the Church to protect God's people from the 'heathens' by Divine intervention; his *Sermo Lupi ad Anglos* (Sermon of Wulf to the English), which, in truth, is no more than an Aesopian representation – the fable of the wolf and the goat! Nevertheless, it sheds a valuable light on the period leading to the year 1000 (the much-feared Millenium) and the breakdown of belief systems. Specifically it condemned the forced remarriages of widows (presumably because they might otherwise enter convents, a recognised protection for single women, and then bequeath their estates to Mother Church), the betrayal and defrauding of 'the poor' (which sounds like a political appeal to the masses) and, of course, the selling of England into the power of foreigners (who, as 'heathens' would not be likely to bribe Providence with rich donations). On the plus side, he claimed that the rights of freemen were being taken away and the rights of slaves restricted, a broad appeal to all classes and an interesting confirmation that the old Laws of Alfred were still supposed to be in force and offering some protection to slaves. 'Free men may not (now) keep their independence … nor may slaves (now) have property,' he claimed, whether goods derived from their own labours or from the grants of the Godly.

He very properly inveighed against oath breaking and pledge breaking, and then he says (the cloven-hoof slips out): 'God's dues have diminished … sanctuaries violated and stripped', with the 'heathens' showing more respect to their holy men than Christians did![7] Obviously the heathen gods were receiving more from temporalities (estates) than did the True Church. He paints a devastating picture of the evils committed by the heathens. Slaves (he says) defected to the pirates, men who then enslaved their former masters, with slaves also killing their former masters, also that a slave so killing his former master paid no wergild but a master slaying his former slave *would* be required to pay. 'Devastation and persecution in every district again and again,' he asserts, while troops ran away rather than fight. He tells of wives and daughters gang-raped in front of their husbands and of two or three seamen driving gangs of wretched captives 'from sea to sea', of ravaging, robbing, burning and carrying on board. It is a curious mixture of moral outrage and of political manoeuvring, of truth and of design.

In 975, King Edgar died and was succeeded by his son Edward, still a minor. There was a brief dispute, influential factions forming for both Edward and for his younger brother Æthelred, but Edward's eventual succession still saw considerable internal unrest. With the heavy hand of Eadwig removed and politics cankered by peace, nobles and powerful men had now grown restless and greedy and the attitude of the Church did not promote unity. Perhaps predictably this culminated in the murder of the young king. In March 978, he was set upon 'at the gap of Corfe' and slain, probably by his half-brothers' retainers and at the instigation of Ælfthryth, Edgar's widow.[8]

So, in short order, came to the throne Æthelred, one of the least esteemed of the English kings (it seems) and portents were subsequently noted. He had barely two years in which to enjoy his kingship so dubiously acquired for other eyes were now watching this Kingdom of England, grown fat and lax on peace. The storm was again about to break and yet again from the north, and in 980 it arrived along with Millenarian claims that the Second Coming would herald the end of the world in the year 1,000. The political structure was failing through the schism of Church and civil polities, whilst doom-laden predictions were hardly likely to offer the consolation of religion. Yet the Apocalypse, when it came, was not to be the one predicted.

Notes

1. Wright (2014), pp.36–42; also Wright, *Raising the Dead* (2021).
2. Q.v. Martin Ryan in *Anglo-Saxon World*, p.341.
3. Wright (2014), pp.118–122.
4. Wright (2017), pp.90–102.
5. Anne Savage (trans.), p.128.
6. Q.v. Andy Orchard in Blackwell's, p.495.
7. See Anthony Clarke, 'Some Belief Systems in Works by Bede and Wulfstan' (part 2) in *Wiðowinde* 198 (2020), pp.23–27, though the interpretations are my own.
8. Sean Miller in Lapidge et al, p.151.

Chapter Eighteen

Gradual Collapse

As the Jelling stone says, King Harald, 'won all Denmark and Norway and made the Danes Christian'. This was King Harald Bluetooth and his son, Sweyn Forkbeard, who established an administrative system that enabled him to build fortresses and a formidable military reputation in Scandinavia. These fortress camps provided for and trained fighting forces at Trelleborg, Aggersbord, Fyrkat and Nonnebakken,[1] and though not primarily destined for England (as some historians have suggested) they provided a truly competent element in any invading force. Here was an organisation fit to compete with English military institutions and, inevitably, it did.

In 980, a ship force fell upon Southampton and most of the town dwellers were either killed or enslaved. The slave markets of Scandinavia and Ireland were back in business. Next the Vikings fell upon Thanet, so, not to be outdone, a northern (probably Irish) ship force then ravaged Cheshire. The following year, St Petroc's at Padstow was ravaged and slavers were operating all along the coasts of Devon and Cornwall.

In 982, three ship sokes of Vikings entered Dorset, an old incursion route, and then ravaged the Isle of Portland, which would then make them an ideal Viking refuge for raiding along the coast. Where were the English ships that had once served Alfred so well? There is no known answer to this or to the powerlessness of the English land forces but there seems now to have been a very general disregard for royal authority, as the case of Wulfbald (in Kent) apparently illustrates. This Kentish thegn, who died before 996, not only plundered his stepmother but also stole a kinsman's lands, ignoring repeated commands from Æthelred to vacate his ill-gotten estates. In spite of a royal judgement that he be dispossessed and placed at the king's mercy, he continued to retain possession until he died and no one intervened. Following this his widow and his son continued to resist royal authority and concluded the affair by killing a king's thegn and his fifteen companions! Society had lost much of its cohesion in a very short time, as far as we can tell. Then, to round off a successful year, the Vikings also burnt London.[2]

Meanwhile, King Æthelred was busy appropriating Church lands, pleading that he had been misled by his early counsellors, now giving these confiscated lands back to his nobles whilst his kingdom fell apart. Were these the actions of a strong and confident monarch or a weak one in a precarious position? It sounds as though he had exhausted all other inducements to loyal service and was falling back on the usual expedient of plundering the Church. In 986, he ravaged the bishopric of Rochester, an action that strongly suggests local resistance or opposition to his will; this was hardly a proper course of action when faced with renewed Viking incursions. Is it possible that relative peace had persuaded the English landholding class that no such holocaust would ever be visited upon them again?[3]

In 988, the Irish Vikings returned to ravage their old favourite, Watchet on the north coast of Somerset, and the *Chronicle* notes that Goda, the Devonshire thane, was killed along with many others in a battle that might not (all the same) have been a complete English disaster. Well, worse, much worse, was yet to come. Olaf Tryggvason, probably with Sweyn Forkbeard, King of Denmark and son of Harald Bluetooth, were making preparations for something larger in 991 and, as a result, this was to become a pivotal date for both England's security and, in the much longer term, for her political development. The events of this year were to give birth to a unique English institution whose existence changed the course of English history for more than one hundred years and it was, finally and paradoxically, one that gave her national security.

Quite by accident, or so it seems, the emergency that arose in 991 and afterwards, combined with the king's own lack of royal responsibility or honour, gave rise to a novel and unique form of tribute payment. Necessity, the mother of invention, created a burden that was to plague English landholders for years to come and until a foreign ruler put it into proper application – recasting it as the means by which to end this endless rapine. It illustrates the law of serendipity in human affairs, also known as the law of unexpected consequences.

In all these disasters it is not difficult to discern the influences that would have worked on Wulfstan and which, in fact were, in the next century, to be repeatedly condemned by religious writers, men levelling equally damaging charges of 'cupiditas' at the memory of William the Conqueror. So we have seen Æthelred appropriating Church lands and then giving them back to his nobles. Well, the next chapter will tell us just *why* his nobles needed land and, indeed, the need for (even more) land that increased during his reign. It was needed in order to increase their revenues and they needed to do this in order to meet the king's demands for money. King William, later on, did much the same when faced with the need to raise money for military purposes. He also plundered Church property on more than one occasion on the basis that the Church was as much a target for an enemy as anyone else and not above hiding the assets of wealthy benefactors.[4]

The specific charges made by Wulfstan, that freemen were made slaves and slaves deprived of the little they had, may be directly linked to the needs of noblemen/landholders (and ultimately the Crown) for money in order to hire and equip local defence forces or to pay off Viking attackers. What we might well ask, however, is how far Wulfstan's own advice to the king contributed to the creation of this chain of evils, a chain he then condemned in his *Sermo Lupi ad Anglos*. Read on and I hope that the camouflage that so easily shrouds causes and effects in a jumble of half facts and opinions will begin to fall away as our story unfolds.

Notes

1. Q.v. Loyn, *Vikings*, pp.70–72.
2. For an overview of this political chaos see Martin Ryan in *Anglo-Saxon World*, pp.342–3.
3. Ibid.
4. Wright (2020).

Chapter Nineteen

Duty, Defeat and Heroism

The devil, they say, finds work for idle hands to do but King Sweyn's expedition had a modified operational plan, one that now meant that the devils were very busy everywhere. The idea was a series of lightning strikes at selected targets, slaving, looting and spreading terror, knowing that no effective local defence could mobilise in time. First Folkestone, then Sandwich, the old hunting ground of Lympne that their fathers had known so well, and then the southern exit of the Wantsum Channel to target shipping from Thanet and, no doubt, the Isle of Thanet itself. To round it off, this Viking fleet finally headed for Ipswich, another important port, but this time in Danelaw Anglia. Well there was no favouritism to be evidenced here: all locations were 'fair game' and all who dwelt in England were 'English'.

This ship force, we are told, numbered ninety-three vessels, so now, presuming an improved Scandinavian shipbuilding tradition with larger crews, probably about 4,000 men, and it is unlikely that they confined their activities just to these three locations. The Thames estuary was always a lucrative haunt for pirates with now well-explored coasts on either side, and Anglia would also be part of their communal memory. However, if they were to make the most of this supine England, apparently now devoid of warships, they needed somewhere to strand, careen and service their own ships. Though many were now probably, stoutly oaken-built they were still in need of maintenance if cargoes of captives and loot were to be sent back to Scandinavia. They chose Maldon for this *pied-à-terre*.

More exactly they chose Northey Island in the Blackwater (Panta) estuary, downstream of Maldon, for their shipping yards and holding pens. Why Maldon? Because Maldon lay at the export end of the commercial route for the Essex and Suffolk textile-producing region.[1] Not only was it a thriving port handling high-value merchandise, it was also a source of chandlery. Even the oaken ships still required tar, caulking, cordage for running and standing rigging and 'canvas', and they needed servicing supplies for working vessels. Moreover, the presence of a spinning and weaving industry further inland was itself a bonus for skilled craftsmen were required to weave the sailcloth (probably wool at this date) and would be valuable captives in any seaport.

It is unlikely that they sacked the port, it would be more lucrative to allow trade to continue and maybe some of the citizens had managed to occupy the old burgh for safety. So, instead, Northey Island became a base for their plundering and slaving expeditions. It was secure in the old and traditional sense, the established pattern of marshland and natural defences, and, moreover, was only accessible at very low water via a narrow causeway that could be easily guarded to prevent escapes; otherwise there was a strand and sea approach on the other and north-eastern side of the island. It was ideal.

Essex was part of the territory of the venerable ealdorman Byrhtnoð, and by great good fortune we know something of him from the *Liber Eliensis* and marvellous details of the consequent battle from the rare survival of most of a lay or poem describing what happened.[2] The temptation for every writer who has attempted to follow this description is to revel in the wonderful language of the poem and its opening descriptions, which still come alive when one stands on this lonely causeway. I will attempt to eschew such indulgence and instead describe the events as they are recorded. Suffice it to say that even today this place really is a suitable setting for *The Woman in Black* in the right season, however fair it may appear in summer!

Over the succeeding centuries this island has seen considerable changes, having been largely walled and 'inned' by the late nineteenth century, but now it has been left to revert and so only about one quarter of its former (Victorian) area of dryland remains. Overall it is now probably just over 500 acres but *Domesday Book* gives us a different and very accurate picture less than a century after the date of the battle of 991. In conformity with the rest of this Hundred of 'Witbricteshern', or Dengy, it was surveyed as an entity at *low* water, there being no Ordnance datum by which to fix 'land' at this date and until after Nelson's day.[3] Each coastal hundred had to decide for itself where land ended and water began, whether at high or at low water, so in 1066–86 the total area was given as 1,008 acres but of this only 360 acres could be ploughed and another 60 acres were used for grazing, the rest was subject to periodic inundation and was marsh salting and mud. Nevertheless, even parts of this salting would have been better than it is today and suitable as a strand due to the protective presence of eelgrass beds (zostera), which human intervention has since destroyed. What remains habitable today is, therefore, very close to the area of the island in 991.

This was hardly a camping site for an army and ninety-three ships would be rather crowded in an estuary a mile wide, so I propose that the main force was probably away raiding along the coast or into the mouth of the Thames, leaving a garrison and workforce holding the camp on the island. We do not know how long they were here or whether they intended a wintersetl at Maldon itself but news of their presence certainly reached

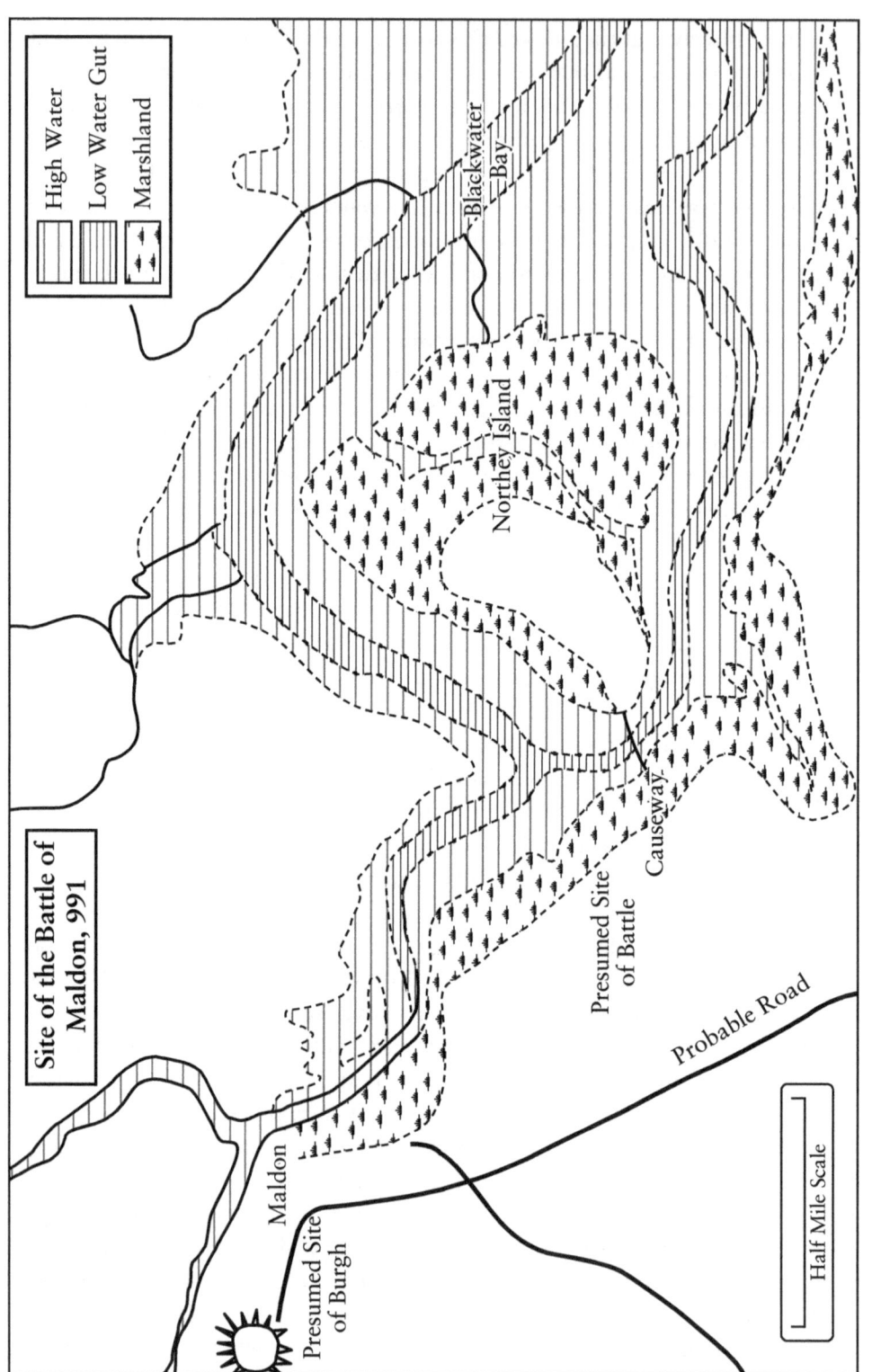

Map 6: Site of the Battle of Maldon.

> Map 6: Site of the Battle of Maldon.
> Though much has changed along this stretch of the river in the intervening centuries, we do know that in 1066 Northey Island was probably only 420 acres of dry land and that the causeway was in the same place as it is today.

ealdorman Byrhtnoð, who was engaged elsewhere at the time. If the island was being used as a prison, then the need to rescue captives would give the situation added urgency and Byrhtnoð seems to have acted with speed and determination. According to the *Liber Eliensis*, Byrhtnoð was also ealdorman of Northumbria, though some historians have cast doubt on the accuracy of this book.[4] That he could have been north of the Humber is not impossible as this region (as we have seen) usually took any chance it could to exploit problems happening elsewhere. His estates by his wife (Ælflæd) were in Essex but he also held estates in the vicinity of Cambridge, in Suffolk, Oxfordshire, Northamptonshire and possibly also in Leicestershire and Warwickshire. He was tall, strong, hardy and proud, in his sixties, and had fought Danes before and the *Liber Eliensis* contains a suggestion that he may have fought more than one battle at Maldon in 991, driving many of the invaders back to their ships. If so, all the more reason for the Vikings to take refuge on an island just downstream when they returned.

News of (a possible second) invasion at Maldon may have arrived late in the season, therefore, we believe it was August when Byrhtnoð hurried south with his hearth troops, calling out the select fyrd as Hollister has suggested.[5] If so, he could also have been hoping to raise the general fyrd once in Essex. Taking the direct route from the Humber along Ermine Street, he came to Ramsey Abbey, to whom he had already been a generous benefactor. Here he sought hospitality and procurement but Abbot Wulfsige protested that he had not sufficient for a multitude and could only feed Byrhtnoð and seven others.[6] The ealdorman's reply was that he did not wish to dine without his people because without them he could not fight, and as they were now in boats on Whittlesey Mere and the original River Nene, they continued to the Wash and made the same request of Abbot Ælfsige of Ely, which suggests that they were heading for Wool Street and so to the Peddar's Way eastwards.

Here, at Ely, he and his men were received with generous enthusiasm, though they seem to have been in some numbers, the basis of a field force. If the 'seven others' stated by Ramsey were Byrhtnoð's chief thegns and he and they were accompanied by their hearth troops then we might have a force in the hundreds. Anyway, in conventual Chapter, on the morrow, Byrhtnoð presented the abbey with 'six capital manors' and nine other places, with all appurtenances, 30 mancuses of gold and 20 pounds of silver, requesting that should he die in battle his body be brought to Ely for burial. Then, as evidence of this nuncupative will, he presented two crosses of gold on two lappets from his gown of gold and jewelled work as well as a pair of skilfully embellished gloves.

Now we learn that upon his arrival in Essex he sent out for his military tenants, but that many were tardy in joining him, which adds weight to a supposition that there had been an earlier conflict and so some may have felt their obligations to have been already discharged.[7] Failure to attend a royal summons of this kind was a serious, even capital offence, but failure to heed an ealdorman's summons was not so serious.[8] So, when the surviving poem begins, we already have evidence for saying that the ealdorman was not adequately supported. Nevertheless, *'navigare necesse est, vivari non est necesse'* – advance we must, we do not have to survive: the ealdorman had *his* duty to discharge.

In the opinion of Michael Alexander, as a work of art '"The Battle of Maldon" is perhaps, within its narrower terms of reference, a better poem than 'Beowulf' ... without doubt the finest battle-poem in English'.[9] For obvious reasons I will confine myself to describing the action and those who wish to read the poem should consult either Alexander or Scragg, though I cannot resist the odd quotation.[10]

Arriving opposite the causeway ('bridge' it is called in the poem) to Northey Island, ealdorman Byrhtnoð drew up his force for a conventional infantry battle, horses driven away from the site (lest they fall to the enemy, or lest they encourage retreat) and hawk released to the woods. Only the ealdorman remained mounted, as he dressed his men in line and exhorted them to keep station before himself dismounting to stand with his hearth companions. On the far shore, a Viking (*sæman*) hailed them, advising them to give tribute (*gafol*) rather than risk conflict: he specifically asked for hacksilver and gold: then they will depart. In return, Byrhtnoð offered spears and swords, for English silver was not so easily won.

As yet the tide still covered the causeway but the English were drawn up in array on the bank and so the two forces faced one another across the 'Panta' (Blackwater), *'Eastseaxena ord and se æschere'*, so once again, these Vikings are the men of the 'ash ships'. Here stood Byrhtnoð and *'þær his heorð-werod holdost wiste'*. As the flood ebbed, three men stood forward from the East Saxon host; for even today the landward end of the causeway drains the fastest. These men now struck down any who dared advance, so that the Vikings began to crave leave to come over to the land.

At this point the writer, and following him many historians, have criticised Byrhtnoð for, of his *'ofermode'*, he gave ground and called for them to come over quickly. This word *'ofermode'* is invariably translated as 'arrogance' or 'pride' but I think this unfair. *'Ofer'* is 'over' and *'modig'* is 'brave' or 'great hearted', and though the poet appears to criticise this action as the mistake that lost the battle, I think the ealdorman had his reasons, good reasons, for his decision to be 'very great hearted'.

In the first place, as the tide ebbed (even Cnut was to fail in an attempt to halt the tide!) the waters either side of the causeway would recede, so the advancing Saxon heroes must, ultimately, have reached the other shore only to be surrounded, and such an attempt at a beachhead would be slow as well as unpredictable. Now the Vikings themselves must have had some warning of the English approach and so the contingent on the island would certainly have sent out flyboats to contact their raiding parties and call for reinforcements, so they needed to play for time. Delay could only favour the seamen, who might already have been reinforced by returning companions. Byrhtnoð could only guess at the size of the contingent he had to face, but it would not be diminished by any delay! With luck it was only a garrison. He redressed his shield wall further back from the muddy foreshore.

'Wodon þa wælwulfas, for wætere ne murnon,
Wicinga werod, west ofer Pantan, ofer scir wæter
Scyldas wegon, lidmen to lande linde bæron'...

['Waded then the slaughter-wolves, the Viking host, caring nothing for the waters, bearing their shields the sailors came to land over the shining waters, west over the Blackwater.']

They crashed into the shield wall and swords, spears and bows were busy; the ealdorman himself driving his spear right through a mail hauberk or byrnie. Very possibly they attacked with a *'cuneus'*, or wedge formation, an exploitative shock formation and, no doubt, one designed to take out the ealdorman. He was a target for spears and for glory hunters, thanks to his splendid accoutrements, and then his sword arm was *'amyrde'*, disabled, and amid his defending thanes he was hacked down and, as was usual, decapitated. Now many of the English leaders ran, took their horses (one took Byrhtnoð's) and made for the safety of the woods, but other thegns pressed forwards for revenge, calling to one another to remember their oaths of allegiance, sworn to die with their lord. Among those stalwarts was a Northumbrian hostage and he also remained loyal, shooting his arrows as long as he might. Byrhtwold has left us the most memorable message of all as he steadied the remaining forlorn hope:

'Hige sceal þe heardra, heorte þe cenre,
mod sceal þe mare, þe ure mægan lytlað.
Her lið ure ealdor eall forhe "a" wen,
got on greote. A mæg gnornian
se ðe nu fram þis wigplegan wendan þenceð'

'Courage shall be more resolute, heart the keener,
Mind shall enlarge, as our strength lessens.
Here lies our leader all cut down,
Laid in the dirt. He will rue the day
Who now from this battlefield intends to run'

And so the poem ends and the seamen 'had the power of the day',[11] but if the *Liber Eliensis* is right, they had many fewer men to man their ships. Moreover, Ely kept their promise and although his head was never found, the loyalty of his hearth troops ensured that the ealdorman's body was recovered and remained intact and it was taken to Ely for burial, where the head was replaced by a ball of wax.[12] His widow also gave the church at Ely a gold necklace (perhaps part of the ealdorman's earlier promise) and an embroidered hanging figured with the deeds of her late husband.

In reality this was not a major or a remarkable battle, just one that we have recorded. Neither side displayed any real tactical ability, it was simply shield wall on shield wall and neither side was at full strength. The battle was *not* lost because of a single tactical 'error', for it was inevitable that the tide would ebb and the two sides eventually meet; there was never any prospect of simply sitting at either end of the causeway and waiting for one's opponents to go away! The suggestion of tactical error made by a monastic scribe or (most likely by) his abbot simply underlines the unreliability of such 'historical' accounts.

The real cause of this defeat lay with King Æthelræd, who was either too cowardly to lead an army in person or too *'unræd'* (ill-advised) by his counsellors to take the threat seriously. The fact that Byrhtnoð was holding the north for the Crown and was then expected to simultaneously hold the south speaks volumes for the state of Æthelræd's polity and governance. Secondarily, Byrhtnoð was betrayed by his retainers, many of whom did not respond to his summons, yet this was (in truth) a royal betrayal for had the king himself made the summons, well he had the ultimate sanction by which to compel attendance. Penultimately, the thane who stole Byrhtnoð's horse and so made him appear to flee very probably unstrung many of the English force, only too fearful of the consequences of losing the fight and, finally, it has been observed that those who fled had Danish names.[13]

The Vikings may have had 'the power of the battlefield' but I wonder if they remained on Norsey Island? The recovery of the ealdorman's body surely suggests that there were English survivors who retired in good order,

Porlock Bay in Carhampton Hundred, as seen from Exmoor. This was the site of early and repeated Viking landings. (*Courtesy David Young, Shutterstock*)

Looking from the lower slopes of bat's castle towards Aller Farm at Carhampton. (*Courtesy John Grehan*)

Victorian idea of a Viking landing, a persistent image that, like horned and winged helmets, was not accurate. (*Courtesy Morph art Creation, Shutterstock*)

The *Helga Æsk*, a replica of the *Skuldelev 5* drakkar; light, efficient and equally suitable for internal waterways. One of the collection of ships at the Roskilde Ship Museum.

The fearsome dragon prow of the *Helga Æsk*. (*Courtesy Russell Scott*)

The Old Harry Rocks outside Studland Bay, scene of a major Danish disaster in 876 when their fleet ran into a gale. (*Courtesy Sasha Samardzija, Dreamtime.com*)

The Athelney memorial, all that now remains of King Alfred's elaborate wintersetl of 878. (*Courtesy John Grehan*)

Ethandun, Battlebury Camp today from the north. (*Courtesy John Grehan*)

Canvey Island today, from the air and looking north, now covered by urban development and no longer a marsh. (*Courtesy Thomas Nugent, Creative Commons*)

The Devil's Dyke or Ditch looking south-east from Stetchworth, now overgrown but still impressive. (*Courtesy Keith Evans, Creative Commons*)

The Saxon tower of Barton-upon-Humber, St Peter's. The top storey is a Norman addition, probably replacing a 'Rhenish-helm' roof. Like others at Wootton Warwen, Barnack, Stoke Mandeville and Kirkby Hammerton, this was originally a 'turriform' church.

Earl's Barton church tower, from a Victorian engraving, another stone-built 'tower' stronghold. The timber parallels that still exist at Michelmarsh, Perivale and Brookland seem to indicate prototypes for timber 'castles' such as we see on the Bayeux Tapestry, which are supposedly 'Norman'.

'Ulfberht' inlaid sword blades, highly sophisticated products that replaced pattern-welded blades. However, research suggests that many such blades were cheap and untrustworthy imitations. (*Courtesy Fosterginger, Vintage News.com*)

Attack on the shield wall: re-enactors demonstrating the hand-to-hand fighting required to dislodge a fixed infantry formation. Such conflicts do not tend to be protracted, though slaughter of the defeated could take longer. (*Courtesy Dreamtime.com*)

Northey Island causeway today, at low tide. In 991 it may have been more like a ford. (*Courtesy John Grehan*)

Though some consider such illustrations as this one, from a Victorian engraving of an illustration in a Harleian manuscript, fanciful, I see no reason why the lodge built at Portskewet for King Edward should have been any different. It clearly shows a building sporting antlers and with bath house, a presence chamber, a chapel and works of charity suitable for a royal visitor.

and surely the Viking garrison, being badly mauled, would have been apprehensive of a follow-up by the general fyrd and other select fyrdsmen? We should recall that the death of a commander does not always determine abject defeat; Nelson was a good example of death in victory. Moreover, it is not impossible that the English took the island and released the captives for no one tells us that the English force was slaughtered. Historians have always presumed a total defeat, but there is no such evidence.

It is notable that these Vikings were calling for gafol, tribute, in order to go away. This perhaps suggests that they had their quota of prisoners (you can flood any market) and did not feel secure enough to remain in wintersetl, although England's defences were clearly in a deplorable way by 991. According to the *Chronicle*, it was on the advice of Sigeric, bishop of Kent, that Æthelræd agreed to pay a gafol of £10,000, an enormous sum (2,400,000d, or pence) and even to 'sponsor' Olaf, probably at Winchester under bishop Ælfheah. What is significant is that this appears to have been the very first geld paid, the first stated sum and in specie, replacing the older demand for gafol of hacksilver and gold.

This decision to pay the tribute was initially a disastrous decision that was to have enormous consequences in the century to come, setting a precedent, not least because it was (apparently) speedily paid. No doubt the real fear was that these Vikings would attack London itself. Yet this particular delivery (this geld) was made possible by an entirely novel fiscal mechanism, because it was a tax on landholding, one that then became an institution and which ultimately transferred it from a curse to a blessing. However, we have first to deal with the disaster; we have to explore the curse before we can discover its metamorphosis!

Notes

1. Wright (2014), pp.373–381; also Wright (2020), pp.175–177.
2. For the 'Liber Eliensis' see *Liber Secundus*, Cap.62, E.O. Blake (ed.), 'LE', Royal Historical Society Camden 3rd series vol. xcii (1962), pp.133–136. For criticism see E.D. Laborde, *Brythnoð and Maldon* (1937), pp.92–93 and 98.
3. Q.v. Wright (2014), pp.78–79.
4. J. Benham, *The History and Antiquities of the Conventual Cathedral Church of Ely* (Norwich, 1812) containing information on the opening of his tomb in 1772.
5. C.W. Hollister, *Anglo-Saxon Military Institutions* (1962), p.93.
6. *De Brithnoto Comite*, Lxxxi of Ramsey.
7. For 'two months provision' see Hollister, p.86.
8. Hollister, op. cit. 90 and 94.
9. M. Alexander (trans.), *The Earliest English Poems* (Penguin), 1966 and 1977), p.113.
10. D.G. Scragg (ed.), *The Battle of Maldon* (Manchester, 1981).
11. *Anglo-Saxon Chronicle*.
12. *Liber Eliensis*: the earlier translation of his remains: in 1771 given as 1154.
13. Q.v. E. Bjorkman, *Nordische Personennamen in England* (Halle 1910), pp.99–100.

Chapter Twenty

A New Economic Model

It was not the outcome of the Battle of Maldon but the consequences that arose from it that elevated this event to probably the most important status of any battle in the period that we are now examining, and the chain effect is something we still feel today. Maybe without this battle, or with a different outcome, England's greatest World Heritage achievement would, or could, never have been constructed, but we will come to such matters at the end of this book. For the present we find ourselves in an age of decline away from the sunlit uplands of the Alfredan heritage and into the shadowlands of concatenated crises.

Why did Æthelred decide to pay gafol rather than to fight? That is an interesting question. Of course, we can always blame his advisors, that is what kings themselves always do, but I think that much of the English hierarchy was now cankered by peace. Too much security had left the rich and powerful unwilling to risk life and lands and that is why no other ealdorman stepped forward to assist, or then to avenge, Byrhtnoð. Even the king, who could call out both the select *and* the general fyrd, *on pain of death* in need, refused to fight! But it is also the case that a convenient solution to gafol had been found and, just maybe, these 'aristocrats' were foolish enough to believe that the seamen would now leave them in peace. Let us look at the solution.

The convenient solution was coinage. Up to now 'tributes' had largely been paid in scrap, as the seamen had put it, (hack) silver and gold. In the case of the Staffordshire Hoard, we can see that at an earlier date this comprised pieces of many treasured religious and secular artefacts. Why this bullion scrap? Well, because normally small transactions would be in kind, in commodities and especially in agricultural produce in this largely subsistence society, but it takes time (and mining) to transform beeves and eggs into coinage and time was a commodity victims of seamen could ill afford. It was necessary to see them off as quickly as possible. Besides, who would buy excess produce in a subsistence world where perhaps 98 per cent of the population produced both their own food *and* everyday goods, and how could one be sure that any coinage was not debased or even fake? So, such 'tributes' fell heavily on the rich laity and the religious, but not yet on *all* men of substance, because the obligation required instant transaction and scrap was a quick solution unless specie could be raised.

However, by 991 there was in existence both a high-value, specie coinage and a database of surveys and landholdings, all thanks to King Alfred in the first instance and then to King Eadgar's 'reform' coinage. Because there were now measured landscapes, with such records one could devise a more equitable system of taxation than had ever been possible with hacksilver treasure and in kind deliveries, so one could collect silver pennies from a wide range of landholders and even tell them what they *should* pay.[1] Moreover, the Crown benefitted because the specie coinage was the monarch's personal perquisite and all money strikes for indigenous coinage were paid to the king for licences to strike money at registered mints. With such an assemblage of component parts it was, then, only one more step to progress to an equitable form of taxation, that is to raise specie (in the form of silver pennies of guaranteed purity), on, or against, the amount of land a free man held, whether a rich man or merely one of modest means: so much on each hide of land. If a man did not possess the specie required he had only to take his hacksilver to the nearest moneyer, pay his fee and have pennies struck from it. 'Freemen', by definition, were 'in' the money economy, they had to be in order to pay for the arms with which to discharge their legal obligations, so they could not escape this payment.

This solution once organised, meant that specie could be readily collected and the pirates sent speedily away. It also meant that the pirates themselves could distribute 'returns' among themselves with greater facility than having to weigh out, assay and agree relative bullion values, so it was convenient to them. However, in practice it *was* often inequitable, for a man with extensive arable holdings would enjoy higher revenues than one with extensive marshes, moors, or even woodlands, yet the assessment was made on acreage not on income. There was also the problem of the Danelaw, where men did not measure in 'hides' but in 'carucates', and though a carucate was half the area of a hide, it was in many cases a measurement of arable land alone. That, I believe, is why we find comprehensive 'extents' also entered in the Danelaw districts, so that no one could escape their responsibilities. Nevertheless, this was Europe's first specie-only taxation and also the first land tax in many a long century, a revival of the Capitatio Terrena of the Roman Empire.[2]

What we see evidenced later for these 'extents', in the pages of *Domesday Book*, is a form of equitable adjustment, what we might call a mechanism, by which to level up the gelds paid by carucated (Danelaw) shires with those given in hidated (English) shires, though it is impossible to say how old this adjustment was. It might, of course, have existed prior to the regular levying of Danegeld but, equally, it could have been created post-991. So it took the form of 'extents', which some historians have identified as 'leets'.[3] That these units relate to the collection of geld is not in doubt, but such sources were wrong to identify them solely as financial assessments for they were clearly areas of land: they occur in carucated shires, some more comprehensively than others, and serve to verify the size of the areas with which they are associated. They were also at times superseded by local developments by 1086, but they nevertheless form an interesting record of landscapes ante-1066.[4] In Suffolk and Norfolk they were comprehensive but we also encounter them in Lincolnshire and Yorkshire as part of the 1086 audit process, comparing past and present statistics, and so it seems that even as early as Æthelred's reign there had occurred a formal unitary linkage between land and geld assessment. We should not minimise its importance as a unifying factor between Danelaw and English jurisdictions.

Yet of all Æthelred's foolish, or 'ill-advised' decisions this was (on the face of it) surely the worst – the decision to pay protection money. It opened the route into decades of misery and terror: how could any kingdom afford, let alone so rapidly raise, such tributes time after time? The obvious conclusion for outsiders was that where this had come from there must be much more, more to be had. They did not comprehend specie taxation, much less the taxation of land. It did, however, provide ethnic unification in England through joint misery.

Where did the idea of a geld, a specie-only land tax, come from? The answer can only be speculative but from the Laws of Ine, King of Wessex (688–726), onwards we know of the existence of feorms, food rents or renders, so much each of a range of food stuffs according to the number of hides held by a landholder. This tells us of the pedigree of the hide. It seems likely that this established system of equitably requisitioned food renders would have formed the basis of Alfred's system of supplying his alternating field forces, enabling a Wessex (and then a joint) army to remain in the field for as long as necessary. Whether any part of this was commuted at any time, in order to pay fyrdmen for extensions of their service, we cannot know but it was obviously but a short step to convert the value of food and drink feorms into specie if required, and then to conceive such newly established 'rents' or 'dues' as fixed cash sums made variable in precise quantity by the operation of necessity, which is to say that when commuted in this way the amount paid could be varied as so many pennies on each hide.

Yet however much was raised as a specie-only gafol by this new geld, the Crown still clawed back a premium (percentage) through the system of licensing moneyers (to strike the pennies) and through regular reissues of coin types. In the much earlier 'age of gold' (which we see exampled in the Staffordshire Hoard), tributes had fallen on the very rich, usually evidenced by scrap taken from publicly paraded ostentation such as sword hilts and processional crosses, but now the value of even minor landholders (the money generators) could be assessed and their contributions actually quantified.

So the advantage to the Crown was that instead of emptying the royal treasury, to pay a 'lion's share', the Crown now declared a specie tax (specie land tax) that obliged both rich and relatively poor landholding freemen (of whom there may have been between 4,000 and 5,000, perhaps more) to contribute 'according to (theoretical) means'.[5] The overall burden of the tribute could be divided among them. Not surprisingly, from 991 onwards we cease to hear so much of tributes, instead we increasingly hear of gelds, heregelds or Danegelds, as this new tribute tax was variously called. But, of course, taxes (just like feorms) are raised by the Crown, so it was soon realised that as a principle and because subjects pay taxes *to* the Crown, the Crown does *not tax* itself. Thus, whatever the burden on the population, the treasury need not now be depleted by any sudden demand. Æthelred was 'laughing all the way to the bank'!

How then did landholders discharge this burden in a society that was largely self-sufficient, basically a peasant subsistence economy? Succinctly, they had to do it through goods and services. Of course, in a subsistence economy the opportunities for selling agricultural produce are limited, though hunter-gathering and speciality production offer openings. Similarly, the building of structures, creation of everyday artefacts and clothing remain mainly within the domestic and estate spheres, except for a few specialisms, such as stonemasonry, English cloth and cloaks, instrument-making and metal working (of all kinds).[6] This last slides neatly into industries.

As early as the eighth century we hear of lead working and exporting, so any landholder lucky enough to possess minerals in his soil could mine, cupel and refine.[7] So we hear of lead, tin, copper, iron, silver and gold production from a number of areas in England. Some of these may have also produced very specialised artefacts, such as jewellery, goldsmithing and armaments.[8] Along the south and east coasts we also see extensive salt-making by 1066 in areas with tidal marshlands (for fuel), a lucrative industry and one possibly very closely linked to fisheries and meat preservation.[9] Salting provisions added value, for they would then 'keep', so not only did salt equal cash but 'salt horse' and herrings could also be sold.

I have speculated elsewhere on the very specialised products of the Weald. Though it was once the fashion to end all Wealdon iron production with the fall of Roman civilisation, a lack of archaeological evidence for Saxon workshops does not prove that they did not exist. Forty years ago I drew attention to the similarity of pattern-welded blades found in south-east Essex and in Kent, and that patterns were probably indicative of given workshops. Since then more knowledgeable scholars than I have drawn attention to the 'growing evidence for sword blade production in England and especially Kent, during the 6th and 7th centuries'.[10] As another researcher put it, there are, 'good reasons to think that many of the swords found in England were made here', especially as there was, 'a sophisticated trade in types or iron alloys'.[11] Certainly our known entrepôt for luxury items (including those from the north) was Thanet. Although some scholars have proposed (against all practical considerations) the export of English wheat at this date as the foundation of England's wealth, the production of quasi-religious, magical, status symbols such as pattern-welded blades and efficient tools of war would have offered a far greater return and one that would have been realisable in ships of that time.

The establishment of a defined specie coinage was not only of assistance to trade and industry – and the emergence of true taxation – it encouraged the establishment of internal markets. Some of these, as we have seen, were probably created early on in the larger (and therefore secure) burghs, where as well as trading, individual trade workers could operate, people who needed to purchase food and drink from others, often (one suspects) thanks to a money economy based on payments made to troops. As a result service sectors could develop in hospitality and marketing. Incessant conflict would also encourage mercenary service with armed forces and, I suspect, the development of such groups, serving for specie reward, progressed and was stimulated after 991, with both the Crown and ealdormen (and bishops) recruiting in order to supplement their fyrdmen. Of course, such developments are likely to have undermined the old 'loyalty' ethos of Anglo-Saxon society, especially when fyrdmen were also paid in specie in order to extend their period of service in the field.[12] At this point honour gave way to mercenary considerations.

From now on, we can say, we expect to see greater reliance on mercenary forces in military activities, with this in its turn stimulating commutation and change, moving away from service obligations alone. Moreover, the convenience of specie coinage was not lost upon the aggressors, so their demands increased and consequently so did the pressure on landholders to improve their goods and services, those sectors of their estate economies that provided them with specie with which to pay Danegelds. Now the stage was set for a considerable change in the conduct of war but it also saw the emergence of a new economic system.

Notes

1. Wright (2014 and 2017) for details of hidations, carucations and extents.
2. Wright (2017), pp.120–121.
3. The great exponent of (the unprovable) fiscal 'leets' was J.H. Round assisted by Miss B.A. Lees, both in *Feudal England* (1895) and in the relevant Victoria County Histories, being then repeated and commended by H.C. Darby in his *Domesday Geography of Eastern England* (1957) for lack of any other hypotheses.
4. See Wright (2014, 2017 and 2021).
5. Approximately 5,000 men owned land in 1066 (*Domesday Book*), q.v. Higham and Ryan, *The Anglo-Saxon World* (Yale, 2013 and 2015).
6. Wright (2020), pp.175–182.
7. Ibid., p.180.
8. Ibid., pp.178–180 and 188; also (2019) pp.106–107.
9. Wright (2017), p.82; also (2020), pp.189–190.
10. *The Sword in Anglo-Saxon England from the 5th to 7th Century* (Anglo-Saxon Books, 2019), p.42, Paul Mortimer and Matt Bunker, citing also J. Lang and B. Ager, *Swords of the Anglo-Saxon or Viking Periods in the British Museum: a Radiographic Study* (Chadwick Hawkes, 1989).
11. B. Gilmour, *Developments in Iron Smithing and Decorative Welding Techniques found in Anglo-Saxon Swords and Related Edged Weapons* (PhD Thesis, University College, London, Institute of Archaeology, 1990).
12. Q.v. Hollister op. cit., pp.27–9.

Chapter Twenty-One

Chaos, Cowardice and Cupiditas

In 992, King Æthelred ordered all important ships to be gathered in the Thames at London, obviously anticipating a further attack. Here he appointed ealdorman Ælfric, eorl Thored and bishops Æscwig and Ælfstan to lead the troops and, if possible, trap 'the force' out at sea. So the ealdorman sent an assembly warning to 'the force', and then he escaped to 'the force'! As a result of this, only one enemy ship was taken by the combined London and Anglian fleets, but that was the ship on which the treacherous ealdorman was escaping. The *Chronicle* draws attention to the miscreant and makes no censure of the king, though we know nothing of the ealdorman's reasons for such blatant treachery.

The following year, 'the force' destroyed Bamburgh (Northumbria) and then moved down the coast to the Humber estuary and 'did much evil, both in Lindsey and Northumbria'. Meanwhile, King Æthelred wickedly ordered that ealdorman Ælfric's son be blinded and yet, despite this depravity and though he then ordered the gathering of a great army, its leaders (Fræna, Godwine and Friðegist) fled rather than fighting. Clearly English morale was crumbling away and we can only suspect that it was the king's 'lack of leadership' that dismayed his nobles and undermined their will to fight. However, as 993 was to prove, Englishmen would still defend their own, given half a chance.

In December 993, Olaf and Sweyn sailed to London with ninety-four ships, perhaps 3,000 men, meaning to fire the city, but now the town dwellers drove them off, apparently with some slaughter. In response, they burned, ravaged and killed all along the coasts of Essex, Kent, Sussex and Hampshire and no royal army opposed them. Then they took to horse and rode widely, spreading terror, until the king and his counsellors sent to them for terms, promising tribute and provisions if they would cease harrying. 'The force' then came to Southampton, took up winter quarters there and were given copious provisions by Wessex and £16,000 (3,840,000d). Supposing that there were 2,000 pirates remaining, the average would be almost 2,000d per man! Quite speculatively (of course) if each 1d = £50 in modern purchasing power, this was an average of £100,000 per man though, of course, pirates never make fair divisions of booty. The lion's share always goes to the leaders.

So King Æthelred sent bishop Ælfheah and ealdorman Æthelweard to King Olaf to conduct him, in pomp, to Andover, where he received 'kingly gifts' of the English monarch. In turn he swore never again to come to the English people in enmity and so there was peace, for a while. Why, we should ask, was no army sent against the pirates and why were the king's nobles and counsellors so loath to accept command, even if the king would not fight for his people? The answer must surely be in the inadequate provision of munitions, provisions and ships, presumably consequent upon budgetary considerations, combined with the royal preference for paying 'protection money'. Such things would demoralise the fyrdmen and cause the general fyrd to adhere strictly to their obligations in law. The recourse for ordinary people, at least in Wessex, would be to take to the woods and wilds further inland, to wait until the Vikings had passed on. However, when these pirates took to horse, unopposed, then the situation really came to a head: there was no hiding place now that the enemy had acquired local knowledge.

Once again, in 997, the 'Danes' (Vikings) sailed around Devonshire to reach the mouth of the Severn, ravaging Cornwall, Wales and Devon as they passed. They put into their old haunt, Watchet, presumably looking for slaves among the mining communities, and then they returned, around Land's End, and went into the Tamar estuary. Here they followed the course of the river through what became the Tamar Mining District (at a later date), probably as far as Launceston, where they struck eastwards to reach Lydford, on the edge of Dartmoor. So any refugees who had fled southwards from Exmoor to Okehampton (seeking safety in the moors) would have found themselves confronted, once again, by the slavers travelling northwards. Maybe this was a deliberate strategy designed to capture a given group of slaves? The Vikings then seem to have returned by following the Tovy, burning down Tavistock monastery on the way for good measure. No doubt their 'indescribable plunder' included metal ingots taken in this rich mining district.[1]

In 998, they sailed east to the mouth of the Frome, around Portland Bill, and then went inland as they pleased, ravaging Dorset. As fast as defending troops were gathered to oppose them, they ran away and so the pirates went looting and slaving wherever they chose, ending up on the Isle of Wight, terrorising Hampshire and Sussex. The following year they entered the Thames Estuary and then the Medway to Rochester, only to meet Kentish troops. Now we are told that these men were (for once) resolute but, nevertheless, they 'moved too quickly and fled because they did not have the help they should have had',[2] which sounds as though the scenario seen at Maldon was being played out all over again. And the king, 'ever but in time of need to hand', was not in evidence!

Once again the seamen seized horses and 'rode as widely as they wished', ravaging nearly all West Kent but, apparently, careful not to penetrate the Weald. So the king and his counsellors advised that they should be opposed by land and sea, 'but when the ships were ready there was delay from day-to-day, which exasperated the wretched people who were waiting on the ships and always, when things ought to have advanced, so they were more delayed from hour to hour and always they let the enemy's numbers grow; always men drew back from the sea ... so at the end it availed nothing... but was oppression of the people, waste of money and an encouragement to their enemies'.[3] This sounds like poor and timorous leadership combined with parsimony but it does not sound as though Crown revenues had diminished.

Finally, in 1000, the king decided to go into Cumberland and ravage it. His ships that went out around Chester, in order to meet him, instead of doing so ravaged the Isle of Man, a Viking settlement that became part of the thalassocratic 'Kingdom of the Isles' and was probably a transit point for slaves and loot between Ireland and England. Why had the king now 'taken to the field', well, because the seamen had decided to ravage Normandy instead of England and so there was no risk of meeting a Viking army! From the account it sounds as though the king's naval commanders had gone a-Viking for themselves and, moreover, they seem to have got away with it. After all, 'heathen' captives could certainly be sold as slaves and Ireland was close by. It was every (rich) man for himself.

Then, in 1001, the Vikings returned, thereby justifying the dismal hysteria of the millenarians, men such as Ælfric of Eynsham and especially Wulfstan the Homilist, who did his best to destroy general morale with his *Sermo Lupi ad Anglos*, making the nation's misfortunes the 'will of God' punishing an immoral people. Such men had nothing else to offer and needed to explain why God did not protect his chosen people. Perhaps if these people could give more to the Church they would be deemed less sinful? No, to the chagrin of many others, the world had not ended in 1000, instead Vikings ravaged the land and travelled inland to Dean, apparently the Hampshire Dean, north of Fareham, for here the men of Hampshire met and opposed them, losing two high reeves and several other notables among eighty-one casualties. In spite of a claim that they killed even more of the enemy, nevertheless the Vikings once more 'had the power of the battlefield'.

So the Vikings now went west to Devon and here the traitor Pallig (brother-in-law to Sweyn) defected to them with all the ships he could gather (though he had been greatly honoured and rewarded by King Æthelred) and together they burnt Teignton and other estates. One suspects that Teignmouth was even then concerned with the export of metals extracted on Dartmoor, just to the west, and so in the money economy in a big way. Then they entered the

Exe and travelled to Pinhoe (just east of Exeter), where Kola and Eadsige, the king's high reeves, met them with whatever troops they could gather and were put to flight with many killed. They burnt Pinhoe and Broad Clyst and then sailed off eastwards to the Isle of Wight, where they burnt Waltham (to the south of Dean) and other villages in a campaign of terror around Meon and Portsmouth until the locals treated with them for peace and offered tribute. What, one might ask, was so attractive about the Meon Valley? Once again I think our answer can be found in *Domesday Book*, for this source suggests a very active fishing and processing (salting) industry in the area of Portsea and Hayling Islands.[4] Cornering the salt fish industry would turn the Vikings a pretty penny as well as providing immediate sustenance.

Clearly this had now become a pleasurable and profitable business for those involved in terrorism and raiding, for now all concerted and organised resistance, presumably all royal authority, had completely dissolved, all the Alfredan legacy had been lost and so, in 1002, we see king and counsellors offering provisions and a further £24,000 as Danegeld. We can only stand astonished that such serial sums should have been handed over to freebooters and pirates, surrendered to protection rackets, rather than invested in defence of the realm.

Notes

1. For the mining areas in 1086 (*Domesday Book*) see Wright (2014), pp.365–370.
2. Anne Savage (ed.), *The Anglo-Saxon Chronicles*, p.147.
3. Ibid.
4. Wright (2020), pp.189–190.

Chapter Twenty-Two

From Atrocities to Despair

In 1002, Wulfstan the Homilist became both bishop of Worcester *and* archbishop of York, held in plurality. I wonder why he was so rewarded? The same year saw the St Brice's (or St Bricius') Day massacre. The *Chronicle* tells us that King Æthelred had received intelligences that 'Danes' intended to murder him, together with his counsellors and so he ordered all 'Danes' in England to be put to death on 13 November.

It is, of course, quite improbable that he was referring to the now settled inhabitants of the Danelaw, instead this was an attack on all the Viking elements, including royal mercenaries, who seem to have infested certain locations as wintersetls and become little more than robber bands. The inference is that such intruders, whether local terrorists, or mercenaries of dubious loyalty, were living off the fat of the land and that the temptations of easy fortunes to be made in this way, 'sprouting like cockle among the wheat', had finally been recognised by the Crown. I think that the only way to explain the prevailing situation is to draw an analogy with the later condottieri. These hired 'defenders', this security organisation, had realised it could prey on its hirers by holding them to ransom, by threatening to join (or even at times joining) the enemy and so going and doing as each band of brigands chose.

We might also, perhaps, look back to the situation in post-Imperial Britain when Saxon 'foederati' had been employed and who seem to have been employed by various (local) provinces to guard the borders of their little empires.[1] I wonder, do we see here a parallel devolution with major landholders (including the king) employing local Viking bands to defend their personal estates, a fragmentation of the new English kingdom in response to the king's refusal to defend his kingdom? These mercenaries then seem to have taken over the very provinces and populations that had employed them. Maybe someone had been reading Gildas's *De Excidio Britanniae* as a result of increasing arrogance by these proto-condottieri and pointed out the danger of a takeover such as Gildas described in AD 490 to 500. The 'plot to kill the king' sounds as if it was a post-hoc justification for a seemingly expeditious solution to political instability. I wonder what it was that Wulfstan advised and whether it had anything to do with his elevation?

At Oxford the 'Danes', or Vikings, so targeted sought refuge in St Frideswide's minster, but such was the hatred the townspeople had for them that they burnt the church down with the Vikings inside, testimony indeed to the misdeeds of this contingent! Further archaeological evidence of massacres has come to light in mass graves at St John's College and from Ridgeway Hill, Dorset. In 2009, Oxford Archaeology excavated an execution pit at Weymouth containing fifty-one decapitated Scandinavian males and dated to AD 910–1030.[2] No doubt there were many other such 'final solutions' but St Brice's Day seems possible. These massacres were certainly not unpopular with Englishmen, presumably at all levels of society, men who saw their produce and their silver drained both by criminal gangs and by mercenaries, so this was Æthelred's chance to do something 'positive' and politically popular while the main enemy force was in wintersetl. Letting the oppressed take the law into their own hands is always popular, but it is also dangerous. Undoubtedly the relatively innocent suffered along with the guilty, such is always the consequence of such retributive hysteria.

At this time Emma (now renamed Ælfgyfu), of Normandy, the teenage daughter of Count Richard of Normandy, came to England to marry King Æthelred. The *Chronicle* tells us that in 1003 her reeve, a 'Frankish peasant' named Hugh, was then somehow responsible for the destruction of Exeter by a returning Viking host under Sweyn, but we know no more. Sweyn's own sister is said to have been one of the victims of St Brice's Day and so he was exacting retribution. In response to this a large army was raised from Wiltshire and Hampshire and it was led by ealdorman Ælfric. When the two armies were close enough to see one another this unworthy ealdorman feigned sickness, retching and vomiting, leaving his men bewildered and scattered, awaiting further orders to form up and engage. On seeing this, Sweyn led his force into Wilton and Salisbury, presumably from Southampton Water, ravaging and burning. It seems that no orders for combat were ever given and that Ælfric slunk away!

The following year, Sweyn descended on Norwich and burnt it down, and in response Ulfcytel of Anglia and his counsellors at first advised buying peace, having been taken by surprise, so they made truce with the enemy. After this the Vikings, true to form, stole away to attack Thetford. The angry Ulfcytel, in retribution, ordered that the Viking fleet should be hewn apart where it lay beached, but in the event his agents failed to do this, no doubt fearing reprisals. Though he now quickly gathered troops, 'the force' arrived at Thetford three weeks after ravaging Norwich and burnt it down; nevertheless, Ulfcytel caught them as they turned to regain their ships. Once again, because the king of England did not summon the host, the Anglian force was under strength, but their resolution to fight won praise from their enemies, though they lost many important men in the attempt.

Sure enough, in 1005 there came famine: St Brice's Day had not come soon enough or hard enough to conserve essential supplies. The time delay involved marks the cumulative effect of tampering with the supply of essential and core commodities. Though the weather may have played a part, the excessive consumption of seed corn and of plough beasts would have exacerbated the tragedy. Indeed, conditions were so bad that the Viking ship force betook itself to Denmark for this year, seeing there was nothing to gain in England, and did not return again until after midsummer in 1006, when fresh harvests were gathered in.

Meanwhile, ealdorman Ælfhelm of Northumbria had been slain on the king's orders and his sons Wulfleah and Ufegeat were blinded, apparently in a 'palace coup' in some degree orchestrated by one Eadric Streona (from 1007 ealdorman of Mercia), who subsequently married princess Edith.[3] So we see a background of famine, misery, want, social disintegration and murderous court intrigues under a callous king too afraid to even defend his kingdom in person, and it is no surprise to read that the Vikings came again, this time to Sandwich, ravaging, burning and killing. Now the king called out the armies of Wessex and Mercia, so that they stayed out throughout the autumn – but to no avail, for he did not lead them and with the advent of winter these men went home.

After the beginning of November, 'the force' took the Isle of Wight and lived off the fat of the land. As Southampton was later the terminus for the Gascon wine trade, this may have influenced their decision as much as the good fishing and good hunting in adjacent territories. At Christmas, the *Chronicle* grimly records, 'they went to their ready entertainment' in Hampshire and Berkshire as far as Reading, lighting 'beacons' as they went![4] They were obviously following the lower Icknield Way and then they switched to the Thames, perhaps on boats taken at Reading, for they then went to Wallingford and burnt it down. From here they marched across the Berkshire Downs following the Ridgeway (path) without any impeder, to East Hendred and 'Cwichalmaslæw' or Cuckhamsley Hill,[5] for they had been told that if they ever reached this spot they would never return to the sea and they were determined to prove this wrong. Not only were they now supremely confident, they could 'cock a snook' at popular superstition and at the king in order to complete the demoralisation.

The army had gathered at Kennington, just south of Oxford, and the Vikings seem to have now followed the Thames thence to meet the English and put them to flight. Maybe the fight was tougher than the *Chronicle* suggests for the Vikings did subsequently retire southwards, probably along the Thames to Reading and then to the south part of the Icknield Way and past Winchester, close enough to that city for the inhabitants to see them heading boldly and unchallenged for Southampton Water. Meanwhile, King Æthelred had gone north for Christmas, to Shropshire, from where he and his counsellors (safely) deplored the ruin of the land that they had abandoned to the enemy.

Manifestly the Viking's strength was now their ability to strike fast and accurately, bolstered by their success. Here we can detect two elements that had improved their strategy. First of all the use of Scandinavian ship types, vessels of oak and with higher gunwales but, most important of all, sailing ships, for their mobility on the waters tells us they were no longer using 'ash ships' alone but vessels like the *Oseburg*, *Gokstad* and *Skuldelev 2* types. Indeed, there were now larger vessels capable of carrying 100 men that have been termed 'troop carriers', ships like those replicas the *Sea Stallion* and *Draker Harald Hårfayra*.[6] However, I suspect that smaller and more manageable ships still accompanied them in order to undertake inland work. Secondly, on land they now moved with assurance, with local knowledge, making best use of main roads and waterways but also relying on locations they had familiarised long before. In this last they may well have been assisted by defectors and brigands, and because success breeds success, so defeat breeds defeatism and the English were now thoroughly demoralised at all levels, taking their despair from the fear and fatalism so often displayed by their leaders, including senior clerics, safely ensconced elsewhere.

Once again the royal debate centred on yielding tribute, protection money, and the finest of provisions. In 1007, 'the force' was given £30,000 (7,200,000d). Yet and finally, the king also gave instructions for defensive measures for he now had records by which to apportion these Danegelds, records that (someone had realised) could also be used to provide munitions. So he ordered a ship to be found from every 310 hides (74,400 acres) and a helmet and byrnie from every eight hides (1,920 acres). In theory, over an area of 24 million acres, which is the total entered in the final list of the Tribal Hidage,[7] this would yield 322 warships and 12,500 properly armed men, giving us a convincing, if averaged, ship capacity of almost thirty-nine crew to each vessel.

By 1009, so we are told, these ships were ready, which surely means that a proportion of them were already in existence when the order was given for shipwrights do not grow on trees! Contemporaries marvelled at the size of this fleet, now gathered at Sandwich, but some questioned whether England had either the luck or the honour for this fleet to acquit itself. Here, on these flats today, there are about 5 miles of strand and flats, adequate space on which to draw up such a fleet and to camp an army, a site covering the south of the Wantsum and also the Narrows, and so able to deploy vessels either to the Thames mouth or along the south coast if an enemy was sighted.

Yet again the weakness and undoing of these preparations was not the men but their leaders. Once again accidie and intrigue set in as they lay camped and waiting: Brihtric, brother of ealdorman Eadric, accused Wulfnoth Cild, the South Saxon, to the king and had him banished. In response, Wulfnoth won over the crews of twenty ships and himself went 'a-Viking' along the south coast. To stop him seemed an easy task, so Brihtric, in order to increase his standing, took eighty ships in pursuit. Then, apparently when rounding the South Foreland, his fleet was met with a great wind that dashed them ashore and so Wulfnoth, presumably on the fleet of the same wind, came up and burned the wrecked and beached ships. Now the king's counsellors were destroying themselves and the kingdom's military resources.

It seems that pandemonium then broke out at Sandwich and the king went home, and so did counsellors and ealdormen so, not to be outdone, the troops also decamped and went with them to London. The remains of the splendid fleet lay abandoned on the long beach at Sandwich Bay and news of this debacle was not slow to spread. At the end of July, Thorkell's fleet sailed east to Sandwich and took possession of the prize in order to ravage along the south coast. We can hardly doubt that his force of Vikings now found ready recruits in England with which to fill these newly acquired ships. Why not when the kingdom's pride and salvation had been handed as a gift to the enemy?

Off they went to Canterbury, but the citizens gave them £3,000 to buy peace (720,000d), so they made for the Isle of Wight and ravaged and burned as they chose in Sussex, Hampshire and Berkshire. Hysterically, King Æthelred ordered all men to resist them everywhere, but it made no difference, so in desperation he finally marched with his army and cut them off from their ships. We do not know what happened, except that it was ealdorman Eadric's fault that they escaped.

Around the middle of November the 'force' went to winter quarters in Kent, on the Thames, living off Essex and neighbouring counties. Though they often assayed London, they always came off worst so, after Christmas, they followed the Thames to the Chilterns and then on to Oxford, where they burnt down the town. Returning on both sides of the Thames, they were warned of an army waiting for them at London so they crossed over at Staines (their old stamping ground at the confluence with the Colne and the Mole) so that in spring they were again in Kent, repairing their ships.

In 1010, they sailed, after Easter, to Ipswich and directly confronted Ulfcytel and his Anglian troops: these fled but the men of Cambridge stood firm. Here died Æthelstan and other nobles, many good thanes and countless folk when Thurcytel Mare's-Head fled. Now the 'Danes' were horsed and so took control of the Fens, burning down Thetford and Cambridge and killing men and cattle before turning south to the Thames valley. Here they met their ships and went quickly westwards into Oxfordshire, thence to Buckinghamshire along the Ouse to Bedford and their old stamping ground of Tempsford, burning as they went. Now they had complete mastery of the landscape, knowledge gained during years of raiding and accumulating local knowledge, and no one dared oppose them or to presume to predict their intentions.

Notes

1. Q.v. Ken Dark, *Britain and the End of the Roman Empire* (2000), especially pp.50–53 and 103–104.
2. Reported by the National Geographic (2017) and identified by Jane Evans of the NERC Isotope Geosciences Laboratory of the British Geological Survey.
3. Simon Keynes, *The Anglo-Saxon World*, p.349.
4. Savage, p.149.
5. Now called Scutchamer Knob.
6. *Havingsten* (Sea Stallion) from Glendalough, a Roskilde replica of *Skuldelev 2*, which sailed from there to Dublin in 2007, and *Harald Hårfayre* (Harald Fairhair), the largest draker yet built (2010–13) and out of Vibrandsøy, she sailed to the east coast of the USA in 2016. She could make 11 knots under sail but the size of the sail required considerable management skill.
7. Q.v. Wright (2014), pp.120 and 130.

Chapter Twenty-Three

The Kingdom Overrun

'When they scattered to the ships the troops should have come out again ... Then the troops went home.'¹ So complained the *Chronicle*, that when 'the force' was in the east the troops were kept west, when they were in the south the troops went north – and the implication is that no one intended to confront the enemy. 'There was no head man who would gather the troops but each fled as he might ... no shire would help the other next to it.'² England was completely demoralised. And why would the king sanction (or maybe even command) such behaviour? Because in a last resort the army would be needed for his personal protection, that is one conclusion.

The Vikings overran Anglia, Essex, Middlesex, Oxfordshire, Cambridgeshire, Hertfordshire, Buckinghamshire, Bedfordshire, half of Huntingdonshire, much of Northamptonshire, Kent, Sussex, the territory of the Hæstingas (Pevensey lagoon and Hastings area), Surrey, Berkshire, Hampshire and much of Wiltshire, so that the king and his counsellors had few places of safety remaining and the state of the wretched inhabitants (both English and Danish) can hardly be imagined. 'Bad counsel' said the circumspect chroniclers, for it is never wise to blame a living king. Then there was the problem and excuse of tribute not promised in time. 'Nor were they (the Vikings) withstood', English leaders only making truce 'when most evil had been done', a formulaic complaint repeated later on. Yet the truth was that for all the truces, treaties and tribute made and given the raiders went everywhere and did as they liked. The situation was hopeless.

So in 1011, in September they besieged Canterbury and by deceit they took the city when abbot Ælmær betrayed it. Here they captured the king's reeve, the archbishop, abbots, bishop and many holy people and thoroughly plundered the city. When they retired to their ships they took archbishop Ælfheah with them to hold for ransom. By Easter (13 April) 1012 the counsellors had agreed to pay £8,000 (1,920,000d) for him, yet the archbishop forbad anyone to give ransom for him. Members of 'the force', being incensed by this and drunk on 'southern wine', then murdered him. And *still* the king did nothing. Well, to be fair, God had done nothing either.

Then, in 1013, the king appointed bishop Lifing to be Ælfheah's successor and before the month of August 'king' Sweyn and his fleet arrived at Sandwich. From here they sailed around Anglia, Sweyn entrusting the fleet and the hostages to his son Cnut. Then Sweyn had his army horsed in order to work evil along Watling Street and then they apparently took to the Fosse Way, arriving at Oxford. Both Oxford and Winchester now submitted so he moved east to London but was repulsed, for Æthelred and Thorkell were there, Thorkell having now pledged himself and forty-five ships to Æthelred, so giving the king no room to prevaricate further.

Though events and accounts are confused and confusing, the most likely explanation, in the labyrinthine intrigues of Æthelred's court, is that he and Thorkell had received advanced intelligences of Sweyn's coming: it would be impossible to keep the demand for chandlery and men secret along the western seaboard of Europe. This being the case, perhaps Thorkell felt he was in danger of being displaced. There being nothing to gain by two Viking forces disputing among themselves, Sweyn now withdrew to Wallingford and thence to Bath. Here ealdorman Æthelmær and the western thanes bowed to Sweyn and gave him hostages. Following this acceptance as de facto king, Sweyn returned northwards to his ships and to Cnut, and now the Londoners, fearful of his wroth, submitted and gave them hostages.

Thorkell now lay at Greenwich, on the south bank of the Thames, opposite the city of London, and both he and Sweyn (on the north bank) demanded full provision and tribute for the winter from the English. Nevertheless, both forces still did as they chose and nothing went right for the wretched people. Æthelred, for his own safety, lay with the fleet on the south side of the Thames but sent his queen, Ælfgifu, and their sons Edward and Alfred, to the queen's brother Richard, in Normandy. At Christmas, the king was on the Isle of Wight, Thorkell's stronghold, but subsequently he too felt it prudent to follow his family across the Channel.

This was a perilous time for Æthelred, who had now reaped the whirlwind of his own making. His safety depended on one Viking faction, probably the least powerful of the two, and continued protection depended on his ultimate usefulness to Thorkell. Neither Viking force knew where all this river of silver came from, it seemed endless and Æthelred had to continue to pretend that it was, though in fact the country was now bankrupt. Part of his trouble with his English nobles and leaders was probably caused by the massive demands he had made on their resources, both in specie and provisions. Perhaps at first, back in 991, most landholders had presumed that the tribute, gafol, the new Danegeld, would come from the royal treasury, the 'hordere' but, of course, it depended instead and absolutely on this Danegeld being a specie-only land tax on all freemen, and this was also an alien concept to them.

Peasants, of course, as bondmen and subsistence farmers, produced provisions for their 'lords', their landowner, as well as giving them labour and 'service'. They were not part of the money economy but their lords had to be, not least because they had to purchase the sinews of defence that went with their status: armour, swords and ships did not grow on trees or in fields. Payment was required for anything outside the local and subsistence economy. The rich had the cash, the silver pennies and gold oras, they also controlled the money-making industries, such as mining and armaments.

Fortunately, the districts producing gold, silver, iron and skilled smiths tended to be in out of the way places, such as rugged Pennine uplands, West Country wildernesses like Exmoor, Dartmoor and the Mendip Hills and wooded wastelands such as the Forest of Dean and the Weald. There was also money to be made from salted provisions (including fish) and specialist textile production, provided these more obvious districts were not ravaged.[3] Defence was also an industry, for royal revenues had to be expended on armaments, ships, provisions and mercenaries. What had happened to the system of burghs, once the bulwarks of the land? When money is in short supply it is always tempting to reduce the infrastructure, the system that quietly supports more obvious activities, and so it seems they had not been maintained.

This massive demand for silver had to be met in one of three ways, either by serendipitous finds, through commerce or by industry. The discovery of treasure, of 'dragon's hoards' or 'ants delving in the earth' should not be lightly discounted.[4] The Provinces of Britannia had been wealthy and today we still find amazing treasures, both accidental and archaeological. Commerce depended on the export of finished and luxury goods, in an age when foodstuffs were almost impossible (in most cases) to export, and also on the security of trade links, by now virtually destroyed. As for industry, that could only function if its locations remained inviolate and preferably obscure.

It is, of course, impossible to estimate England's silver resources at this date, though they appear to have been formidable; our best guide comes from evidence of later and of Roman silver extractions known from the Mendips, South Wales, Shropshire, Derbyshire, Flint, Wharfedale, Nidderdale and Swaledale. Typical recovery of silver from lead ore in Derbyshire in 1847 was between 2½ and 7oz per ton, as recorded.[5] At Llantwit Major in Glamorgan a Roman specimen actually yielded 170oz the ton but such exceptions can never have been the rule.[6] We must conclude that supreme efforts were being made in processing (which also suggests heavy production of lead) but that expectations were no longer met by supply.

So, by *c*.1010 not only had all reserves been used up, the means of replacing them were failing rapidly and, as a result, major landholders were disinclined to pay the increasingly heavy taxes demanded by the Crown whilst small landholders, such as thegns, were disinclined to fight as well as having to pay out, and they could all, now, afford fewer hearth troops; and, of course, without cash, mercenaries could not be purchased to make up the deficit. As for the peasantry, they were desperate for viands for themselves, disillusioned by the lack of traditional defence forces, apathetic and probably resigned to the 'will of God', just as the Church now preached, in order to save face. Moreover, the Church was still hanging on to its money in spite of everything, witness that (in 1013) Ælfsig, abbot of Peterborough, in exile and safe at Boneval, could still afford to buy St Florentine's body from his hosts for £500 (120,000d)!

If we accept the figures given in the several versions of the *Chronicle*, then the 'tributes', let us now call them heregelds or Danegelds, paid by the Crown alone (without supplementary local agreements, such as were made by Canterbury in 1009 and 1011) came to £134,000 between 991 and 1012, some 32,160,000d! It is difficult to give any approximation in money values but if we accept Barlow's appreciation of one silver penny as the equivalent of a pre-Second World War half sovereign, or my own suggestion of one silver penny as something like a modern £50 note, then we are looking at £1,608,000,000 in recent purchasing power.[7] The number of landholders was possibly between 4,000 and 6,000 (4,000 is the usual 1066 estimate but there may have once been more). At 24 million acres or 100,000 hides, a 4p levy on each hide would only raise £1,666 13s 4d (400,000d) and a twelve pence levy £5,000.[8] So if every hide paid (which was not the case) *and* paid at the high rate of 12d on each hide, then these twenty-one years of successive 'tributes' actually represented 26.8 years of heregeld.

Of course, there are historians who do not want us to believe such sums and others who pour scorn on the totals of ships and their men given by the *Chronicle*, but if we are to pick and choose the figures we *want* to believe, how shall we believe any of the *Chronicle*'s statistics, or even its events and characters? 'Pick 'n' nix' is all very well for religion but we must be, or try to be, more accurate and scientific with history, even when we doubt some of the contemporary glosses and opinions appended to such figures. Over the course of twenty-one years a 12 pence, continuous, levy would only raise £105,000 (25,200,000d) and then *only* if everyone paid on *every* hide! That this was not the case, that tax evasion was rapidly evolving, we know from both the County Hidage, the Northamptonshire Geld Roll and from

Domesday Book.⁹ A levy of 24d per 240 acres (hide) generally seems much more likely as a practical tax return *and* this on top of providing the best provisions in copious quantities for thousands of men.

The search for wealth is a search for power, but when the prospect of enrichment becomes elusive, so sadism supplies the exercise of power. There were now thousands of armed mercenaries scouring the countryside for provisions with rapine, pillage and arson, destroying the very people who fed them and also the means of creating provisions. All these brigands had been promised the 'dream ticket' of loot, but where was it? The concept of a specie taxation based on a solidarity (in this case land) was a complete novelty and hidden mystery to men accustomed (in the past) to hacksilver and gold, and so they must have been desperate to find the magical source of England's wealth. But without an English king who at least knew the fundamentals involved there could be no bureaucratic machinery put to work to gather the tax. Indeed, with so many brigands infesting everywhere it would have been impossible to raise or to deliver it. So we may be certain that frustrated mercenaries rapidly went out of control looking for loot and for provisions. Yet the more stotts (plough oxen) they slaughtered, the fewer ploughs were available for surviving peasants to employ in ploughing, so cereals and other arable crops also failed. We are not told much about disease in the *Chronicle*, though Ælfric of Eynsham[10] identified diseases, but malnourished peasants would be particularly susceptible and armies have always been breeding grounds for disease. England's misfortunes were, in reality, nothing to do with respecting monastic life and failing to make heavy donations to Mother Church, much less to the need to improve popular 'morality'. Cowardice and rampant greed, manifested on every hand, were to blame!

Those landholders and nobles who could held on to what they could with their hearth troops, hoping to avoid a major descent by one band of brigands or another. All was chaos with churches stripped of all valuable fragments, senior clergy either fled abroad or now riding with hearth troops of their own for safety. There were daily apprehensions of large troop movements and the new king, Sweyn was now, no doubt, nonplussed to know how to prevent his own men turning on him for lack of rewards. At Candlemas, 3 February 1014, King Sweyn died suddenly, we don't know how, but it solved his problems and his army now elected his son Cnut in his place. He was now King Cnut, with all the problems that involved.

Notes

1. Savage, p.151.
2. Ibid., p.156.
3. Wright (2014, 2017 and 2020).
4. An illustration in the Tiberius 'B' Calendar, British Library, eleventh century.
5. Q.v. R. F. Tylecote, *Metallurgy in Archaeology* (1962), quoting J.A. Smythe, *Lead* (1923).
6. V.E. Nash-Williams, 'The Roman Villa at Llantwit Major' in *Archaeologia Cambrensis*, 1952–55, 102, 89–163.
7. Barlow (1970 & 1979), p.183; also Wright (2020), p.172.
8. For area of hide see Arthur Wright, *Raising the Dead* (2021).
9. Wright (2014), pp.114–117.
10. Ælfric's homily 'the prayer of Moses': God would reward the vigilant faithful who respected monastic values.

Chapter Twenty-Four

The Real Millennium

At their wits' ends, the English nobles, clerics and counsellors decided to beg for Æthelred to return. No doubt they were desperate to avoid any more demands for impossible tributes and had finally made up their minds to act in concert, so 'they said that no lord was more dear to them than their natural lord, if he would govern them more justly than he had done'.[1] I think that here we are hearing 'the pips squeak': make the taxes lighter, lead us, and we will have you back! Well, without the taxes and (most important) the machinery of tax collection no tributes at all could be paid and then what would happen? A land full of criminals and nothing to oppose them, no protection money, no royal authority to raise it or to raise an army. It was a 'Catch 22' situation, damned if you do and damned if you don't.

In return, Æthelred sent the æthling Edward to say that he would improve whatever they hated and forget all injuries provided they gave him full friendship and outlawed all Danish kings. So in the spring he returned to England and Cnut sat glowering at Gainsborough until Easter when the people of Lindsey gave his force horses, to go harrying, so that (in reality) he could forage and plunder elsewhere. We may note, here, that the full force was *not* already in the field and that enthusiasm for their venture now seems to have somewhat evaporated. Now King Æthelred (or more likely Edmund) struck the first blow and with his full force and the support of the nobles, ravaging, burning and killing in order to terrorise the Lindsey men as a reprisal and Cnut, reluctant to trust to a battle, went out with his fleet leaving the wretched inhabitants to their collective fate.

Furious, he sailed south to Sandwich and there put ashore the English hostages given in 1013, but first he cut off their hands, ears and noses! He also demanded £21,000. I suggest that the mutilation of the hostages was Cnut's psychological attempt to placate his semi-mutinous crews, together with a promise to obtain adequate recompense for their miserable wintersetl. Then to add to the miseries of these years came a great sea flood on Michaelmas Eve, probably a North Sea surge, affecting Lincolnshire, the Fens and East Anglia. What had the people done to deserve such miseries at the hand of God? The Church had no answers.

The year 1015 saw a great council at Oxford where old scores were settled. Sigeferth and Morcær, senior Thanes of the Seven Boroughs, were lured to his chamber by ealdorman Eadric and there they were murdered. The king seized all their goods and ordered Sigeferth's wife to be brought to Malmesbury when, to complete the intrigue, the æthling Edward married her without the king's consent and then went from west to north into the Five Boroughs, taking over Sigeferth's and Morcær's property, so depriving both Æthelred and Eadric 'Streona' (acquisitor) of this prize.

Now Cnut came to Sandwich early in September, when going round Kent to ravage Wessex, finally entering the mouth of the Frome. Dorset, Wiltshire and Somerset were now ravaged, so ealdorman Eadric and æthling Edmund raised troops and joined forces, but Edmund heard that Eadric meant to betray him and the army held back, leaving Cnut to do exactly as he wished! Once again the king's counsellors were the kingdom's enemies and the king himself lay sick at Cosham (Portsmouth) and did nothing. Not one to miss an opportunity, Eadric 'acquired' forty of the king's ships and proved the rumours right by joining Cnut. With this alliance all men bowed to them and this new host was horsed.

Cnut and 'Streona' crossed the Thames (Isis) at Cricklade to enter Mercia by an old and familiar route. By Christmas they were burning and killing in Warwickshire, so Edmund gathered troops to oppose them. Warned by bitter experience, these select fyrdmen insisted that the king should join them in person, with the men of London, so that the general fyrd would be compelled, on pain of death, to also join them, but, as the king did not come, they then took themselves home, each to look after his own.[2]

After Christmas, Edmund gave orders that these men should now report for service or face the full rigour of the law and the king was implored to join them with all the men he could muster. Finally, the king arrived, only to be informed that there was a plot to betray him, so he quickly forsook his army and returned to London! What was Edmund to do? Riding north to Northumbria, he joined up with eorl Uhtred, apparently to recruit forces but, lo and behold, the pair of them decided to go on an expedition of their own. Their men also needed sustenance and rewards and the supply system had (now) obviously collapsed: neither rations nor money were forthcoming! So while Cnut ravaged the south, they ravaged Staffordshire, Shropshire and Chester, but when Cnut had finished with Buckinghamshire, Bedfordshire, Huntingdonshire, the Fens and Lincolnshire he went to Northamptonshire and then turned towards York. Uhtred then turned his coat and hurried north-eastwards to make peace with Cnut, only to be killed all the same.

Putting a puppet eorl in Uhtred's place, Cnut retired south by west, probably on the Fosse Way, taking to his ships again at Easter, probably on the Devon coast. Meanwhile, Edmund returned to London and to his father. Now Cnut sailed for London, after Easter, but Æthelred died before Cnut reached him, leaving Edmund as apparent successor. So the shipmen arrived at Greenwich and now they displayed great ingenuity in siege working. First they dug a great ditch to the south side, cutting off the Bermondsey promontory it seems, so the southern end of the bridge must have been defended, and after dragging their ships to the west side of London bridge they then diked outside the walls so that no one could go in or out. Yet, in spite of all this and determined attacks they were repulsed. They had exhausted themselves, which says much for London's defences and defenders.

Now it was Edmund's turn to carry the war to the enemy, receiving the submission of Wessex. He met 'the force' at Penselwood, near Gillingham, and again at Sherston, west of Malmesbury, but these actions were indecisive and he was opposed by Eadric Streona and Ælmær Darling, who had joined Cnut. Gathering troops for the third time, he returned to London and put the besieging 'force' there to flight. Next he returned to Wessex, only to see 'the force' renew their siege of London, until they finally gave it up and sailed off to the Orwell. From here they may have picked up Wool Street and so to Ermine Street, for they now arrived in Mercia, killing and burning as they went.

Raising an army for the fourth time, King Edmund moved against them, apparently as they returned southwards, going into Kent, driving cattle to meet their ships on the Medway. Crossing the Thames at Brentford, the king drove 'the force' before him in a cavalry pursuit, killing as many as he could overtake, and at Aylesford Eadric 'Streoner' now came over to the king, who was unwise enough to accept his submission. The fugitive remainder of 'the force' now entered Essex and so, once again to Mercia, apparently using Ermine Street and Wool Street, and Edmund raised an army for the fifth time and followed up Wool Street to 'Assendun', Ashdon by Hadstock.[3]

Here the two armies met and Eadric 'Streoner', with the 'Magensæt' or Magansæt tribe from Herefordshire and south Shropshire, fled and so betrayed his lord and king once again. Cnut took the victory and 'all the oldest retainers in England' were slain. Edmund seems to have escaped using the Icknield Way and so across to the Fosse Way via Akeman Street, for Cnut pursued him to Gloucestershire, possibly to the forest of Dean. Now the two kings were reconciled, coming together at Alney (or Apperley), near Deerhurst (south of Tewkesbury). Hostages were exchanged as were oaths and pledges and a tribute was fixed.[4] Edmund received Wessex and Cnut Mercia, and London bought peace from 'the force', who consequently took their ships to London and made it their wintersetl. It was a compromise rather than an outright victory for Cnut, which suggests that both sides had fought to a standstill.

On St Andrew's Day, 30 November, King Edmund 'Ironside' died, suddenly, and his wife and children fled overseas. So, in 1017, Cnut received the whole kingdom of England, placing his lieutenants Thurkil in Anglia, Eadric in Mercia and Eric in Northumbria, though Eadric was killed before the year was out. Then (Ælfgifu) Emma (of Normandy) was brought to him, Æthelred's widow, and he took her to wife, setting aside Ælfgifu of Northampton (ealdorman Ælfhelm's daughter), whom he had married in c.1013. In 1018, King Cnut received £72,000 (17,280,000d) from England plus £11,000 (2,640,000d) from London, in tribute, and some of 'the force' went, satisfied, back to Denmark, leaving forty ships with Cnut.[5]

In 1066, we think there were possibly 4,000 major landholders, so if we stretch our guess in 1018 to 6,000 the burden on them, on all large *and* small, would be astonishing. Then again, we should ask how Cnut, now the King of England, could be both fining *and* paying himself simultaneously? The answer, of course, is that this geld was actually a tax, a specie-only tax on landholders (as we have said), so as 'tribute' a substantial sum (the largest share) could be clawed back by the Crown as Cnut's personal share. Of course, what London paid was quite independent of the geld mechanism and if the population of London, all told, was 10,000 souls then individual contributions were enormous! The remaining (or actually disbursed) sum left after Cnut had taken his share would represent his financial obligation to his captains and their troops, suggesting that he had raised a considerable force with which to meet Edmund, though we are never told how many men or ships were involved. Now he was able to dismiss them safely and send them home.

So we can say that not all the £72,000 was actually paid out from the treasury, even though it was probably (eventually) paid in! However, the £11,000 paid by London, the 'square mile' within the old Roman walls, represents a staggering amount for such a relatively small merchant community and it speaks volumes for the wealth of the pre-Conquest city. These 2,640,000d might represent £13.2 million in today's terms. We should also remember that those paying this tribute were both English and Danish landholders and merchants.

So, not only were all the eldest of the English army and nobility eliminated at 'Assendun' and the fyrds worn down by the attrition of repeated conflicts, the financial resources required for any future recrudesence of resistance had decisively come into Cnut's hands. His would be the largest portion, which he could augment (as king) just as Æthelred had done, so he retained, in England, sufficient resource to enable him to resist any future invasions and foreign challenges. He had not won this conflict and this kingdom in order to leave himself and his people defenceless. The enormous tribute paid did not all flow out of the English royal treasury, and English troops (as we shall see) were still confident and competent if well led. Only the ruler had changed and in accepting the crown he had, presumably, been told the secret of the geld? Who could resist such an offer of unlimited wealth?

Notes

1. Savage, p.100.
2. See Hollister on the roles of select and general fyrds in detail.
3. There are two claimants for the site of Assendun: Ashingdon in south-east Essex and Ashdon (by Hadstock) in north-west Essex. Hadstock (St Botolph's) Church was excavated in 1974 (Warwick Rodwell in *The Antiquaries Journal* vol. 56, issue 1, pp.55–71, 1976) and although likely to be a slightly later structure (as it stands), an earlier one was traced within it, including an associated 'empty grave' of importance. The possibility is that this was St Botolph's monastery of 'Icanho' founded in 654 and possibly the saint's original burial site? A door of very early date has been dendro-dated to *c*.1035 (1040–70?). See also Warwick Rodwell, *Under Hadstock Church* (1974).

    In 2002, the Hadstock Society, with HLF funding, commissioned a geophysical survey of the Red Field site that tentatively identified two *possible* burial pits, q.v. P. Croxton-Smith, 'The Site of the Battle of Assandun, 1016' in *The Saffron Walden Historical Journal* 3 (2002). See also ibid. nos 6 (2003) and 9 (2005) for reports on Ashdon/Hadstock Church.
4. Odda's Chapel was not built until 1056 but Deerhurst Priory (now a parish church) seems the obvious site for the accord as it was built in the eighth century.
5. So, 19,920,000d, which, as I said before, might equal £996,000,000 in modern purchasing power. If there were 2 million inhabitants in England, this would equal (at an average) 9.96d (£498) for every man, woman and child. For the possibility that the population might actually have been greater see Wright (2014), pp.251–269, especially p.266 and the table on p.270, and such calculations of tributes seem to confirm that two million is far too low an estimate.

Chapter Twenty-Five

Deceit and Despair

With England exhausted of everything, King Cnut spent the winter of 1019–20 in Denmark, but he returned to England at Easter. He then held a great Council at Cirencester and ealdorman Æthelward was outlawed. In thanks for his victory at 'Assendun', the new king next ordered a minster (church) to be built, which is presumed on archaeological evidence to be the church at Ashden by Hadstock in north-west Essex.[1] He next outlawed Thorkell and then went to the Isle of Wight with his ships, presumably in readiness for any attacks through the Narrows by other opportunists, or to be closer to the Severn in order to deal with Irish Vikings.

In 1023, King Cnut and Thorkell came to an agreement and exchanged sons, Thorkell becoming Danish regent and guardian to the aetheling Harthacnut, Emma's (Ælfgyfu's) son. In support, Cnut took a force to Denmark in 1026, where he was beaten by a Swedish ship force, losing heavily both in Danish and English troops. The following year he travelled to Rome (no doubt seeking Divine support) and then to Scotland, where King Malcolm 'bowed to him'. He also made generous donations to the English Church and removed St Wystan's body from the reconsecrated shrine at Repton to Evesham Abbey, again, no doubt, to improve his hold on Divine interventions for in 1028 he took fifty ships from England, perhaps 2,500 men, to Norway, where he drove King Olaf from the land, returning to England the following year.

It seems that in the fifteen years under Cnut, England not only recovered her economic stability but her naval and military prowess. When he died at Shaftesbury in 1035, the eorl Leofric with many thegns and Cnut's household (bodyguard) troops from London all chose Harold 'harefoot', son of Ælfgyfu, as king, to hold for himself and for his younger half-brother Harthacnut, Emma's (Ælfgyfu's) son. Eorl Godwine and a Wessex faction were unhappy about this but could not stop it, so they advised that Ælfgyfu-Emma stay in Winchester with Harthacnut and his bodyguard and that eorl Godwine would be her man, yet Harthacnut lingered in Denmark (establishing his power as king there) and Archbishop Æthelnoth may have refused to consecrate Harold.[2] Meanwhile, Emma's children by Æthelred fled to Normandy and Ælfgyfu (of Northampton) campaigned for Harold 'harefoot'.

Once again the political battles consequent upon a disputed accession began to undermine the kingdom. Æthelred's son Alfred was then lured to England by eorl Godwine and Harold 'harefoot', but instead of escorting him to his mother at Winchester (as promised) the plotters imprisoned him and killed some of his escort, while others were blinded, mutilated and scalped and some sold into slavery. Then they took the prince (æthling) to Ely and blinded and castrated him and left him with the monks.

Now Harold 'harefoot' was chosen as supreme king and Emma was driven out in the winter of 1037, with Harthacnut joining her at Bruges. King Harold of England died in March 1040 and then Harthacnut arrived at Sandwich a week before midsummer to be accepted by English and Danes alike. 'He never did anything kingly while he lived,' was the verdict of the *Anglo-Saxon Chronicle* (written circumspectly after his death) and he began by disinterring the body of Harold and casting it into a fen.

The late Harold 'harefoot' had continued with punitive taxation, that much is clear, and Harthacnut followed in his footsteps. When the citizens of Worcester killed two royal huscarles who were collecting such 'tribute' (as it is called), the new king harried the whole shire in 1041 and some lands seem to have passed into Scandinavian hands.[3] Yet his uterine brother, Edward, came safely to England, to be sworn as future king, perhaps as evidence of the continuing power of Emma and her supporter, eorl Godwine? As 'proof' of his non-complicity in Alfred's murder, this eorl now gave the new king a great warship manned by eighty warriors.[4] Well, if gifts worked with the Church then why not the Crown?

The year 1042 was recorded as a great tribulation, with bad weather and diseases of both crops and stock and early in June Harthacnut died suddenly of a 'fit' or stroke, so that Edward now succeeded, being crowned king the following Easter. Immediately he deprived his mother, Emma, of all her lands and all her gold and silver, apparently apprehensive of a Danish invasion by Sweyn of Denmark or by King Magnus of Norway and it seems he did not trust her loyalty. In 1044, King Edward went to Sandwich with thirty-five ships and in 1045 with an even greater ship force, such was his fear of a Scandinavian invasion of some sort. It was not much of an army with which to meet a 'force'.

Meanwhile, famine stalked in England and in 1046 it was compounded by the hardest winter men could remember, with deaths of men, cattle, fish and birds. These things may not be unrelated to the punitive 'tributes' raised and especially to the need to supply the king's standing fleet and his personal army of mercenaries with foodstuffs that, indeed, the peasantry needed most.

Kings had now learned that money can buy security by paying for defence, though this was undoubtedly seen as personal rather than national defence. Such personal forces not only required payment, they also demanded the finest provisions and considerable license, and they encouraged powerful noblemen, like eorl Godwine, to follow suit. Shortages and disease are the natural consequences of such unstructured social changes, their downwards economic pressures and also of garrisons. The misery of the masses can hardly be imagined.

While the king watched his southern kingdom and the Channel, Godwine's son, Swein, who held the Welsh Marches, went into Wales, in alliance with the northern King Gruffydd, and received hostages. On the way home Swein then abducted the abbess of Leominster and detained her at his pleasure, yet he received no serious rebuke from a supposedly devout king – one who also depended on the Godwine family for internal peace and for advice!

When King Sweyn of Denmark asked for help in 1047 against King Magnus of Norway, in the shape of fifty English ships and their crews, a testimony to the continued military strength and reputation of England, the king's advisers counselled against it, all except eorl Godwine, saying that Magnus's forces were the greater. When Magnus defeated Sweyn, that removed one threat to England and when Magnus died, shortly afterwards, that removed another, so that when King Sweyn regained Denmark in 1048, Magnus's successor made peace with England. Here we have England as the balance and arbiter of northern power, if not the broker.

The following year, emperor Henry III made war on Baldwin of Flanders and he then asked for Edward's aid in using his ship force to prevent any escape by Baldwin, so the king took a great fleet to Sandwich until the emperor had won. England was a military and naval power to be reckoned with, thanks to her financial security. Yet, once again, a weak king, one incapable of controlling his powerful nobles, undoubtedly undermined security in the end, while his peasantry groaned under his vainglorious displays.

In this same year, 1049, eorl Swein (Godwineson) asked King Edward for estates of his own, but Godwine's other son, Harold, and his cousin, eorl Beorn, both opposed him at every turn. In response, Swein personally joined his eight ships at Bosham and then eorls Godwine and Beorn left Sandwich (with forty-two ships) and went to the fortress of Pevensey, where there was adequate safe anchorage in the lagoon, to await events and possibly in order to thwart any attempts to seize the Godwine estates on this lagoon's eastern shores.[5] Meanwhile, King Edward sent the Mercian contingent (along with the fleet) home. Now a threat appeared from Flanders and the king was forced to send for his few remaining ships in the Stour, possibly riding at Manningtree. The larger part of this threatening Flemish fleet proceeded to attack the area of Walton Naze and then escaped. As in 1066, Pevensey lagoon and its harbour were a key strategic location. It is strange that this has been so overlooked by historians.

Meanwhile, eorl Beorn at Pevensey was told by his cousin, Swein, that he should go with him to Sandwich where he (Swein) would now swear allegiance to the king. Taking three ship's companies with him, the trusting Beorn rode with him to Bosham, in order to take ship for Sandwich, but on arrival was made prisoner, taken swiftly to Dartmouth and murdered. Harold pursued them, retrieved Beorn's body and took it to Winchester. As a result of this murder, the king and the army declared Swein 'nithing' and he fled to Bruges with only two ships, so perhaps he had been in league with Baldwin of Flanders all along? Now, with Swein out of the southern Marches, the Severn lay exposed and thirty-six Viking ships from Ireland descended on the Usk and Newport, probably slaving in the Welsh commotes with the help of King Gruffydd. Local forces under bishop Aldred tried to oppose them but were taken unawares at dawn, suffering casualties. Once again, court intrigues and jealousies had put the whole kingdom at risk.

In 1045, King Edward had married Godwine's daughter, Edith, a union that was apparently (by their subsequent and joint report) never consummated. The chroniclers commend this, on either part, as chaste and holy, but the fact remains that relations between Edward and his father-in-law Godwine soon deteriorated dramatically. According to William of Malmesbury,[6] Edward was 'chaste' because he hated Edith's father, though Clerk Herman said he was 'piissimus', that is 'religiously elevated'. [7] Barlow, however, commented, 'that Edward's childlessness was due to deliberate abstention from sexual relations lacks authenticity, plausibility and diagnostic value', adding, 'it is typical of that irrationality and ignorant credulity with which the eleventh century abounds', further observing that Archbishop Stigand 'was unimpressed by the king's piety'.[8]

No doubt feeling more secure, or perhaps in a gesture to placate his nobles, the king next paid off nine ships of his household troops, retaining only five and, if we can credit accounts, began to take more interest in ecclesiastical matters than in government but, in both spheres, favouring Frenchmen. He was, after all, in all essentials except paternity, a Breton. Godwine, meanwhile, was more inclined to ally himself to Baldwin of Bruges, by marrying off his son Tostig to Baldwin's half-sister Judith, and he also persuaded the king to pardon eorl Swein. It seems as though Edward was now gradually easing himself out of affairs of state and political conflicts for, as Professor Brookes summarised it, 'he had been bred to hunting and idleness', tastes that never left him, though this was, perhaps, not quite yet his resignation from politics.⁹ There was a crisis yet to come, one in which his fingers would be badly burned.

Notes

1. Q.v. Rodwell, art. Cit. (1976) and note 3 to Chapter 24.
2. Q.v. *Encomium Emmae Reginae* iii, 1.
3. Examples in Bishop Lyfing's Charter of 1042.
4. John/Florence of Worcester's *Chronicle of Florence of Worcester*, c.1120.
5. Wright (2019) for a description of the lagoon at this time, now totally reclaimed as the Pevensey Levels.
6. *De Gestis Regum Anglorum*, i, 239.
7. 'Miracula S. Edmundi' in Liebermann, *Ungedrukte*, p.244.
8. Barlow, op. cit., pp.82 and 84.
9. Prof. Brookes, *The Saxon and Norman Kings* (1966).

Chapter Twenty-Six

Turning the Tables

Count Eustace of Boulogne was King Edward's brother-in-law and in 1051 he visited England, an interesting meeting as Eustace's (Carolingian) family had a strong claim on the French throne. Edward seems to have been at pains to develop a relationship with William of Normandy as well, both William and Eustace being Frenchmen hostile to the de facto (Capetian) French King, Henry I.[1] Whether Edward took the opportunity to promise his throne to either, or both, of these candidates is uncertain, but he may have made such promises to several such potential allies in order to serve his political ends.[2] That he was setting aside the proper English protocol of electing a king via the Witan clearly never disturbed him; in Continental terms the crown was (to him) his to award to whom he chose. An offer or promise to Eustace in 1051 does seem a possibility but one to William, an enemy of Brittany, seems less likely.

Count Eustace was also accustomed to acting in just such a high-handed manner and he regarded English subjects as so many human chattels. However, the English had developed a fierce independence, itself an indicator of unity; they were not just so many abject peasants, they knew their value in conflicts. This foreign contempt for humanity was not compatible with the spirit of unity that had served the English peoples so well when they had combined to eject or even survive foreign invaders. A clash with Eustace's party was therefore inevitable. It occurred at Dover.

Having dined 'not wisely but well' at Canterbury, Eustace and his hearth troops donned their armour ('byrnies') before entering Dover, obviously determined to do as they pleased. One of Eustace's men tried to force an entry into a property and in the attempt wounded the householder, whereupon the householder slew him. Eustace and his troops then mounted and went to the house, broke in and slew the man on his own hearth; then they proceeded to murder more than twenty other householders. The incensed townsmen turned out in force and slew nineteen of Eustace's companions, wounding others and Eustace himself barely escaped with his life and a few men. As a French count he was not used to being thwarted by 'peasants'.

Now he rode back to King Edward and made false report so that the king became furious with the townsmen. He ordered condign punishments – eorl

Godwine was ordered to punish the town – and he refused. The excuse for this high-handed French behaviour made by some historians is that Eustace had been asked to build a 'castle' at Dover and the townsmen objected, but that is not the story the chroniclers tell, neither is it likely, as the English had been building burghs and 'castles' for a long time and the old Pharos was probably already the nucleus of Dover Castle.[3] No, this story is part of the 'Norman supermen' fantasy that has tried to minimise all English (they usually say 'Anglo-Saxon' or 'Saxon' as a pejorative) achievements since the time of Sir Walter Scott and Augustine Thierry, the original authors of such 'history'.[4]

The Breton king, relying on his French coterie, now engineered an armed confrontation with the Godwines and so eorls Leofric, Ralph (Edward's nephew) and Siward, probably fearing civil war, sided with the king. For their own safety, eorl Godwine and Swein were forced to take refuge in Flanders and Godwine's other sons, Harold and Leofwine, in Ireland. Now that he had arranged this purge of the most powerful part of the Anglo-Norse faction at court, Edward set about doing as he pleased. His first action was to send Queen Edith to a nunnery at Wherwell (south of Andover) and steal all her property, then he installed many Norman Frenchmen, at the same time rewarding the English eorls who had supported him by calling out the English fyrds south and north of the Thames on a royal command and refusing Godwine any guarantees of safe meeting. The *Chronicle* is quite detailed and it seems obvious that Edward had chosen his moment carefully and, perhaps, even engineered it! Odda of Gloucestershire was now made eorl in the south-west for he was a rare survival from Æthelred's day and a distant kinsman of Edward. 'Castles' and churches went to 'Frenchmen', thus securing both temporal and religious power to the king and his un-English faction.

Was he attempting to destroy the regional power of 'English' eorls, formerly ealdormen, the system that had served defence so well in the past, doing this in order to create a Continental-style absolutism? Historians have fought shy of such questioning, probably overawed by the saintly accolade bestowed on Edward by posterity, a reputation apparently based on his, not at all certain or proven, celibacy, the holy aura that was later created to surround both him and Queen Edith. After all, he eventually became essential to the Norman justification for the invasion of 1066 through the claim that Edward had 'promised' William of Normandy an English throne, one that was not (under English law) in his gift. Continental kingdoms and aristocrats could not understand that such an inheritance was subject to ratification by any body of counsellors. Nevertheless, the last word lay with the English Witan.[5]

In 1052, eorls Ralph and Odda were set to guard the Narrows and the Wantsum at Sandwich and apparently early in the year, fearing Godwine's return. Indeed, he did finally sail from Bruges to the Yser and at midsummer came to Dungeness, south of Romney, on the Walland Marsh. Immediately the two eorls called out all the land-forces and set out in pursuit with their fleet, but Godwine now put into Pevensey lagoon, a safe anchorage with an impregnable fortress on a peninsular, while wild weather confounded his pursuers and made guarding the entrance to the lagoon impossible. When it abated, he set sail for Bruges again. When the two eorls returned to Sandwich, they were ordered back to London by the king, in order to change crews and commanders (we are told) but possibly, also, because he now feared for his personal safety. Thus it was that all became confusion and the English ship sokes, being composed of fyrdmen and not mercenaries, all went home in disgust.

This news reached Godwine, so now he passed the Narrows again and sailed west to the Isle of Wight, where he harried until he had tribute and provisions. Then Harold arrived at Porlock, on the northern edge of Exmoor, with nine ships from Ireland and set about seizing food, cattle, property and men, killing those of Odda's men who opposed his landing, before sailing around Land's End to meet his father. Together they now rounded up all available shipping on Wight, at Pevensey and at Dungeness, Romney, Hythe and Folkestone. From here they went to Dover, seized more ships and hostages and so to Sandwich, everywhere taking ships, hostages and provisions and certainly recruiting on the way. They then entered the Stour, probably in pursuit of some retreating royal ships, before returning to the Thames, taking Sheppey and burning down Milton Regis. Finally, they chased the king's eorls to London.

Now the king and his eorls still had fifty ships with which to defend the city, but doubtfully enough men to oppose the Godwines, who demanded restitution of all their estates and authority, having been unjustly (they said) deprived. I think that Edward's mood can only be imagined, the tables turned on him so quickly and being so powerless to act, so he did what weak kings (like Æthelred) had always done, he counselled and prevaricated and, no doubt, blustered until his own nobles began to turn against him and Godwine's men grew difficult to control. Yet it was in no one's interest to see London sacked and an accord was finally reached, to the great alarm of all the 'Frenchmen' who had been installed by Edward.

Some fled west to Osbern Pentecost's 'castle' (on the Marches, later known as Ewyas Harold) as fast as they could ride and some north to eorl Robert fitz Wymarc's 'castle' (at Clavering in north Essex). Robert, archbishop of Canterbury, with bishop Alf and their joint hearth troops, went out the eastgate of the city, killing and wounding many as they went, making for the safety of open country. They rode hard until they reached Walton Naze and there took the first ship available, which was unseaworthy, so barely escaping alive to the Continent. There Robert gave up his pallium – 'just as God willed' says the *Chronicle* with delicious irony.

Now there was a great meeting called outside London and eorl Godwine presented his case. Not surprisingly, he was proved guiltless, as were his children, and all was restored to them and also to those who had supported them. Queen Edith's property was totally restored to her and Archbishop Robert was declared an outlaw along with all the other craven 'Frenchmen'. Just after 'St Mary's Day' (8 September) Godwine brought his ships to Southwark for the final accord, though himself unwell, perhaps as a result of confinement on his ship. He had, apparently, taken property from 'many holy places' during his campaign, well his followers needed rewards, and now (the clerical compilers of the *Chronicle* reported) he failed to make sufficient recompense despite this ghostly warning. God was at it again!

The Godwine family was now not only *the* force in the land, they were very probably as wealthy as the Crown. By Easter (1053) the king, the eorl Godwine and his sons Harold and Tostig were all at Winchester. Sitting at feast with the king's eorls, Godwine was suddenly struck down, probably by a stroke, falling against his footstool, powerless and speechless. He died within a few days, leaving his son Harold as the power in the land. Swein had already died in 1052 while returning from pilgrimage to Jerusalem. The Lord, the religious might claim, had sent condign punishment upon the sacrilegious, though he had also and simultaneously set restrictions on King Edward!

Notes

1. Q.v. Wright (2019), pp.90–91; also (2020), pp.61–62; also D.C. Douglas, *William the Conqueror* (1964), pp.44–53.
2. Ibid. (2019), pp.31–33; also Barlow op. cit. (1970 and 1979), pp.214 and 218–219.
3. Wright (2019), p.43; also (2020), pp.18 and 27.
4. Ibid. (2020), pp.1–2.
5. Ibid., pp.20–23.

Chapter Twenty-Seven

The Weakness of the English Crown

The lightning campaign of 1052 not only proved the mettle of English troops, when well led and directed, it also serves to illustrate the competent generalship of Harold Godwineson: local knowledge, unrelenting pressure and versatility of approach all contributed to his success. King Edward, despite his Breton upbringing and French connections, proved to be no political match for the Godwine family and so the king's attempts to overturn the established political system in England met with dismal failure and there was a rapid devolution of kingly powers onto Harold and his brothers. The 'saintly' Edward now retired into conjugal celibacy, holiness and hunting while granting favours to various ladies in 'forest' locations, including young ladies who gained royal patronage for 'feeding his hounds'.[1] It was an age when high-profile devotion by those who could afford it was a guarantee of moral excellence and eternal salvation.

Of course, disturbances and campaigns continued sporadically. In 1053, the English border guards at Westbury were ambushed by Welshmen, and in 1054 eorl Siward invaded Scotland with both land and sea forces, defeating Macbeth and gaining much plunder, though he lost his own son and his sister's son together with a number of huscarles in this enterprise. The following year he also died and his semi-autonomous eorldom of Northumbria passed to Tostig, the brother of Harold.[2] Efforts were also made to bring Edward 'the Exile', Edmund 'Ironside's' son, to England, but he died on arrival (the *Chronicle* appears to be suspicious of his death), leaving only the æthling Edgar (his son) as a possible successor to the throne, a child who was (maybe fortunately) apparently ignored by all but Queen Edith.

With the accession of Gruffydd ap Llewelyn to the Welsh throne in October 1055, the western Midlands border erupted. Ælfgar, nominal eorl of East Anglia, son of eorl Leofric, being outlawed (we don't know why) went to Ireland, returning with nineteen ships (perhaps 1,000 men) to Wales, where he made alliance with King Gruffydd. With a combined Irish and Welsh army, they then marched on Hereford, where eorl Ralph opposed them. The English army fled, we are told, 'because they were made to fight on horseback', which sounds as though being horsed they, in reality, found it easy to flee, though the *Chronicle* also mentions four or five hundred killed.[3]

Perhaps, as at Maldon in 991, the old bond of loyalty was (not for the first time) undermined by the king's absence, with consequent failure of the great fyrd to turn out in full force, though Florence of Worcester accused the king's Frenchmen of cowardice.[4] As a result, Hereford was burnt down and Æthelstan's minster was stripped of everything, including its hangings, and destroyed. Some citizens were killed but others were taken away into slavery in Wales.

Troops were raised in all the adjacent territories and these then gathered at Gloucester and crossed into Wales under eorl Harold's command. They camped beyond 'Straddele' (Ystrad Dwr or the Golden Valley), possibly reusing an old encampment at Longtown.[5] However, further pursuit into the Black Mountains and the Brecon Beacons would have been foolhardy so he retired and built a dyke around Hereford while opening negotiations. Peace was then agreed at Billingsly, just north of the Wyre Forest and south of Bridgnorth (on the Severn). Here Ælfgar was reinstated and so his ship force, with winter setting in, sailed upriver to Chester to await the tribute Ælfgar had promised them, presumably concluding their progress by marching overland from Shrewsbury to Chester, using Watling Street.

Now we should ask ourselves why this treaty was agreed so far inland and why the ships did not, instead, sail back down the Severn and away to Ireland or even to the Mersey, also why was Ælfgar responsible for paying them? Let me provide one explanation.

In the first place they had certainly sailed too far inland and were almost certainly being shadowed by Harold's English army, so there was no real chance of escape. Nevertheless, they could continue to cause trouble unless they were now placated, not least for their commander, Ælfgar. Paying them off would provide for Ælfgar's personal safety and, no doubt, he would be happy to agree to pay them from his now reinstated lands and revenues. Why did they not sail back to the Severn's mouth, well presumably because the English ship force lay there, waiting for these few ships to return and maybe because the pay-out was at Chester. Moreover, so late in the season, these pirate vessels required maintenance before they could safely face the Irish Sea. For the pirates there was no obvious way back, except to abandon their ships and trudge on to Chester, collect their money and find a passage sometime in the spring, back to Ireland. Maybe some 'fell beside the wayside' but whatever happened it had all been a cleverly arranged strategy on Harold's part.

There is no mention in all this of King Gruffydd's army so, perhaps, he had fallen out with Ælfgar's small force and/or he also feared to meet Harold's army. So, Harold had now dealt with the incursion, neutralised the pirates and diplomatically removed Ælfgar. Logically it now only remained to deal with this renegade and traitor in due course, but, for the present, he was eorl Leofric's son and that kept him safe, and maybe he was stupid enough to believe that all had been forgiven.

In 1056, Harold's mass priest, Leofgar, succeeded to the bishopric of Hereford and finally shaved off his warlike moustaches, but in spite of this promotion he then took up his spear and sword again after he had been installed. Just before midsummer, in conflict with Gruffydd, apparently at Glasbury-on-Wye, he was killed, along with his priests and also Ælfnoth the shire reeve and other good men when other Englishmen fled. What followed was chaos, until eorls Leofric and Harold arrived with bishop Aldred and made a frightened Gruffydd swear to be a faithful under-king to King Edward in the future.

In 1057, Ælfgar succeeded his father, Leofric, as eorl of Mercia and without his father's protection there was no longer any need to show him leniency: in 1058, Ælfgar was again declared an outlaw. There seems to have been an old and established hatred between Tostig, Harold's brother and now eorl of Northumbria, and Ælfgar's sons and Ælfgar himself may have been, like Swein Godwinson, a character flawed by the circumstances of his birth.[6] Anyway, in 1058 the outlawed eorl rejoined Gruffydd, giving him his daughter in marriage and making simultaneous campaign with a fortuitous Norwegian invasion (or raid) under Magnus (King Harald 'Hardrada's' son), a raid comprising Vikings from the Kingdom of the Isles and from Ireland as well. The *Chronicle* provides only sketchy references, so it cannot have comprised a really serious threat; on the other hand it was certainly not gloriously defeated. Booty and slaves would seem to have been the purpose, avoiding outright conflict as far as possible and Tostig would have been responsible for dealing with activities in the North, both now and in 1061 when the Scots invaded.

Here we face a lacuna, a long gap in our records, all except those records concerning religious appointments and pilgrimages. It may be that eorl Ælfric was (*pro tempore*) tacitly permitted to govern Mercia, having reached a *modus vivendi* with his Welsh son-in-law, but in the second half of 1062 he altogether disappears from our records. In his place, his teenage son Eadwine was appointed eorl, thus depriving Gruffydd of any possible Mercian support and leaving the way open for the Godwines to finally deal with the menace of the Welsh king.

Tostig had, since 1058, ruled the earldom of Northumbria, which had once, when under Leofric, been brigaded with Mercia. Perhaps the mercurial Ælfgar had been seen as too much of a risk for such volatile border territory and Tostig seems indeed to have governed it with a heavy hand, though Professor Barlow makes a case for this being a benevolent despotism.[7] Tostig was, perhaps, as bellicose as his brother, Harold, but more straightforward, less devious or fickle and better able to keep his own counsel, which is why he is harder to understand.

Anyway, with Mercian intervention no longer an impediment, Harold went, after Christmas, on an audacious campaign against Gruffydd. He descended on Rhuddlan, Gruffydd's 'palace' and burnt it to the ground along with all remaining ships, though Gruffydd himself escaped by sea. Possibly this was in retaliation for renewed raids on Mercia? After Easter in this same year, 1063, Harold took a ship force from Bristol and ravaged the Welsh coast all the way round to Rhuddlan, while Tostig launched an overland attack from Chester. When they joined forces, Gruffydd had again managed to escape but his own nobles were only too anxious to make peace and so he was murdered by his own men. His head was brought, as proof, to Harold and he duly delivered it to the (saintly) King Edward, along with the figurehead from Gruffydd's ship. It is probably not without significance that the late Welsh king's two brothers, Bleddyn and Rhiwallon, were made the new client rulers of Wales. Politics was always a dirty game!

In spite of this, neither Wales nor Northumbria could remain peaceful for long for both the north and the west were perennial trouble spots, borders that remained more or less fluid for centuries. While kingdoms beyond the nominal English borders remained independent and also less affluent, there was always the temptation for petty kings to acquire some part of England's wealth in cattle, people and silver. The same temptations, as we have seen, beckoned other overseas invaders and the recidivism of all these brigands, pirates and ambitious landholders could not, as yet, be prevented by English domination of the seas or the land borders for any real length of time, or by precepts and pleas for internal loyalty that could not be enforced by binding and acknowledged laws. The power structure as well as the organisation for defence was still too weak and relied too much on the unpredictable loyalty of powerful individuals who could set themselves against a weak monarch.

The weakness of the English Crown throughout this period has been all too apparent, despite England's unique specie-only taxation and its obvious potential for better defence. Indeed, it was this geld, land tax, which exercised a major influence on invaders and which also stimulated unrest within the kingdom itself among the powerful, not only in the absence of equitable application but with the simultaneous lure of fabulous riches. We might say that, though a decisive tool for stability had been created, one that had real potential, as yet no one knew how to apply it and so, as yet, it did more harm than good. Still, we can see (what contemporaries could not) that the power for lasting good was now there, if someone could only harness it and turn it into binding law.

Notes

1. Wright (2014) quoting Domesday Book.
2. Lapidge (et al., op. cit.), p.397.
3. Savage (ed.), *The Anglo-Saxon Chronicles*, p.181. Building on the imprecise evidence of the *Chronicle* and of Florence alias John of Worcester's *Chronicon ex Chronicis*, Barlow tried to make this a Norman cavalry battle but I cannot find any solid evidence to support this.
4. Florence alias John op. cit. I, pp.212–4.
5. Opinion of the Longtown Castle Project as reported in 'A Story of Two Castles' *Current Archaeology* 375 (2021), p.41.
6. Q.v. Barlow (1970 and 79), pp.193–4 for the feud.
7. Ibid., pp.194–195.

Chapter Twenty-Eight

A Winter's Tale

Anyone who has studied the Gloucestershire folios of *Domesday Book* will be struck by the picture they provide of a hunting paradise. The splendour and diversity of the landscapes, the diversity of habitats and the potential for game of all kinds, not only to the south of the Severn but also in the Welsh Comotes on its north bank, were then (and for some centuries to come) unspoiled by industry and commerce. King Edward's consuming passion during his later years was hunting and the Godwine's hold on political power depended on keeping the king too pre-occupied with his passion to be interested in politics.

To this end, it seems, in 1065 earl Harold set about creating a sumptuous hunting lodge at Portskewet (Newport, Gwent) in this newly conquered Comote, a lodge adorned and provided with the best. Stripping away modern industrial accretions, the attraction of the area is obvious from the little of the original landscape that still remains. Wentwood Forest stretched from the Usk to the Wye, divided between Gwent Uwchcoed (the above forest) and the Iscoed (the below forest) with marshes and flats from Caerleon to the Newport Wetlands. As work began on this lodge at Lammas, it seems obvious that Harold was aiming for the autumn passage season for hawking over the flats, followed by winter and spring hunting, as the king liked to spend Christmas at Gloucester. 'When all was ready', at the end of August, Caradoc, son of Gryffydd, arrived with a large force and killed most of the workers, seizing everything portable and ruining the surprise.[1]

It might be that this raid had as much to do with hostility to any extension of the royal forests as it did with revenge or ethnicity. Though we know little of any 'forest laws' at this period, the erosion of the ancient right to hunt over untilled land was probably threatened long before the Norman Conquest and, equally, resisted as passionately as in later centuries. Even if the taking of game by ordinary men was not yet proscribed, the abuses consequent upon an influx of wealthy men and their entourages would always have caused friction with local populations. Magnates like Harold also had 'parks' (not, however, 'emparked' or fenced at this date), minor forests of their own. At Odiham in Hampshire we can see in *Domesday Book*'s record that Harold's '80 hides less 1½' were later added by King William to his 'terra regis' (to the south at Neatham, which had a similar set of statistics and had formerly been King Edward's park), and from an analysis of the figures we can therefore deduce that these 11,179 acres of 'preserves' had formerly been Harold's own forest.[2] It seems unlikely that he would have welcomed poachers.

Taxation seems to have been another point of friction, the raising of geld, not only to pay for defence but also for Edward's lavish lifestyle.[3] Once again, many entries in *Domesday Book* tell us that eorl Harold was seriously evading his tax liabilities and, of course, the Crown does not tax itself, so when the tax revenues due from these magnates had to be raised and maintained, the burden fell on lesser landholders. Although English coinage maintained a high silver content after King Edgar's reforms, there were still small differences between mint purities and, in particular, we should note that Northumbrian coinage was rather less pure.[4] The usual consequence of lower purity was a demand to collect more than the nominal amount due, in order to then 'dealbate' it in order to analyse and make up the difference in purity. To the ordinary tax-payer this seemed like an excuse to pocket extra revenue. With such internal pressures on the social system and on individual incomes, rumblings were to be expected and it is not surprising that soon afterwards the 'pips' eventually 'squeaked', which they did in 1065 at a gathering of all the thegns in Northumbria and Yorkshire. This certainly suggests cause and effect.

So here we see, yet again, the independent and rebellious spirit of Northumbria, for while Tostig was hunting in Wiltshire with the king in the autumn they received news of a revolt and conspiracy in the north. The focus of it was definitely on Tostig, for his supposedly heavy and unjust taxation, also for legally removing enemies and, for good measure, for despoiling churches, according to Florence of Worcester.[5] Two murders of probably high-ranking, maybe troublesome, Northumbrians were done at York, and Queen Edith herself had ordered another murder 'for love of her brother', making her blameless and him guilty. Barlow also suggests that the conspirators had intrigued with Eadwine and Morcar of Mercia and possibly with Harold (though he denied complicity).[6] Anyway, the rebellion was certainly supported by a typical piece of political plotting and intrigue.

Early in October, the rebels entered York and murdered many of Tostig's huscarles and servants, plundering his armoury and his treasury. As he was in the south of England, this effectively deprived him of his core select troops and rendered him incapable of acting in subsequent events. The rebels then 'legalised' this revolt by outlawing Tostig, and so they next supported their actions by raising troops in Nottinghamshire, Derbyshire and Lincolnshire, killing and plundering as they went, to be rapidly joined by eorl Eadwine and his troops, including Welsh auxiliaries (or mercenaries). At Northampton, they murdered, burnt houses and corn and reived cattle: we are told that thousands of beasts and hundreds of men were taken and these slaves were carried off northwards. Some of the rebels even reached Oxford, so the scene was set for civil war along the line of the Thames. As had happened so often before, a period of peace ended with an internal power struggle.

Now Tostig, his wife and supporters, went over the waters to eorl Baldwin in Flanders for safety and the rebels demanded Morcar for their new eorl. No doubt in panic but safely ensconced at Britford (south of Salisbury), King Edward agreed and sent eorl Harold to negotiate, obviously backed by the general and select fyrds of southern England, to chaotic scenes in the temporary royal court.[7] In the absence of the king, the actual response to the call to arms was abysmal and the rebels refused to have anyone but Morcar and 'the laws of Cnut'. This last demand might be a hint that Tostig had applied the laws of Wessex to the Danelaw, contrary to the Secular Dooms of Cnut (caps 12 and 15), but I wonder if the real reference was to Cap 69 and the demands for heavy taxation?[8] Cap 80 also gave a man the right to hunt over his own land, though (as yet) we know of no recorded restriction of this ancient liberty. In fact, Cnut's laws were basically those of Edgar and Æthelred II, as compiled by archbishop Wulfstan, and it is difficult to understand how there could have been any major departure in Northumbria from the general rule of law in the rest of England.[9] We are, I think, probably hearing of mob hysteria in these demands, with many men creating their own justifications rather than voicing any justifiable grievances, but maybe with the less than pure Northumbrian coinage at the root of these demands.

It was late in the season and, besides, no one wanted civil war. King Edward made no attempt to lead a royal army in person (which left Harold out on a limb) nor to supervise the negotiations. Fielded basically as the go between, there was nothing Harold could do and the attitude at court seems to have been hostile to Tostig or, more likely, careless of his fate provided further conflict was avoided. Nevertheless, Tostig regarded this as a betrayal by his brother and the feud between them that followed was to end the line of the Anglo-Saxon kings.

Was there any justification for Tostig's suspicions? There are hints that Queen Edith may have preferred her brother Tostig over her brother Harold: as we have seen, she was prepared to murder for him. There is also the problem of the accession, which possibility requires us to step back to 1064 and look at Harold's activities. We also need to take stock of the real character of the 'saintly' King Edward. We think that Edward was born in 1005, so he was not an old man in 1065, for all the dotard image portrayed on the Bayeux Tapestry, yet he seems to have had some misgivings about the succession, for he was childless. If he had misgivings, well it was his own fault, for part of his skill in preventing invasions seems to have been to keep foreign rivals guessing as to who might succeed him and so keep them watching one another for any hostile moves against himself: divide and continue to rule!

Eustace II, Count of Boulogne and master of the cross-Channel trade, had married Godgifu, King Æthelred's daughter, and his ancestors had once been kings of France, so *he* may have been promised the English throne in 1051 when he visited England – when he received a bloody nose at Dover! William, Duke of Normandy, was (when the opportunity presented itself) quick to claim that he had been promised the English throne, that is *after* he had led the joint 'French' forces to victory in 1066.[10] Harold 'Hardrada' of Norway had a flimsy claim but may have been similarly encouraged, and Swein Estrithson of Denmark, Harthacnut's cousin, also claimed that Edward had promised the throne to him. Of course, delivery of the actual throne was not in Edward's gift (though nomination counted), for the English Witan, the council of the mightiest in the land, had that prerogative and the Godwines and their supporters were undoubtedly the mightiest in the land. The question really was, who would they choose, or would Queen Edith trump them all?

Leaving aside the Godwine family and assuming that King Edward, as a Breton not an Englishman, believed he had the right to name his successor, our next step is to speculate what he did in 1064, though why he did it we do not know. Maybe it was the invasion by Magnus, King Harald 'Hardrada's' son, which persuaded him to encourage rivalries, lest one of the 'suitors' should take the initiative, or maybe he was seeking an alliance with one of them? Anyway, in 1064 Edward despatched Harold Godwineson to France with an embassy in order to visit someone, the Bayeux Tapestry leaves us in no doubt about that.[11] What it does not tell us is the original and intended destination, or the projected contact.

Crossing the Channel was never a certain business and the best 'jumping off' point was probably the Isle of Wight, at least that was the favourite start for most English armies for many centuries, but Harold chose to start from Bosham. Perhaps he should have started from Thanet, but maybe he was avoiding the notice of other English ships, for his mission was certainly secret, the Tapestry makes that quite clear. Whatever his planned landfall, he actually arrived in the mouth of the Somme and, getting out on the wrong side, fell into the hands of Guy of Ponthieu, as everybody knows. From here the story (or its factoid) is deemed common knowledge, that is all except for the real purpose of his visit to France.

I have proposed that his real destination was Eustace's territory.[12] When, instead, he found himself an 'honoured guest' at the court of Duke William of Normandy, he half-divulged his embassy to the man in power instead, call it force majeur, presumably it was (to all concerned) the Will of God. The problem that King Edward, it seems, foresaw and the problem for any 'suitor' for the throne of England (including any Godwine) was Queen Edith. Of course, it is in the nature of secret diplomacy that when the diplomacy is discovered, the secret remains hidden and so there have been many speculations as to the real purpose of Harold's embassy. What follows is my hypothesis, based on the evidence contained in the margins of the Bayeux Tapestry and on its main schema.

First of all, Edith was Edward's queen and a Godwine by birth, and she had not only maintained, especially in the *Vita Ædwardi Regis*, her virginity but acted in her marriage 'like a beloved daughter ... the gem in the middle of the Kingdom'. Now in England a woman *could* inherit land in her own right and a daughter *was* entitled to inherit her father's estates, which meant that (unique in Europe) *she* could become an independent queen.[13] Well, independent or not, she was younger than Edward and when she was widowed, who would she then remarry? There would, of course, be no question but that her new husband would rule, so she would certainly have suitors.

As a Breton by breeding and election this would be an appalling prospect to Edward, but it was also appalling to eorl Harold for he was not his sister's favourite brother and, no doubt, he entertained ambitions for himself. William of Normandy was married and happily so, which rendered him ineligible for marriage to Edith, but Eustace of Boulogne was already on his second wife and would welcome any chance to increase his wealth and power, any chance to advance both of these beyond those of the sitting (and to Eustace upstart) Capetian, King of France. Nevertheless, the Scandinavian kings were Edward's greatest fear throughout his reign and even likely to fight one another over Edith and England when he was gone. The most likely recipient of an embassy in 1064, therefore, was Eustace, but then Harold (by the Will of God) ended up in Normandy.

He could hardly disclose his intended destination to William without betraying his king and himself. If Edward needed an ally who would hold the Narrows against Viking fleets and possibly marry or oppose an ambitious widow, it was *not* likely to be William. The Breton–Norman alliance was not a certain or continuous affair by any means for they were in conflict in 1065–66, a conflict in which the 'guest' Harold was then involved in 1065, and Conan II of Brittany was probably poisoned in December 1066 on Duke William's orders.[13] In 1064, Edward the Breton's sympathies were not likely to have been with Duke William of Normandy and, besides, the Normans were not noted as sailors. If they lacked ships and seamanship, how could they hope to stop the Scandinavians? Eustace, on the other hand, controlled the cross-Channel trade and English ship sokes would obey their anointed king.

Remember Ælfgyfu of Northampton and her children by Cnut? Remember Ælfgyfu-Emma of Normandy and her remarriage to Cnut, with children by Æthelred? Well an Ælfgyfu appears on the Bayeux Tapestry and what follows is what I think the Tapestry is telling us. Harold, as an 'honoured guest' (for the winter of 1064–65) at William's court, had to square himself by telling William something and he could hardly divulge that he was on his way to Eustace of Boulogne, looking for an English alliance, so this is the story he told instead.

Standing in the 'mead hall', flushed with wine, he recounted a story, one already known by some, that Ælfgyfu of Northampton's children were *not* those of Cnut. There was clearly scandalised delight all round, just look at the Tapestry. So Harold Harefoot had murdered the rightful king when he murdered Edward's brother, but fate (Providence) had then seen to it that Edward eventually inherited anyway. In private, Harold now takes the moral of the tale further, this for his host's benefit: Ælfgyfu of Northampton had seized the treasury and power once Cnut was dead, leaving Emma powerless, Queen Edith's temperament is just the same and her landed wealth in England is formidable, and so she would make a good royal match for a Scandinavian entrepreneur with something military to offer. Does William want to see a woman on the English throne, an enormously powerful Edith? Worse still, does he want to see this rich kingdom added to another powerful kingdom when he has had to fight so hard to maintain the independence of Normandy? No, of course not, and (secretly) neither does Harold. William can rely on Harold to help him as an ally, when the time comes, if William is prepared to help Harold. Moreover, the Tapestry's margin tells us what the *Vita Ædwardi Regis* also says, that Harold is a sly fox.[14] But, of course, William is even more sly and before Harold returns to England he has become, symbolically, 'that man's man' in Norman eyes and has sworn, at the very least, his friendship on cleverly disguised Holy relics.[15] The story is well known.

Now we have set the scene and the background for a momentous event and for the political claims consequent upon that event. As yet there is no hint (in 1064) that Edward will soon die but Duke William has *already* begun to construct and to amass an invasion fleet even before Harold's visit.[16] He was an ambitious man. Now, as Harold departs, William awaits a favourable turn of events and, in his turn, begins to make alliances, including one with (a no doubt puzzled and angry) Eustace. When dealing with Scandinavian kings it was best to strike first and possession is nine-tenths of the law, so

William needed help. He did not *need* Harold, but Harold's arrival (and departure) was, in the event, fortuitous for, out of the blue, King Edward dropped dead at Christmas 1085–6. Now William could hold England to ransom, maybe then place Harold on the throne to dispose of Edith and, in alliance with English troops, snatch the silver plum of massive English tribute from under Scandinavian noses.

Notes

1. Barlow, op. cit. p.233, repeats a twelfth-century story that it all began with English merchants refusing to pay tolls and Harold committing sacrilege, with the result that Harold was killed a month later. Hardly reliable evidence.
2. Wright (2014), p.223.
3. It is often claimed that 'Heregeld' was abolished when Scandinavian troops were paid off in 1051 but there seems to be no definitive proof of this and gelds do seem to have continued.
4. The subject is complicated, q.v. D.M. Metcalf and J.P. Northover, 'Interpreting the Alloy of the Later Anglo-Saxon Coinage', *British Numismatic Journal* (1986), and the same authors' 'Sporadic Debasement in the English Coinage c.1009–1052', *Numismatic Chronicle* vol. 162 (2002).
5. Florence of Worcester I, p.222.
6. Barlow, op. cit. p.235.
7. Ibid. 237, quoting the *Vita Ædwardi Regis*.
8. Barlow also notices this, p.196.
9. W. Stubbs, quote *Select Charters* (OUP, 1870, 1921 and 1960), pp.86–7. For a deeper discussion see D. Whitelock, 'Wulfstan and the Laws of Cnut', *English Historical Review* 63 (1948); Patrick Wormald, 'Æthelred the Lawmaker' in D. Hill (ed.) *Ethelred the Unready: Papers from the Millenary Conference* (BAR ser.59 OUP, 1978), pp.47–80; Pauline Stafford, 'The Laws of Cnut and the History of Anglo-Saxon Promises' in *Anglo-Saxon England* vol. 10 (CUP, 1982).
10. Q.v. Wright (2019 and 2020).
11. Wright (2019), pp.19–26 et seq.
12. Ibid., pp.91–94 in particular.
13. Q.v. Barlow, pp.299–300 and Appendix A pp.292–3; also p.249 for Edward's dying speech in the *Vita Ædwardi Regis*.
14. Q.v. David Howarth, *1066: The Year of Conquest* (2008).
15. Wright (2019), pp.42–43 and *Vita Ædwardi Regis*.
16. Ibid., pp.146–147.

Chapter Twenty-Nine

Fulford and Stamford

Flying in the face of a long-cherished tradition and quasi-religious belief, I am *not* going to nominate the Battle of Hastings as *the* battle that made England 'great'. We have already seen enough of the genius of several English kings to give them a share of the credit, just as we have seen the disastrous effects of weak and cowardly kings. In 1066, England already possessed formidable resources and (whatever some people have said in the past) famous troops, as well as the mechanism by which to raise a nation in arms, and if Hastings tells us anything it is of Harold's complete mastery of military command.

On 4 or 5 January 1066, King Edward was 'alive *and* dead'. He probably died of a stroke, leaving Edith in Harold's care. She was Domina, Harold her servant and protector, pending a decision by the Witan. Was Edward of sound testamentary capacity or were his mental processes impeded, did he actually make the lucid speech subsequently attributed to him in the *Vita Ædwardi Regis* and bequeath the management of the kingdom to Harold? If so, Harold had every right to be nominated as king of England. On 6 January, King Edward was buried with great honour and on the same day Harold was crowned king. The meeting of the Witan must have been both remarkably expeditious and unanimous, but no one was richer than Harold and he needed to forestall any move by Edith.

Edward's translation to saintly status was initiated by the 'Vita' and promoted by the Norman kings. They made no objection to his dying testament but authors like William of Poitiers laid heavy emphasis on Duke William's 'long-before' promise of the English throne and Harold's perfidy as the sworn vassal of the duke's, a man sworn by receiving a gift of arms he did not need (but could not refuse) and by his oath on the (hidden) relics – whatever that oath might actually have been. If we were writing such a political intrigue and such a palace coup today it would not read with any improved veracity. The victors always write the history, but that does not provide us with facts.

That history is not always honesty, let alone reality, the details of Edward's reign bear witness. This had been yet another king afraid to lead his troops against their foes, incapable of plotting to effect, given to 'hysterical expressions of disgust for the theatre of the world ... bizarre trappings for an efficient government', hysterical proems to charters, a king who was not a just judge and who 'weakened himself in England by imprudent actions' and whose diplomatic promises, though cheap, only put off invasions and conflicts to another day and the next reign.[1]

The chroniclers wrote a fulsome encomium for Edward after the invasion (with an eye on their new and Norman masters), which included praise for his military prowess, for just as imperfect kings are betrayed by their bad counsellors, kings betray their good counsellors and generals by stealing their glory. It does, however, confirm that Edward was wise to commit the kingdom to Harold.

The acquisition of good, even holy, standing with the Church was not at all difficult for a rich man, he did not even have to sell all he had and give it to the poor, he simply purchased the Kingdom of Heaven (and a good reputation on earth) by 'good works'. Such 'good works' invariably involved generous bequests to the Church, founding conventual houses, enriching bishops and abbots and making great show of piety. In return, the living turned a blind eye to all peccadilloes and the Divinity pardoned all human failings. As the Church thus approved the late King Edward, it was not difficult for the Norman chroniclers to improve on the myth.

Perhaps the last words should be given to Professor Brooks, who observed that English kingship survived Edward's reign, 'yet this is a tribute rather to the strength of the institution and to historical circumstances than to Edward himself ... a medieval king neither by temperament nor by upbringing ... bred to hunting and idleness, and these tastes stayed with him all his days'. He was not an English king, rather he was a Breton, and 'there is not much to suggest that he was himself a man of learning or an intellectual'.[2] Yet, for its rich and faithful patrons, the medieval Church was invariably creative and in Edward's case (which was not an isolated one) it created a saintly cult.

It looks as though Harold and King Edward had been planning to take the rebellious northern thanes in hand after Christmas 1065 and that this campaign was not postponed by the funeral or the coronation, for we next hear of King Harold returning from York to Westminster for Easter of 1066. That was when men saw the portent of the 'hairy star' shining for seven nights and soon after this eorl Tostig and his household troops arrived at the Isle of Wight. It appears that he had attempted to solicit men and ships from Duke William of Normandy, which must have been interesting intelligence for him but (with his own preparations under way), William could spare none.[3] Nor, according to the *Chronicle*, was Harold himself unaware of the duke's plans, but then it would have been difficult in 1065 let alone in 1066 to have kept the demand for chandlery and provisions quiet, all along the Atlantic and North Sea seaboard. In preparation for William's arrival, Harold had been gathering a great land force and ship force himself in at least the first months of 1066 and possibly before.

Driven from the south coast, Tostig seems to have acquired more ships and perhaps some ne'er-do-wells as he rounded the Wash and harried Lincolnshire: he had sixty ships by the time he entered the Humber estuary. Here he met eorl Edwin's land force, which drove him back to his ships, apparently with some losses for he next arrived in Scotland with only a dozen 'small' ships. Taking the Orkney route, King Harald 'Hardrada' of Norway himself now arrived in Scotland with 300 ships and Tostig became his man. It seems that King Harald (like Duke William) had also been making preparations before 1066. Undoubtedly, Harold had also heard of these. A newly crowned king could expect all sorts of opportunists to test his mettle.

The combined enemy force then sailed up the Humber and the Ouse, landing at Riccall early in September and advancing on York. In 1086 (and so also in 1066), Riccall was a reasonably prosperous vill of 4,000 acres with 960 acres under the plough and 3,000 acres of meadows and wood pastures to attract these foragers. At Fulford, just outside the city, the Norwegian force met the brothers Edwin and Morcar and their local fyrdmen on 20 September, even as King Harold of England was marching north to their support, and Edwin and Morcar were heavily defeated.

There is no really hard evidence for this battle but Snorri Sturlasson in his (less than reliable) *Heimskringla* provided details at a later date. Morcar may even have retreated afterwards with a small fleet up the Wharfe to Tadcaster, awaiting Harald Hardrada's next move, and Brooks suggests that this was why the Norwegians stopped at Riccall.[4] Here their main force took to the land in order to march the short distance to York. Two miles from York were the vills of 'Water' and 'Gate' Fulford and here Edwin and Morcar drew up their levies across the road, apparently with their right flank on the Ouse and their left on fenny ground with ditching. In *Domesday Book* (combined) Fulford is given an area of 3,000 acres with 1,245 noted as under cultivation, so fenny ground and even scrubby wasteland (Elvington Moor?) may have existed, with the name 'gate' implying some sort of passage through woody or difficult terrain.

Harald apparently chose to throw his army's weight (his left) onto the English right wing, by the river, which may have been the firmest ground, while the English used their local knowledge to attack across the fens with their left. In a hard-fought battle, the Norwegians turned the English right, rolling around to take the English left in their flank: it appears that these men were then caught in their own fenny trap, floundering to escape.[5]

Edwin and Morcar escaped and I wonder if Morcar regained his fleet as the Norwegians gave up their pursuit and entered York?

The invaders then passed through the city, and although they did not sack it they undoubtedly now helped initiate the economic disaster that was to befall it and its hinterland two years later. It had already it seems, been ravaged by King Harold earlier in the year and now it had to provide for another army. Four days later, Harold arrived once again with his army to find the city supine, the cupboard bare and Harald Hardrada and Tostig departed for Stamford Bridge, a place to the east of York.

King Harold's immediate problem surely was to find provisions for his army but having force-marched his army at something like 30 miles a day, and so arriving quite unexpectedly, he instead forbore and pressed his advantage by following up his enemies, and this was an astute decision. As part of the accord with the city, Harald and Tostig had agreed an extensive exchange of hostages, with offers of support from the north and east Ridings perhaps, and it was onto this formal ceremony at Stamford Bridge that Harold's English army was now descending. Because they did not expect trouble, no doubt anticipating great hospitality from the city's fathers on a hot day, a large number of the Vikings were without their armour, especially their byrnies, though carrying their weapons. The advantage to the English is obvious.

How had King Harold achieved such complete surprise? In the first place, he had wasted no time in setting out, although he probably expected Edwin and Morcar to be able to hold off the Norwegians, pending his arrival. In order to cover so much ground each day, his army must have travelled light and, as his men were no more supermen than their enemies, this means that they had a large baggage train to transport their armour. It also suggests that his army was mounted, at least those who had furthest to travel, and that the road north, Ermine Street, was in good condition.

To cut the Norwegians off from their armours (left either in York or in Riccall when they were gathered to the east of the city), the English army must have passed through the city and, being mounted, were able to neutralise any attempted warning from there. In order to neutralise the Norwegian disembarkation point on the Ouse, at Riccall, where there would have been men guarding the river boats, Harold either took them by surprise or he followed the Roman Ridge to Castleford and then struck east. Had he crossed the Humber due south-east of York he would have come between York and Stamford Bridge, an effective and swifter interposition but with the risk of being seen at his crossing point by the largest of the Norwegian warships, now confined to the Humber.

However, it was that he accomplished it, it was a fortunate stroke and, as they say, 'fortune favours the bold'. Armies do not move silently and long

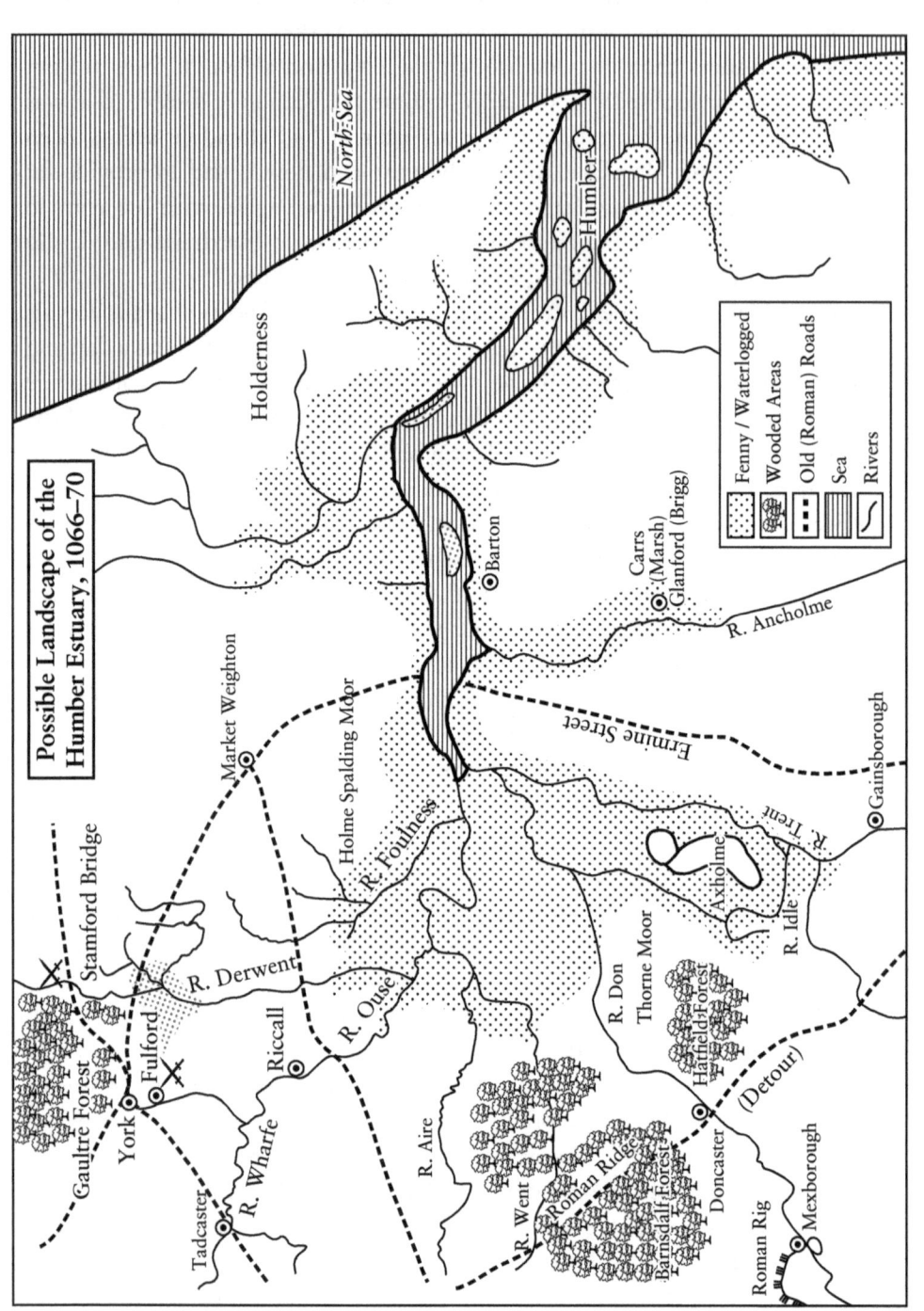

Map 7: Possible Landscape of the Humber Estuary, 1066–70.

> **Map 7: Possible Landscape of the Humber Estuary, 1066–70.**
> Note that viable landing sites were limited, so the Norwegian Army sailed confidently up the Ouse to Riccall. In this way they exited the marshy terrain and arrived at the gates of York fresh for battle. By 1069, however, well-placed piquets could observe both the estuary and landing sites, having the advantage of cavalry response, especially if a landing had been attempted at Ermine Street or movement observed on the Trent or the Ancholme. At both dates the mouth of the Estuary and the Holderness shore were much more open to winter gales, with Spurn Point less prominent than it is today, making pelagic movements very dangerous in the flimsier raiding craft. So in winter time it was essential to campaign before the onset of gales.

columns can be seen, especially as dust clouds, and heard. Moreover, the English needed to don their armours before approaching their enemies and finally deploying, all of which takes time. King Harald Hardrada is credited with 300 ships in the *Chronicle* and given that, by now, some of these were large and impressive, ocean-going, warships, his force may have been 12,000 men or more, so at this battle he probably mustered at least 10,000 men. King Harold can hardly have arrived with fewer and yet he needed to remain undetected until the last moment.

To the immediate north of York and stretching eastwards lay what was soon to be recorded as 'the forest of Gantres', or Galtres, and in 1066 this may well have wrapped around the eastern hinterland of the city's circuit.[6] This is to say that the road to Donnington may then have passed through Stockton Forest, even as far as Helmsley Gate, though in 1066 Stockton itself comprised only 1,000 acres and had *no* woodland. Helmsley, on the other hand, covered an area of 36,000 acres, of which only 12.8 per cent was cultivated at all.[7] The implication is that the majority of this area was primary or secondary woodland, heath or scrubland and so, even if 'Great Burnham Wood to Dunnsinane' did *not* go, there would be plenty of cover and little likelihood of dust, as well as the woodlands dampening all sounds. As late as 1845–52 (1904–05 revision) the area east and east-nor'-east of York included twenty-one moors, commons and woods.

The River Derwent has also undergone changes at Stamford Bridge, with a fresh channel cut in the eighteenth century and a new bridge erected in 1727 downstream of the old bridge, which had formerly run over 'the Shallows', an area fordable in very dry weather.[8] Over the water on the left or east bank of the Derwent the ground sloped gently uphill for 50ft and beyond that levelled out to the 'Battle Flats', as they are called on the Ordnance Survey Map.[9] The one inch 1913 map calls this area the 'Hatkill Field' (battlefield?) and shows 'Mill Sike Beck' to the south and 'Flawith' and 'Barton' beks (streams) to the north, which all helps us dictate the confines of the action.

The action seems to have begun on the west bank of the river with Harold's army taking Harald's army by complete surprise, so cover must have been available almost to the river. Immediately there was a rearguard action it seems, for as Vikings crossed the bridge to join their main assembly the story has it (in one version of the *Chronicle*) that one valiant and mail-clad warrior with an axe held the bridge, hewing down all who attempted to cross. Then an Englishman, hiding in a boat (or a salting trough) floated under the bridge and thrust his spear upwards between the planks to dispose of the defender in a most unheroic manner!

This allowed the English army to pour across and fan out and, if there had been mounted men among them, they could have forded the shallows now that the former defenders on the bank were scrambling upslope to the protection of their own shield wall. Snorri speaks of horsemen and archery and has Harald Hardrada killed by an arrow through the throat. Although this sounds uncharacteristic for a Saxon army (so we have been repeatedly told), one Old English rune poem includes the stanza 'yewbows are useful for youths and veterans of warlike skill: wieldy mounted, they are favoured by those who fight from horseback.'[10]

Eystein Orre, Snorri says, was now despatched on horseback to bring up reinforcements from Riccall, a distance of at least 20 miles and involving a crossing of the Derwent lower down. Even if the battle had begun early in the day, there was hardly time for him to return with many more men as the road trip would take seven or eight hours for men on foot to arrive. Finally, Tostig also fell but Eystein, we are told, did arrive with reinforcements for a last stand in the dusk of the day, a fine, heroic and Norse ending to the tale that might just be true.

The *Chronicle* says, 'the English struck them fiercely from behind until some of them came to ship. Some were drowned, some were burnt, some perished in various ways, so that there were few left …'[11] This sounds as though the 'hot trod' continued into the following day, chasing fugitives back to Riccall and firing the fleet there into the bargain. Styrkar the Marshal escaped on a horse, apparently attempting to pass himself off as a local, while Harald's son, Olaf, asked terms of Harold and, with his bishop and the earl of Orkney, he was allowed to depart with twenty-four of his 300 ships. Presumably (at best) no more than 8 per cent of the Viking army had survived the invasion, a significant victory indeed.

I wonder if Eystein actually made it back to Riccall but was then penned in by Morcar's fleet entering the Ouse? This would have effectively blocked the main escape route for the Norsemen and it would help explain the burning and drowning of fugitives, with both the fleeing fugitives and the remaining boat guard caught between the hammer and the anvil! Moreover, an 'immense booty' was recovered from the battlefield, presumably taken from York, as if the site had been chosen for a major Viking stronghold. Indeed, I feel certain that more would have been made of this battle by chroniclers, more would have been written and recorded for posterity, but for the interposition of the other great threat far away in the south. With Harold occupied in the north of England, the north wind that had plagued Duke William of Normandy for so long dropped and favourable airs opened the undefended backdoor of England to his well-prepared and opportunistic enterprise.

Notes

1. Barlow, p.159, quoting Sawyer's *Anglo-Saxon Charters*, the Royal Historical Society (1968), no. 1006, itself from Kemble's, *Codex Diplomaticus Aevy Saxonici* no. 774; also ACW (2017) p.176. As a judge vide Barlow, pp.178–9 and p.103.
2. Christopher Brooke, *The Saxon and Norman Kings* (1963), pp.139–140.
3. Odericus Vitalis.
4. Q.v. 'The Battle of Stamford Bridge', F.W. Brooks (East Yorkshire Local History Society, 1956), p.10.
5. K DeVries in *The Norwegian Invasion of England in 1066* (Boydell Press, 2003), who identifies the 'Fordland Swamp' but I do not know how sodden the terrain was in September 1066.
6. Later estimated at 100,000 acres.
7. Phillimore's *Domesday Book* vol. 30, 1 and 2, also John Speed's map (1611–12) 'North and East Ridings'. The 1845–52 survey is the O.S. one inch map 63 (revised 1904–05) 'Vale of York'.
8. Brooks, pp.17–19.
9. Sheet CLVIII (six inch).
10. Rahul Gupta (trans.) 'Linguarum veterum septentrionalium thesaurus grammatiocriticus et archaeologicus' (Oxford, 1703–1705) vol. I, p.135, in *Wiðowinde* 195, p.31.
11. *The Anglo-Saxon Chronicles* (trans. Savage).

Chapter Thirty

The Affair of England

In contemplating his 'affair of England' in 1064 (or before), Duke William of Normandy faced a series of extraordinary challenges. In the first place, he needed men, but then he also needed the ships in which to carry them. He could not know how many ships until he knew how many men, but while ships can be berthed until required, men cost a great deal of money when kept idle in camp for any period and cantonments (especially in summer) breed sickness. Above all, he needed money to pay for men and ships, but how much money would that be? That depended on the quality of the troops and to defeat the English fyrdmen, especially hearth troops and select fyrdsmen, he needed the best. In fact, he needed more than the best, he needed something revolutionary.

Of course, he was personally wealthy, but an invasion was an enormous undertaking so he needed the assistance of his avaricious brother, Odo, bishop of Bayeux, and his other brother, Robert, he also needed everything he could get from his subordinate lords, great and small. Yet still he needed more money and the only solution was a joint stock venture, but whoever joined him with such a financial contribution must be trustworthy, the plans must not leak out. This was easier said than done as such massive demands for chandlery (for this fleet) could hardly be kept secret on the western seaboard. For a start, the Norwegians were making similar preparations, which were already pushing up prices and straining resources. If everyone knew everyone else's intentions and the target was obvious, then the fine details of invasion must certainly remain secret.

Once on English soil the problem then would be how to beat the experienced English troops. This was a technical and tactical problem. The English often rode to battle but they, like the Scandinavians, fought on foot. In France and Flanders, and especially in Normandy and Brittany, the idea of mounted men had been developed beyond simple convenience and speed of movement, or scouting. Here there had been the development of special breeds of horses, large and heavy horses, horses and riders specially trained, trained to attack. They do not seem to have developed the technique of couching and lancing with their spears but they had certainly discovered that the combined weight of horse and man, over half a ton for each horse alone, was very effective in crashing through shield walls. All you needed was level ground on which to build up speed, aggressive horses and riders with courage and resolution. Once through the shield wall, the height advantage of a mounted man gave long swords advantages of weight and momentum, just like a mounted policeman's baton.

William's other tactical discovery seems to have been a geographical one: at the southern end of France, from the Camargue and Iberia, the Basques hunted whales. Now Basques also had ships, so what more natural than to hire ships and men from them and, moreover, these whalers seem to have developed their own specialised archery. Of course, all armies had archers, they were very useful for galling and disabling static enemy lines, for provoking men to break formation in order to teach the pests a lesson, but bows were not particularly powerful and the main tactic was the close-range delivery of mass missiles, not fancy shooting. The Basques, however, used crossbows for whaling, slower to fire but powerful enough to penetrate a Right whale, weapons one could easily aim and which were powerful enough to fire projectiles (bolts) in flattened trajectories.[1]

Now men are easy enough to transport and tranship, not so horses, especially mettlesome, large and very expensive horses. Whether it had been done before with such 'destriers' we do not know, but certainly the removal of at least 1,000 such beasts across stormy seaways, their loading and unloading, their safety and the security of the vessels that carried them, these things would break new ground. Moreover, horses can be seasick and these horses each weighed at least half a ton and were aggressive and powerful. They would take time to load and needed both provisions and mucking out. No suitable ships existed, they had to be converted and the loading of them was equally technical and novel.[2]

Ships do not build themselves, neither are they made of sub-standard materials. Sometimes the timbers used need to be seasoned, and construction can take months because it has to be staged. Shipwrights cannot be created overnight nor sails woven, cordage has to be created and the best, the preferred walrus hide plaited thongs for standing and running rigging, were enormously expensive. The caulking and tarring cannot be completed until the hull has dried if 'green' construction is employed for the strakes, and then there are sea trials. Despite the convincing picture of industry on the Bayeux Tapestry and the accounts written by landsmen many years later, most of the ships in the invasion fleet were hired or bought and those that were newly built needed at least a year, maybe two when in bulk, to complete. This fleet was not built in six months!

Count Eustace II of Boulogne was *not* a Norman, he was a Frenchman of the best pedigree and, like the Count of Ponthieu , he was generally at war with the Duke of Normandy. However, he controlled most of the cross-Channel trade and so was enormously rich and could obviously call on ships and seamen as well. He also had a long-standing family grudge against the King of France. It seems inevitable that he, and Guy of Ponthieu, should be drawn into the joint stock scheme. They now joined the principle potential beneficiaries of the joint stock proposal to bankrupt England.

However, the ship list that survives totals 776 ships and there were probably between 770 and 1,000 vessels of all sizes involved, a sufficient fleet to transport the size and type of force involved.[3] Moreover, the *Brevis Relatio*[4] says that this fleet was gathered from fourteen Norman barons, which at least suggests that the preparation of an invasion fleet was being distributed, camouflaged and kept partly secret, as it would need to be if it was commenced in 1064 or before. The possible omission of Eustace of Boulogne from this list of contributors might also suggest that he was involved at a later stage, possibly in order to finance recruitment and provisioning of the delayed invasion force. That he was required to give surety for his inclusion in the joint stock scheme is suggested by Bridgeford,[5] who observes that William required Eustace's young son to become his hostage, given into the custody of Odo, Bishop of Bayeux, as a guarantee of good behaviour. What Eustace was promised in return is a matter for speculation and we will come to it later.

By the spring of 1066 the secret was certainly out and it may be, as later writers were so vociferously to claim, that William did proclaim himself King Edward's heir before arriving in England. There seems to be evidence for a (now lost) presentation to the Pope on these grounds,[6] though whether the Scandinavian claimants made the same presentation in a bidding war we do not know. Writing the history (after the event) is a very good way of creating 'factual' future history! I am inclined to think that the invasion was initially a means of raising money on a scale like that of the late Cnut. Anyway, the net result was that King Harold of England 'gathered together the greatest naval and land forces that any king in (this) country had ever gathered before' and from May onwards these forces watched the south coast, waiting for the invasion.[7] England was prepared.

William was now recruiting with a vengeance and from deep war chests. He needed a large force if he was to meet English infantry on their own ground and, for all his tactical inspirations, he still needed a great deal of luck, not least to simply get across the Channel. His many converted horse transports would not have been especially well found and manageable, and the English had a long history of naval conflict and success. Moreover, to have any chance at all he needed the weather in his favour, but favourable weather would also warn the English to take to the waters and catch his armada at its most vulnerable. How was he to achieve a safe crossing?

By August, William was ready, with perhaps 12,000 men, camped at Dives-sur-Mer and consuming vast quantities of food, drink and fodder with the attendant sanitary and health problems that any medieval army faced, yet still the wind blew from the wrong quarter and rain pelted down.[8] All William could do was grit his teeth, pray, continue to pay and provide and depend on the English army being the first to run out of supplies. Surely they would need to disperse with the onset of the harvest season, in order to return home and 'carry' the essential winter and spring food resources? Meanwhile, his mercenaries and 'feudal' vassals were munching their way through money and seed corn, anything on four legs (other than horses), including the essential plough beasts, was being consumed and Norman peasants were slaving at their harvests and secretly cursing the prospect of their own starvation the following spring.

In mid-September the wind changed to a (helpful) southerly, but then to a westerly. William ordered his fleet to sea, only to see it floundering and wallowing into St Valéry with, it appears, losses of both ships and men. What had caused such apparently precipitate action, was it frustration, starvation, recklessness? Most likely it was intelligences, for by the end of the first week of September, King Harold was standing down his coastal forces and thereafter desperately marching north, whilst on 20 September his lieutenants were deploying for battle at Fulford. The Bayeux Tapestry plainly tells us that a fifth column now sent agents to William and my guess, it can only be a guess, is that the ship shown on the Tapestry left just after 8 September to tell him that the south coast garrisons had gone.[9]

These men brought William the welcome and astonishing news that Pevensey was virtually unguarded: both the Bayeux Tapestry and the *Chronicle* agree that this was where William actually landed, *not* at Hastings. Here, they reported, on a fecund lagoon surrounded by supplies lay an intact, stone-built, fortress on a peninsular, covering a principal harbour with the essential wharves for horse transhipment and it now had little or no remaining garrison.[10] This was a godsend, a Divine intervention, and then the wind itself changed and fell light, ideal for the passage of the vulnerable fleet. On the night of 27 September 1066, the Franco-Breton-Norman and mercenary fleet slipped across the Channel unopposed.[11] In the morning they made harbour at Pevensey, seized the impregnable fortress (built by the Romans) and set about the arduous process of unloading horses and supplies.

Notes

1. Wright (2019), pp.111 and 119–120.
2. Wright, 'That Which Must Inevitably Happen: Wyrd' in *Wiðowinde* 197 (2021); also op. cit. pp.51–52, 57 and 144–145 (2019).
3. Wright (2019), pp.143–7 for detailed analyses.
4. Bodleian Library and see Appendices B and C to C Warren Hollister's, 'The Greater Domesday Tenants-in-Chief' in *Domesday Studies* (1987).
5. Andrew Bridgeford, 1066, *The Hidden History of the Bayeux Tapestry* (2004), p.190.
6. Q.v. Morris, pp.140–9, for a persuasive picture (2012 and 2013).
7. *Anglo-Saxon Chronicle*, version 'C'.
8. See Wright (2019), p.145, estimating 1,200 horses, 6,000 armoured men and 6,000 unarmoured men.
9. See Wright (2019), pp.46–47.
10. Ibid., pp.53–60.
11. My own estimate is that loading the horses would require that half of their transports 'waited on' at sea for twenty-four hours, so loading began on the 26th and they arrived on the morning of the 28th.

Chapter Thirty-One

Harold's Strategic Genius

I have written before, at some length, about the actual invasion process, the beachhead, the subsequent battle and, indeed, the subsequent reign of William the Conqueror.[1] I am now going to review what happened in terms of battles in order to complete the process of English unification, but without all the detailed background I have set out elsewhere, for we are now drawing together all the threads of our argument, the final pieces of evidence.

Two days after the battle of Stamford Bridge, a messenger arrived with the news of Duke William's landing at Pevensey. Next day, King Harold and his exhausted men were spurring their horses southwards, sending on ahead curt commands to call out the furloughed fyrdsmen, all in the next few weeks. Already on the south coast and in Sussex and Kent, local forces were steeling themselves to conflict, awaiting the arrival and the further instructions of their king.

William, in his turn, soon created a demilitarised zone and seized all the provender he could from it. He now dominated the ancient and separate territory of the 'Hæstingas', with the lagoon itself, and his army was recovering from the crossing and discovering the local topography – with the assistance of 'collaborators' on the western side of the lagoon – for there were, of course, *no* maps. The invaders needed to know the topography they had now found themselves in just as much as they needed to know what their enemy would do next. If the enemy did nothing, what would that mean and what would the invaders need to do? Detailed local knowledge was essential to any future strategy and deployment. Consolidate, consider and play cat and mouse, but who (in truth) was the cat and who the mouse?

News of the victory at Stamford Bridge apparently arrived at Pevensey with Robert fitzWymarc, a Breton (though one of the royal household of the late King Edward), according to the account written by William of Poitiers,[2] a few days after the landing. It was not good news to William; Harold had had the victory and was on his way south. The choice of the fortress had been wise for on its peninsular it was impregnable, but William had to give battle sooner or later and later would mean an increasing English strength. Meanwhile, Harold tarried in London, maybe waiting for stragglers, probably issuing commands. His family now urged him to hold back until all his forces could be assembled but, the story goes, he was set on providing a trap for the invaders, a night attack, a ship force attack, something of the sort. As we shall see, his plan may have included a night assault designed to follow attrition.

For his part, William knew the danger of having his fleet trapped in the lagoon but he had also, now, discovered that the lagoon with its fens and saltings was a sure defence against surprise attack from the land. Only one road led around the lagoon (from the east down to the south-west) and then eastwards along the narrow peninsular to the fort, and the inhabitants on the Anderida, or fortress, side of the lagoon were sympathetic to his cause and knew the secret waterways through the fens. To the east, on the Hæstingas (or Hastings) side of the lagoon were Harold's estates, all the richest farmlands, so these William wasted and plundered. To the east and to the north of the lagoon he created a buffer zone devoid of sustenance for any attacker. Moreover, his men now knew the area well, they had scouted and ravaged diligently. If Harold came down the road from London he would have to traverse the east and north sides of the lagoon in order to reach the causeway itself and to the south of Anderida were other impenetrable marshes and Beachy Head. The downlands above Beachy Head were ideal cavalry country and William had already seized and burnt the royal hunting lodge there, commandeering all the provender that had been laid up there for the royal stud on the Downs.

Between 11 and 13 October, Harold advanced from London to the place we now know as Battle and here he halted. This was probably a site he had noted long ago, as the best generals do. William's troops were stood to in patrols in the buffer zone and English troops would have been foolish to enter piecemeal and challenge the Norman-French cavalry pickets and vedettes. While Harold prepared for a standing battle and prepared his fixed position, William employed a chord *across* the lagoon, to ferry his infantry forwards while his cavalry scoured along the road on the north side to Ashburnham and Ninfield, ready to take any English advance in the flank and, thankfully, not required to tranship again.[3] By dawn of 14 October, the Norman-French army was probably within a few miles of Battle, on the other side of Telham Hill. They could not risk moving northwards and so becoming entangled in the dense Wealden woods, impossible cavalry country, so it was from here they must make a frontal attack. At daybreak they moved into relatively open country and onto Battle Hill, where their scouts had seen enemy scouts: the Bayeux Tapestry gives us a lively incident at this point. So far the prospects looked good for an easy cavalry battle.[4]

Harold, for his part, had witnessed French heavy horse at work in 1064–65. He therefore chose his position very carefully and the margins of the

Bayeux Tapestry provide us with a running commentary, moreover one that confirms the researches of Grehan and Mace that our traditional battle site, on Battle Hill, is entirely mistaken.[5] The position chosen by Harold in October 1066 was, for very good reasons, Caldbec Hill, a mile to the north of Battle Hill, a position focused on the Hoar Apple Tree.

So, on the morning of 14 October, the Franco-Norman-Breton army, now deployed in three vans, easily crested the ridge of Battle Hill and to their great satisfaction saw the English army drawn up in infantry formation on the next hill along the London road. A gallop down the reverse slope and a charge up the rougher, facing slope of Caldbec Hill should have ended the engagement in fairly short order, but it did not. The Breton heavy cavalry crashed into the finest of English axe men embedded in the shield wall across the road and causeway, while their left came to a floundering halt in the boggy ground on the English right flank. The Norman heavy horse met the same fate on the east side of the road, while the Franco-Flemish heavy horse wallowed in bog and muddy streams under a steep slope.

Imagine Duke William's horror, as leader of this joint stock scheme, as his carefully prepared shock force was channelled into one, narrow killing zone, slowed to a walk by the steep slope with the rest of them sinking deeper into the churned up morass they were themselves creating, his men barely making the steep but firmer ground above on which the English shield wall awaited them! Cavalry soon churn up wet ground into a bog, making it impassable for infantry. The Norman chroniclers, though writing at some time after the battle, still emphasised the shock experienced by this Breton attack. I think we can now supply the details missing in their accounts. This was going to be a long day.

Notes

1. Wright (2019), also (2020).
2. William of Poitiers, *Gesta Guillelmi Ducis Normannorum et regis Anglorum*.
3. This being the most difficult of operations q.v. Wright (2019), pp.51–52 and 143–147; also Wright in *Wiðowinde* 197, pp.10–13.
4. Ibid., pp.67–69.
5. John Grehan & Martin Mace, *The Battle of Hastings 1066: the Uncomfortable Truth* (2012), following Jim Bradbury, *The Battle of Hastings* (1998).

Chapter Thirty-Two

The Jaws of Defeat

The Breton cavalry, having careered down the back slope of Battle Hill exhilarated by their good fortune, then thundered along the causeway, or they sank into the soft ground either side, those on the hard standing barely retaining momentum as they met the English shield wall, slowing on the uphill because of the steep and rough terrain. Succeeding waves pitched into the stalled line in front of them, which was being systematically axed, while fetlocked and hocked horses and riders either side of the causeway tried desperately to turn around, or to escape to the left (where the ground was worse). More riders followed behind them, men cursing comrades who were thereby flung onto their croups and thighs, biting, slashing, some falling only to be trampled on. Yet the infantry were following behind, to exploit the opening made by the cavalry and they, in turn, were then trampled by backing cavalry or held by the mire. Soon this maelstrom of thrashing and treading turned the soft ground into a bog, whilst the English axe men cleared the causeway itself with grim efficiency and while screaming, kicking, agonised and terrified horses piled into a barrier of carnage that prevented all further attempts by the cavalry to renew their attack.

Not only was momentum lost, the Bretons panicked and turned tail; there was no way they could advance. Some of the English followed, those who could get around the wall of dead and dying, hewing their enemies from behind. The Norman heavy horse, themselves bemired, compressed and in confusion, saw the chaos to their left and also pulled back, though at least taking a chance to cut down English pursuers, for how could they effectively charge such a slippery slope? On the Norman right, the Franco-Flemish van faced not only a bluff with boggy runlets below but, buried in these mires (as the Tapestry shows) 'lilies' – sharpened stakes – or a *cheval de frise* just at water level, undetectable until man or beast fell on them, the aqueous equivalent of caltrops. So William's right also retired in order to consider a fresh attack.

As the invading army rolled back to firmer ground, leaving a wall of dead and dying, the English line partly retreated upslope and, with the advantage of elevation, poured a hail of arrows, darts and rocks, on their retreating enemies. Franco-Norman archers shot back with dropping shots, for they were at extreme range below the hill. All was confusion, a dismal prospect for the stock holders and demoralising for their troops. Here at Caldbec Hill they had encountered a natural fortress, yet they dared not retreat, for where would they go with the English in jubilant pursuit? How would the leaders escape the fury of their own troops? To survive they *had* to prevail, retreat was not an option for any but the cavalry, and it was doubtful even for them.

The English weakness was that they *must* hold their position, they could not descend to the firm ground while the cavalry remained. Moreover, local pursuits were dangerous for them, for the same wall of dead and dying that obstructed further attacks also impeded their return when they sallied. Nevertheless, for them it was a matter of waiting for night, when local knowledge would help spread further panic among a frustrated and fearful enemy surrounded in the dark. In fact, Duke William did not even know for sure whether yet more English troops were not marching on the 'hoar apple tree': the longer the day drew out the greater was the risk of overwhelming English reinforcements arriving.

Now, surely, the battle became one of infantry attrition. Writers such as Colonel Lemmon have speculated that William now threw his cavalry at the English lines, but this could only hold good if the battle was fought on Battle Hill, and if it was, then the whole picture and detail of the Bayeux Tapestry is wrong.[1] The Tapestry tells a tale that can *only* fit Caldbec Hill and logic supports it.[2] Now William had instead to conserve his cavalry, either for a final push and forlorn hope or as a screen to protect the escaping stock holders. To this end the infantry were expendable and they were the only ones who had a hope of breasting the English lines beyond the causeway. Archers on both sides poured fire on their foes, but the English certainly could not retrieve their long-distance shots and it is possible that the Franco-Norman forces were instructed to conserve fire and retrieve as much as possible. English missiles could not last for ever.

So the day dragged on, three or four times as long as such a battle should take, the horses growing more aggressive as their essential water supply ran out: another reason for holding the heavy horse back and not distressing them further. Besides, holding fire and holding back the cavalry would help to persuade the wasting infantry that some grand plan was afoot! Nevertheless, cavalry were required at intervals when the English sallied forth, probably in wedge formation, onto the firmer ground, attempting to cut off retreating Franco-Norman infantry. The cavalry still had their uses!

The Franco-Norman force included both archers and crossbowmen but whilst arrows were reusable, bolts (quarrels) were not, especially as the weapon was unknown to the English. The English could drop effective fire by their archers onto attacking masses with some results, for although their bows would not pierce shield and hauberk, an advancing man is vulnerable to a descending arrow where the hauberk is open at the neck. The *Carmen de Hastingae proelio* also mentions stones on sticks, missiles we appear to see on the Bayeux Tapestry, and I take these to be heavy missiles, not unlike 'throwing the hammer' and involving a similar technique. Flung high over the English front rank, again as dropping shots, these would be formidable weapons.

What we need to remember is that neither side had an inexhaustible supply of missiles, so each relied on picking up expended arrows. The suggestions we have in the later *Chronicles* that the English made sorties and were thereby bested at times, sounds as though they were overconfident but it might equally indicate a desperate need to descend to enemy lines in order to retrieve arrows and stone hammers. Thus when the English retired upslope and closed ranks, the Franco-Norman archers could retrieve both their own and their opponents' expended arrows. As for the crossbowmen, they were surely under orders to be economical as their supplies could not be augmented. We will shortly see why they were to become so important.

The English right, covering the causeway and the only firm-standing approach, contained the select troops, the gesiths of hearth troops, select fyrdmen, huscarls and mercenaries, and it was essential for them to maintain their position. Attack after attack on them only piled up the cadaverous obstacles, while on either side the morass became impassable. As the day drew on, Duke William had only one recourse, to attack the English left on its steepest slopes, where the general or great fyrd was posted, for here there were Englishmen shown on the Tapestry as lightly armoured. When they too withdrew upslope, they left a little steep but firm ground on the other side of the boggy valley whose streams lead eastwards to the River Brede. It seems that a possibility now opened in William's mind. Could this inexperienced English wing possibly be turned?

Notes

1. Lieutenant-Colonel C.H. Lemmon *The Field of Hastings* (1957 and 1977); see also Wright (2019).
2. Q.v. Grehan and Mace, op. cit. (2012).

Chapter Thirty-Three

The Master Stroke

The Franco-Flemish heavy horse, probably under Count Eustace 'Gernons' (so called for his moustaches) struggled through the boggy stream and the 'lilies' and filed along the narrow front of the regrouped English left, ready to face left and charge uphill, but the space was so narrow that they could hardly walk, let alone canter, and the fyrdmen were a hedge of spears. The horses shied away and skittered or plunged, and darts and arrows came at them point-blank, maddening the unarmoured mounts, and in desperation the cavalry continued to ride to the right, escaping eastwards, or instead they fell down the slope and onto the 'lilies'. In the panic, some rode to the left to collide with the Norman horse and Bishop Odo who, with his marshal's 'baculus' (club) 'encouraged the young men', that is he forced them back to the right in the hope of making a front.

Yet in this debacle there was hope, for even as Duke William rode into the chaos with his helmet pushed back onto his head and in full view, beside him Eustace pointing to the leader and holding his gonfanon aloft, someone who had ridden further to the east returned with startling news for the duke. Certainly he mentioned water and the horses were desperate for water. Seizing this opportunity, William ordered both the vans to send their heavy horse behind him and to follow him eastwards, which their foes greeted with derision – surely they were running away! So it must have looked to the forsaken infantry as well, watching them in horror.

The duke was ahead with the count and, yes, it was true, here were fresh streams, here was water for the horses and briefly they were allowed to slake their thirst. Looking back towards the English left, refused on the slopes above, the cavalry now saw before them a fold in the ground and an easy traverse that would take them, half hidden, behind the English line. Quickly orders were passed back: it seems that Odo was given the important order to take over the field and reassure the infantry while all the heavy horse from two vans, maybe more if Breton survivors joined them, rode east and then swung northwards, up the slope of the shallow valley.

Distraction was now required, just for a short time. Though the English left could not take the processing cavalry in the flank without falling into their own marsh obstacle, the whole English front, flanks and centre needed to be made to focus on the 'Norman' centre. So Odo (it seems, for he did not figure in the later cavalry action) ordered the crossbowmen forwards with the archers behind them, picking up as they went and with ground quivers stacked behind them (as the Tapestry shows). No doubt the English, looking down on them, now anticipated a frontal attack and were all attention.

They advanced to the wall of the dead and the archers loosed a terrific rain of parabolic fire (see the Tapestry, which shows them drawing to the chest) onto the heads of the English troops. Simultaneously, as the English raised their shields for overhead protection, the crossbowmen fired point-blank at the front rank. According to the *Carmen*, William had ordered his crossbowmen to fire at the faces of the English troops, which, given the flat-trajectory accuracy of the weapon was quite possible, but even those who ducked behind their shields would find the crossbow bolts penetrating clean through them at this range!

The English had expended all their missiles and could find few to pick up, that is until the 'blizzard' hit them! Under this tremendous storm, they focused on the main front and it is possibly now that King Harold was seriously wounded, probably by an arrow that penetrated next to a clavicle. For essential minutes no one looked eastwards but the leading heavy horse were now up on the plain behind the English lines and forming front ready to charge. In front of them was the English left flank, formed of the general fyrd, 'freehold' farmers and householders defending their homes, not really men of war and so, line abreast, the cavalry cantered, galloped and charged.

The hapless fyrdmen were hit by a wall of 500 or 600 tons of heavy horse. The alert ones ran for the proximate shelter of Andredasweald, the Wealden woods, but the terrified main body was propelled into the centre of the English line, which in turn collided with the English right wing and now Breton, Norman and French infantry surged forwards over the walls of dead and dying with a tremendous roar. Horseman stabbed, hacked and slashed at now defenceless groups of spearmen, whilst the axe men, the huscarls, closed around their dying king. The English army was, therefore, caught between the hammer and the anvil for irresistible force left them no chance to about face and form their spearmen into a hedge, even if they had possessed such resolution. Shock and utter surprise totally demoralised the main force and the slaughter was horrific. Those who attempted to run were caught in the mud and the main body of the English army was compressed to helplessness and systematically butchered.

According to Guy of Amiens, Harold was cut down by William, Eustace, Guy of Ponthieu and one Gifford.[1] Had he been shot in the brain with an arrow, as William of Malmesbury claimed, I doubt he would have been able to fight on, especially if it was a crossbow bolt.[2] As I have said, following the original evidence of the Bayeux Tapestry (before it was restored), I believe a dropping shot penetrated his clavicular area, causing massive blood loss when he pulled it out and disabling an arm, rendering him more or less helpless.[3] Anyway, the news of his death spread rapidly and as his brothers had also died, so the English *sauve qui peut* began in earnest for those who could find any avenue of escape.

By now it was night and so the pursuing Franco-Norman cavalry (according to William of Poitiers)[4] tumbled headlong into a ravine later termed the 'Malfosse', and here Count Eustace was wounded.[5] This may have been no more than a condign accident consequent upon darkness falling or it may have been a 'last stand' by English fugitives using a fallback position, but here the Tapestry fails us. In the darkness, given the similarity of armour and dress on both sides, it would have been difficult to distinguish friend from foe unless by speech. And around their fallen king lay the loyal flower of English thegndom, to rise no more.

Notes

1. *Carmen de Hastingae proelio*.
2. *Gesta Regum*, c.1120, rather 'after the event'.
3. Wright (2019), pp.84–85.
4. William of Poitiers, *Gesta Guillelmus Ducis Normannorum et Regis Anglorum*.
5. Proposed as the Oakwood Gill by Bradbury and also by Grehan and Mace.

Chapter Thirty-Four

A Kingdom by Default

No English reinforcements arrived on the morrow of the battle, so William allowed five days of recovery, the minimum essential time for his horses, while remounts were brought up from the stud at Eastbourne.[1] Now if we discount the established, traditional and uncritical tale that William had been promised the throne of England and was now claiming it, and if instead we follow the evidence of far earlier preparation for invasion than 1066, then the purpose of the joint stock holders was at this point to obtain 'tribute', no doubt a 'tribute' at least as large as that given to Cnut. The problem was that no one had appeared to offer it by the end of five days, so, where to next? Should it be to London or to the ancient capital of Winchester and who would eventually respond?

The truth was that there was no one to respond. The flower of English nobility had successively died at Gate Fulford, Stamford Bridge and Hastings; the king was dead, so who would or could negotiate terms or authorise a geld? Moreover, who would collect it and who was there left to pay it? The essence of the geld was rapid payment but most of the major tax-payers were dead, many of the minor ones too, and who could unlock the 'hordere', the royal treasury (and its bureaucracy) at Winchester, even if anything could be collected? Of course, the working of this administrative machinery was unknown to the invaders, they thought the supply of silver inexhaustible and had no idea where it came from, but unlike the situation with earlier gelds, the whole spectrum of tax-payers, north, south, east and west, had now been erased from the practical account. Survivors from the battle were making for the safety of London and its walls but surely, as William must have reasoned, there was someone who could organise further resistance? Even he could not have comprehended the extent of English noble losses and the demoralising effect this would have. The recourse, no doubt, seemed to him to lie with stern measures, in order to concentrate English thinking, and essentially these measures would include provisions and comforts for the troops.

The Wealden wastes and woods were dangerous and to be avoided, not suitable terrain for cavalry or even for foreign infantry with fugitives abroad. The inhabitants of Pevensey had, so far, collaborated, perhaps Rye had too, so William's next move was to burn out Romney. This left Sussex's port,

Rye, to dominate the wetlands and harbour here, just as Pevensey dominated its lagoon. Perhaps the men on the Kent side, at Romney, were suspected of sympathising with the English fleet, for surely that was somewhere and it must now be denied supplies and chandlery?

Next came Dover, to secure the cross-Channel route and also the 'castle' based on the ancient Roman 'Pharos' and attached church. It had a strong garrison but it capitulated and now William had secured the whole south coast. He also had to deal with a serious outbreak of dysentery among his troops, consequent upon the battle at Battle, in addition to perhaps 30 per cent losses to death and disability. Disease is always the biggest killer in an army, so now he was possibly down to 50 per cent or less efficiency and his army was dwindling alarmingly fast.[2] This was a truly alarming prospect should the English now reform another host. He was not to know that this was now impossible, so he needed to use his small force decisively.

Objective Canterbury quickly followed and it wisely submitted, putting the Archdiocese and the archbishop's caput under William's control, so he despatched a flying column to Winchester, ancient capital of Wessex and the seat of the dowager Edith. She and the city's fathers capitulated and, no doubt, some money and treasure now fell into William's hands, essential in order to secure the loyalty and obedience of his many mercenary troops. Finally the target had to be London, financial or trading seat of England and refuge of all escapees. If anywhere was going to resist his demands it was London, but I doubt even he realised that he was a victim of his own success. How should the Duke of Normandy understand the machinery of the unique English tax system? In Normandy and France they did things very differently.

With recourse to the time-honoured terror technique of ravaging, the Franco-Norman (surviving) forces swept through to Southwark, found London bridge down and the city inaccessible and so set the place on fire before driving on through Hampshire, Berkshire, Hertfordshire and Middlesex (in addition to Sussex and Kent). At Wallingford they paused, no doubt to strengthen and garrison the very large, ancient fortress, and here Archbishop Stigand came to make his peace. Such as remained of a Witan, such as could be scraped together and now in London, had elected the Æthling Edgar but Stigand was *not* among them and, just maybe, he explained the English predicament to William, maybe he even explained it to all the joint stock holders. The support of the Church, in England, was now secured and, just possibly, Stigand had hinted at more.

Swinging north-east, the army now took the burgh of Berkhampsted: whether this was as an agreed meeting place or an accidental one we do not know. The eorls Eadwine and Morcar, who should have supported the boy king Edgar, had now departed for the safety of their northern territories, leaving the Witan leaderless, so the surviving members of the Witan escorted Edgar to Berkhampsted to meet William, to renounce the crown and to offer it to him in person. The kingdom needed an effective king if it was not to descend into chaos and if the collection of any tribute was to be commenced, otherwise it lay and remained paralysed.

Here was a problem. William's immediate overlord, his feudal overlord, was the boy king Phillipe of France, while the best claimant among the joint stock holders was Count Eustace, but William was the commander and he had his brothers Odo and Robert to support him. Edgar had not been crowned, the army needed its promised rewards (if it was to remain amenable to discipline) and the country needed to be governed by a strong hand. Even so, William hesitated.

Eustace's son was (we think) Odo's hostage, the English Witan was imploring William for peace, law and order and his soldiers needed to see him crowned both as proof and so that they could be rewarded and kept under control. This was the real situation and the one air-brushed out by generations of historians dedicated to the post-hoc justification of 'a promise' of the English throne by Edward. In the end, William agreed. It was an astonishing outcome and conclusion, though not unlike Cnut's earlier predicament. Though William's advance guard now met some opposition from survivors of the battle who had sought refuge in the city, the general response was acceptance. This was the will of the Witan and obviously the will of God.

The feeling of security was underlined when William took up residence in the new Palace of Westminster, at the west end of the City, whilst ordering a 'castle' to be built outside the east wall. Presumably this was to cover any approach up the Thames by other hostiles. Generations of historians have represented this as repression of the Londoners, no doubt forgetting that the docklands did not yet exist! Just how, we should ask, was one new burgh going to subjugate a whole walled city from outside the walls?

Crowning was essential to the Franco-Norman force for that was how European kingdoms recognised kingship, so William was crowned on Christmas Day 1066, by Ealdred, Archbishop of York. This in itself proved that the 'other' archbishop also agreed with the nomination, so ensuring that there should be no opposition from York. Once again we encounter a misrepresented event, for the indiscipline of some of William's mercenaries (celebrating his kingship in the usual mercenary way) is traditionally represented as Norman soldiers fearful for their lord's life – in which case, why did they not attempt to rescue him?[3] Instead they went to their usual amusements of arson, rape and looting.

That it was growing difficult to restrain his troops is reflected in the *Chronicle*, which commented that Edgar's party and the Witan only made peace 'at need, when most harm was done and it was most unwise that no one had gone before', and though William promised to a be a good lord 'his men plundered all they could'.[4] After all, they were the victors and now they wanted their reward. They had not fought for altruistic motives nor yet for sympathy with the duke's supposed claim to the throne; a claim that officially came later. Now he was king to the English by virtue of the Witan and to his followers by virtue of his crowning so, as king, he made haste to accumulate as much treasure as he could, largely from English 'gifts' (in every sense protection money) and then he rapidly paid off a substantial element of his army in order to keep the promised peace.

Not unnaturally, the new king now returned to Normandy with a mort of treasure in order to make a triumphal tour, handing substantial donations to the Church in order to buy their acknowledgement and God's forgiveness, as all successful generals did. Eadwine and Morcar had submitted to him before he left, so he prudently restored their lands to them but took them with him to Normandy, for safety. Unfortunately, he left his brothers behind to rule in his stead and this misplaced trust, in itself, initiated a pattern that was to dog the remainder of his reign.

Notes

1. Wright (2020), pp.15–17 and (2019), p.95.
2. For further details see Wright (2020), pp.16–19.
3. See Wright (2020), pp.21–23.
4. Savage (trans.), *The Anglo-Saxon Chronicles*, p.195. See also Loyn (1977), p.86, quoting an earlier passage in the *Anglo-Saxon Chronicle* for 1011.

Chapter Thirty-Five

The Abhorrent Vacuum

The one unhappy party among the joint stock holders was Count Eustace II of Boulogne. He had surely been looking forward to securing both ends of the cross-Channel route across the Narrows, maybe he had been promised as much at Berkhampsted or even when he joined the confederacy. Instead he was now fobbed off with extensive estates well inland, while William's half-brother, Bishop Odo of Bayeux, received Kent and the strongpoint of Dover 'castle'. Count Eustace, therefore, returned home and commenced his preparations.

Odo of Bayeux and William fitzOsbern (the latter at Winchester) seem to have acted, and allowed their soldiers to act, pretty much as they pleased during 1067, though, to be fair, they needed to keep order along the Welsh borders where local bandits and Welsh kings appreciated that nature abhors a (power) vacuum. Needless to say, these troubles and raids on the English are always referred to as 'English revolts' by historians but no one told these raiders that there were no Normans around, so the English peasantry suffered.

Later in the year, Eustace arrived at Dover with a force of his own. You will remember that his earlier experiences here had not been pleasant yet, once again, we are told by historians who follow William of Poitier's account that the English invited him and he was happy to help them! In fact, his invasion seems to have been a half-baked affair with very poor planning and it was certainly insufficient for the obvious objective. It may be that Odo had been approached to join him, if so we have a possible reason for the creation of the Bayeux Tapestry, but Odo was circumspectly absent from Dover when Eustace's force arrived.[1] After all, given Eustace's track record here at Dover it would have been prudent to see how events really went before committing oneself to treason.

In the event, in the absence of Odo, his garrison at Dover decided to teach the invaders a lesson, a lesson that the local inhabitants supported and Eustace was lucky to escape when many of his men did not.[2] Odo, earl of Kent, was therefore able to represent his garrison's loyalty to his brother as his own compliance with the duty laid upon him. Meanwhile, Countess Gytha, Harold's mother, and her grandsons arrived at Exeter, apparently with Irish mercenaries, and took over the city and, not to be outdone, Northumbria decided to enlarge its reputation for troublemaking by murdering William's regent there.[3]

Despite the winter weather, King William returned late in 1067 to take command with his usual energy. The Godwines, Gytha and her boys, were sending envoys to the Danes as well as to other towns, which tells us that they lacked strong local support, so William raised a heavy geld, then raised an army and called out the English fyrd.[4] After all, his invasion force was now down to a mere shadow in the field thanks to the additional need to provide garrisons at key points. The citizens of Exeter sent an offer of surrender to William but when he arrived he found the walls manned against him. This, I think, we can explain as an occupation by an alliance of Gytha's mercenaries and Damnonian rebels from Cornwall, which was still very much an anti-English colonial shire.[5] Once again this tells us that she had no other alliances she could rely on.

We are told nothing more than that the siege was long and bloody until Gytha and her grandsons slipped away, leaving the city and their erstwhile supporters to their fate. The citizens were not badly treated, it had hardly been their fault, and William pursued the escaping fugitives into Cornwall, restoring the Anglo-French colonial estates here, so that by Easter he was at Winchester and the army disbanded. At Whitsun, Mathilde arrived to be crowned queen and peace seemed to have been restored.

Along the Welsh borders, William now established a military buffer zone, but some powerful men had other ideas. Eadwine and Morcar made alliance with Welsh kings, while in the north Maerleswein, Gospatric, the bishop of Durham and the æthling Edgar made a Northumbrian alliance. Raising yet another army, presumably once again with a large English contingent, William marched north, securing his advance with 'castles' as he went. These do not appear to have been like many of the older 'burghs', designed to shelter populations, but more the modern English understanding of the word, that is smaller ringworks and strongpoints, designed to aid flying columns of troops and to delay enemy movements along lines of communication.[6] William was climbing systematically northwards with typical thoroughness, determined to secure his ascent.

The 'revolt', as many term it, collapsed quickly. Some nobles sued for peace, while others fled to Scotland, but such was the size of the Anglo-French army that Malcolm of Scotland swore fealty and allegiance to William as soon as he arrived in York. Meanwhile, three Godwine youths from Ireland who landed in Somerset, to plunder and take slaves, were confronted by local forces under Eadnoth and then they quickly retired to Ireland with their 'liberated' captives!

I think that by now King William had positively advanced his justification as the 'nominated heir of Edward', no doubt to gain the moral high ground over any further claimants, and in this apparently peaceful period he took the opportunity of ridding himself of more of his mercenaries and those who wished to return home. For those who wished to remain there were offers of land, estates forfeited by those who had died in 1066, not forgetting the forfeited Godwine empire. A large Franco-Norman force just did not exist by 1069, quite apart from its casualties of war, because it was not necessary and the money to pay it was running out. Selling off Northumbria was one way of raising money but the purchaser-commander he now sent there with a mercenary hearth troop appear to have been out of control once they were out of royal oversight.

With the advantage of a heavy snowfall, a discontented and abused Northumbrian faction entered Durham to massacre this outpost and, knowing that after this there was no going back, they moved south onto York. The opportunists Mærleswein, Gospatric and Edgar joined them, as did the Yorkshire thane Archil, and though York's Norman governor was murdered, the 'castle' held out. As had happened so often in the past, once a king and his army departed southwards, promises and allegiance meant nothing in this border region, nor for that matter on the Welsh Marches.

I doubt whether King William could have moved so quickly, yet again, without the English fyrds but now he marched to the relief of York. On his arrival, the insurrection disappeared, so he built a second 'castle' at York and left his trusted lieutenant fitzOsbern in command. In midsummer 1069, Harold's sons again arrived from Ireland with sixty-four ships, perhaps 2,000 pirates, entering the Taw and going inland on the Barnstaple (west) side of Exmoor. It is difficult to discern a purpose for this other than to take slaves and metals from mining communities, but eorl Brian came upon them unexpectedly with a large local force, killed many and drove the rest back to their ships, so the survivors went back to Ireland.

And now there should have been some peace and stability, but nothing is so persuasive as success and imitation is a sincere form of flattery. King Sweyn of Denmark now declared that he too had been promised King Edward's throne and, as invasions are not planned or prepared overnight, King William must have already received some intelligences of his preparations, knowledge that was perhaps to others the real reason for renewed Northumbrian restlessness. Was fate about to favour the perfidious?

Notes

1. Wright (2019), pp.90–94 and 96–97; also (2020), pp.27–28.
2. See also Bridgeford (2004), pp.200–202.
3. See Wright in *Wiðowinde* 195, pp.20–22 and Wright (2020) pp.28–29.
4. Ibid. (2020), p.28.
5. Ibid. (2017), pp.67–72; also (2014), pp.360–362 and 371.
6. Ibid. (2020), pp.29 and 49–51.

Chapter Thirty-Six

Axholme and Stafford

Late in the summer of 1069, King Sweyn of Denmark despatched 300 ships, under his brother Osbeorn, to England. Historians have always represented this as an invasion designed to support the desperate pleas of 'the English nation' but I doubt that philanthropy was involved at all and, of course, nationality did not exist for centuries to come. I have to ask what 'national body' issued such an invitation and from where? Was there a secret underground headquarters for the English maquis? Well, armies do not feed themselves but they do amuse themselves and so they are always 'bad news'! Arriving in the Channel, this fleet then turned north, according to some accounts, which sounds as though there was an English ship force protecting the Thames mouth and Narrows. Such a force would, indeed, be English for we have already seen that the Normans were not sailors. Now the Danish fleet steered for the Humber, perhaps merely a coincidence or perhaps, as yet, not aware that the revolt had been quelled.

The garrison at York was, however, made aware of their coming as they sailed past the Wash and along the Lincolnshire coast and, in panic at the thought of meeting 10,000 or 12,000 troops, they tried to clear the approaches to their castles, in which attempts they set the city on fire. The Danes arrived while they were fighting the fire, caught them in the open and massacred them, then they looted whatever they could and retired to their ships. Next they entered their old haunt, the Trent, and from there went to the 'Isle of Axholme', an area of marshes, fens and islands bounded by the rivers Trent, Don and Idle, probably leaving their 'troop transports' in the Humber estuary and using smaller craft to penetrate the inland fens.

Today and in recent history, this area, north and east of Doncaster, has changed dramatically from its aspect in 1069. In 1911, there were only 47,000 acres of the 'Isle' remaining but *Domesday Book* entered the entire area as a total of 120,000 acres of fens and islands, presumably including Ditch-Marsh and adjacent wetlands even to the Foulness valley, an extensive wetland area.[1] Clearly the Danes intended to follow their ancient, established pattern of a wintersetl and strand on the marshy main island, with raiding parties ravaging Nottinghamshire, Yorkshire and Lincolnshire, following the several watercourses available. It was a good choice and one their forefathers must have discovered long before, one close to our supposed site of Brunaburgh. Of course, the presence of such extensive wetlands would have seriously diminished the water speed of the rivers that approach confluence with the Humber here, making travel up the Trent in particular much easier. The Humber estuary was therefore always the ideal back door into midland England.

William seems to have raised a fresh army in a remarkably short period of time for he was already marching north again as the enemy dispersed to Axholme. I suspect that a considerable part of his army was composed of English fyrdmen and 'king's thanes' (as *Domesday Book* styled them), for the Franco-Norman army of invasion had, by now, dwindled to a shadow of itself. I think that the heavy horse, the 'miles', and the crossbowmen would be retained wherever possible but there was hardly the money, let alone the time, to recruit fresh mercenaries. I further suspect that William, like the rebel eorls, had long held an anticipation that the Danes were outfitting for England and so he was careful to keep a nucleus of men standing to after the Northumbrian revolt. His English ship force would have been able to provide sightings and intelligence even when the Danish fleet was still out of sight of the land.

In the event, King William was now able to surprise the Danish army by attacking Axholme, no mean feat in itself. In fact this was, in my opinion, *the* major battle of this campaign, though completely overlooked by contemporaries. The Anglo-Norman army seems to have followed Ermine Street and then taken the route to the west of Gainsborough to come around from Doncaster and so take their enemies by complete surprise. Once again, this was territory well-known to the English, as far back as Brunaburgh, while William's acquaintance with fenland warfare certainly went back as far as the Pevensey Lagoon in 1066.[2] What was all the more remarkable was that this was not cavalry country at all, so the troops involved were probably predominantly English infantry. The onslaught was so fierce that it drove the Danes clean back to the Trent and the Humber, and it is a pity that no near contemporary thought to set down a few details of this remarkable victory – but then clerics were not interested in means, only in political ends.

But the news of a Danish invasion had reached other ears and those ears presumed that William would be occupied in the north for some time, so Eadric the Wild and his Welsh allies took the opportunity to attack and invest the English city of Shrewsbury. When an Anglo-Norman force under fitzOsbern suddenly appeared here they scurried back to Wales, so this relief column then moved on south-westwards to reinforce local forces at Exeter, who were also experiencing opportunistic attacks. As soon as this column

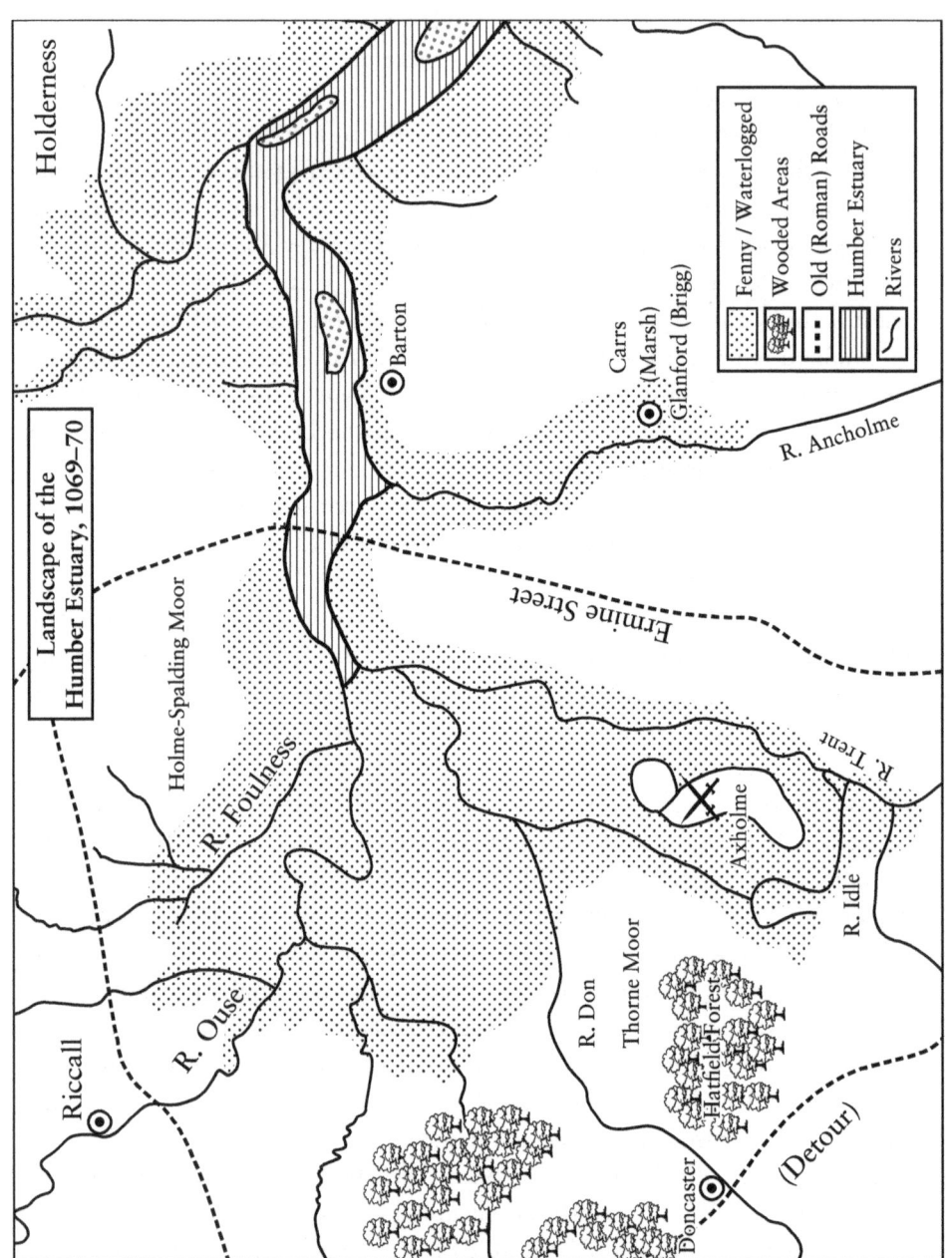

Map 8: Landscape of the Humber Estuary, 1069–70.

> **Map 8: Landscape of the Humber Estuary, 1069–70.**
> The real battle, one we know nothing about, was on Axholme Island in 1069 and was surely an amphibious operation, perhaps a simultaneous attack across the Trent and also from Thorne Moor? Driven out of their marshy retreat in this way, the Danish Army had no escape but by ships and back to the Humber, where the Anglo-Norman Army could take possession of all landing sites on either side of the estuary. Consequently, detachments in force could cover each likely landing spot and did not need to be spread out all along the banks.

was safely out of the way, back came Eadric (like Boh da Thone) from the Marches to harry Staffordshire.

Meanwhile, William appears to have covered the more vulnerable banks of the Humber with what must have been a considerable-sized army, at least as large as the Danish army, confining the Danes to an area around York and to their ships. No doubt they made raids for supplies as winter drew in but the Anglo-Norman army seems to have provided fairly adequate cover. It was in their interest to protect food supplies. All in all, York and its environs were now in poor shape and not much of a headquarters for anyone. Turning briefly from his Dane-harrying, King William now seems to have cleverly marched a very strong contingent south and west along the Trent to Stafford, where they fought a bitter battle with Eadric and the Welsh raiders.

The Welsh and brigand army appears to have been taken from the south-west and driven north for their fleeing remnants dispersed across the Staffordshire moorlands and into Derbyshire, some then going south to pick up the Trent route and others being driven north-east.[3] The *Domesday Book*'s records reveal their depredations as they dispersed to seek safety. The main Anglo-Norman pursuit seems to have been along the Don or the Aire, for they possibly crossed at Pontefract and as they did so were opposed by the fugitives.[4] Of course, as William's army increasingly neared the Humber, so he would have met his brother, Robert, who was harrying the Danes, so many of these fugitives would have been caught between the hammer and the anvil at this point, which explains why they chose to stand and fight here.

Now it was a matter of chasing marauding bands of Danes out of north Lincolnshire and southern Yorkshire; no doubt they were hoping to make the remains of York their wintersetl but as soon as William appeared they took to their ships on the Humber. It was now December and no English ship force could sit out the winter gales and watch the mouth of the Humber, but no more could the Danish fleet and army put safely out to sea, especially as they had had no strand on which to maintain their many smaller ships. They were temporarily safe on the waters of the Humber but they could not leave, and neither could they come ashore for supplies or to service their ships.

King William now made his headquarters at York but he also appears to have set garrisons and patrols on either bank of the Humber, on Holderness and on the 'Ageland' coast. Had he retired to a more comfortable wintersetl, the Danes would certainly have come ashore and in the spring the endless pursuit would have started all over again, so William decided to sit tight in a landscape already devastated by the actions and needs of 20,000 men or more, over the last five months (let alone the earlier Norwegian invasion), and to let the invaders either starve or be drowned. Should they attempt to land on the Holderness coast, a dangerous undertaking in winter for longships, they would need to move circumferentially, whereas William's cavalry were operating along a chord. Moreover, this coast, even inland, was very marshy in places, not easy for strangers to negotiate, and the Lincolnshire ('Ageland') coastline opposite was even worse. I suspect that King William was using the knowledge of local fyrdmen.

Trapped in a saltwater estuary, the overriding need would have been for fresh water, but with round-the-clock surveillance by strategically located outposts, themselves connected by cavalry patrols, any attempt to land at the few available landing spots would have been extremely risky. Foraging for food must have been virtually impossible once the Anglo-Norman army had requisitioned local supplies. All the Anglo-Norman forces needed to do was to clear the immediate coasts of provender and to cover all available landing spots and sources of fresh water, then sit back and watch and wait. This was certainly not the wintersetl the Danes had anticipated!

That winter cannot have been an easy one for the watchers and patrols on such an exposed coast but it was far worse for the Vikings, starving, freezing, sick and some of them wrecked by winter gales. Maybe they ate their prisoners? For the Anglo-Norman army, provisioning was a matter of scouring the wastes of Yorkshire beyond the barren south and beyond the Forest of Gaultres: men and horses needed shelter, fuel and food. Billeting in outposts made sense to the military mind but discipline was impossible to enforce under such conditions. Over large areas, wretched peasant populations starved and froze to death but, politically, there was more than just Yorkshire and Lincolnshire at stake. If these pirates escaped, many shires inland would be betrayed. This, then, was the reality of the so-called 'harrying of the North': Whilst wretched refugees were streaming southwards, the Anglo-Norman army was either watching the shores or hunting down brigand refugees from Staffordshire and otherwise stray Danes. No one was enjoying this winter campaign.

Of course, no one was keeping records, no one had either the machinery or the expertise and there was nowhere to gather such information, either for preservation or presentation. Claims, therefore, that 'tens of thousands' perished under 'Norman brutality' are quite obviously nonsense, political fantasies that should never have been repeated by more recent historians. The army so involved in defence of the realm could not have been formed without a major English contribution and the stunning victories achieved would never have been possible if only a thousand or two surviving Norman 'supermen' had, in reality, now formed William's force and were galloping over bogs! Most persuasive of all is the lack of information about these two brilliant victories if we are to suppose that the chroniclers who set down this 'history' were pro-Norman. The fact that they were clerics, absent, ignorant of military matters, biased against royal taxation of any sort and determined to draw suitable moral tales, or even miracles, from every entry does not explain why these two singular achievements were all but erased from the record by both Orderic Vitalis and William of Poitiers, both of them Normans. Perhaps, just perhaps, it was because they were not 'Norman' but largely English victories.

In the end, the devastation so liberally bestowed by modern historians, elaborating on the clerical drama for political effect, is also fictitious, but if the chroniclers did not know about the real victories it is equally obvious that they did not make or keep records of collateral casualties and all such claims are and were no more than propaganda. We have already seen how this landscape in northern England had been fought over again and again for several centuries, how mangled it was by events in the eleventh century alone, even before 1069.

Domesday Book's Yorkshire folios, the primary source (at least if we discount Vitalis's hysteria) of embellishment of William's 'ruthless harrying of the North' for so many historians, does *not*, emphatically *not*, record simply the events of 1069–70. Such claims are pure inventions. If we only look at the very recent history of Yorkshire in 1066–86 we see that William's opposition of the Danish invasion was *only one* factor to contribute to this area's miseries. In 1065, there had been an invasion by Scots and Northumbrians, which spilled into Midland England, then we have a hint that King Harold was campaigning here, once again, early in 1066. Certainly in 1066 the Norwegian invasion had seen two massive armies deployed and foraging around York, and in 1067 King William had had to march against a Northumbrian alliance occupying and plundering the North Riding and York, and moreover he had had to march northwards twice over with armies living off the land! Then in 1069–70 came the Danish invasion and battle of Axholme, with a winter campaign to follow. Nor should we forget that in 1072 the Scots invaded and in 1075 the bloodthirsty Bishop of Bayeux 'pacified' the Northumbrians yet again. Looking back on the records from 1086, I wonder which of these plagues of locusts had really done the greatest damage to Yorkshire or even Lincolnshire before the *Domesday* reckoning was ever made? No, William's campaign in 1069–70 was *not* the single cause of the devastation of the North.

Overemphasis has certainly been given to destruction in the Yorkshire entries by the process of adding *every* fortuitous absence of ploughs to those entries stating *actual* diminution of plough totals (for whatever reason) and then counting both categories as 'wasted'. If we look at Derbyshire, the devastation was certainly piecemeal, not at all general, and it appears to have been effected by the retreat of fugitive rebels defeated at Stafford, and probably also by their pursuers, which (as with the 1067 and subsequent 1069–70 campaigns) had included Englishmen in the supposedly 'Norman' army.[5] Peasant agriculture can be surprisingly resilient, but it cannot work miracles. Totting up the 'wasta', the wasted, entries in *Domesday Book*, here and in Yorkshire, does *not* help us to pinpoint 1069–70, it only tells us of the longer-term miseries of so many ordinary people, people subjected for so long to the invasions and political games of powerful lords and their brigand or mercenary soldiery. What was needed and what eventually came, was freedom from such capricious elements, it is called security. Soon we will see how this was finally achieved but at least, for the present, a determined king had saved many lives in the Midlands.

Notes

1. Wright (2020), p.34 and especially note 13.
2. Q.v. Wright (2019), pp.101–108.
3. Wright (2020), Map of Derbyshire's 'wasted' areas, pp.42–43.
4. Q.v. Morris, p.228.
5. Q.v. Wright (2020), pp.37–45.

Chapter Thirty-Seven

Maintenance of the Aim

Had King William abandoned the chase or had he abandoned his imprisonment of the Danes he would have done nothing, could have done nothing, for the Yorkshire peasantry but he would have opened the door to Danish ravaging and slaving right across all the northern shires at the least and almost certainly have encouraged not only brigands like Eadric to follow suit but the Scots as well. Now and for centuries to come the broad borderlands with Scotland were the province of reivers and moss-troopers, and we have already seen the imperfect Northumbrian legacy that had plagued it. Imprisoned in this winter campaign of 1069–70, even the English troops involved became mercenaries, having their service extended by payment, and mercenaries are always difficult to control under such conditions.[1] By maintaining his aim and his purpose, King William was remaining true to his (English) Coronation Oath to protect his peoples from slavery, sex, murder and arson.[2] Such is the primary duty of any government, monarchical or otherwise.

Here we see both 'maintenance of the aim' and 'economy of effort' applied practically as the finite resources of Denmark rotted in the Humber estuary. The fleet included ships provided by Maerleswein and Waltheof but the Danish crews included mercenaries from Frisia, Saxony and Poland, including men who were probably not sailors. When King Sweyn finally arrived in the spring, hoping to lead his army to victory, he found it starving, sick, debilitated, demoralised and drowned; instead of a large ransom he found he even needed a seaworthy fleet to carry the remnants of his army home. William (we are told), astutely, offered the fleet commander a 'large tribute '(though whether real or fictional we do not know) if he would leave and furthermore gave permission for the remaining Danes to raid the coast of Lincolnshire for supplies as they left. How could starving men refuse?

So, in the early spring, perhaps before it was really safe for the English ship force to sail northwards, the battered, leaking and sodden enemy fleet limped out to sea and sailed southwards, rather than face a large and relatively well-fed and fit Anglo-French army on land. No doubt they welcomed the chance to take fresh supplies, even on such a barren and marshy coastline as Lincolnshire, yet the permission was, in reality, condign and cynical. In their condition these Vikings could hardly hope to survive contests with determined local resistance when they attempted to land at the few available places, and the Anglo-Norman army would have been shadowing them on Ermine Street! Not all battles are fought on battlefields, even when they involve attrition.

This was no skip along a sandy shore looking for a fast food outlet. Seamen would have had to leave the safety of their ship, risking being stranded in an emergency, or beach it with the risk of not getting off in time. Starving men, mad with thirst, suffering from pneumonia, lice, skin infections, dysentery, maybe starvation oedema, and with muscles and sinews weak from inactivity, would have needed to wade through marshes, mire, unknown saltern guts that could be running at several knots and as deep as a man, and even then the fenland desolation spread for miles with little or no habitations. They dared not stray too far inland lest they meet English flankers. True, the area abounded in fish, fowl and eels, but these take time to catch and would merely provide another psychological misery; the only hope for the remains of the fleet was to keep convoy and rely on mass. The English ship force was out there ready to pick off stragglers, even if King William had ordered it not to fully engage. 'Economy of effort' is a Principle of War.

Now these survivors dropped down to enter the Wash, shadowed by William's land and sea detachments, and once in here they took over the Isle of Ely. Meanwhile, Anglo-French flying columns on land were flushing out brigands who had hitherto escaped and were in hiding, and one of these refugees from the battle of Stafford may well have been the 'wolf's head' Hereward, for now he turned up with a band at Peterborough. In an act of patriotism and piety, this band razed the town and sacked the abbey before joining the Danes on Ely. The newly appointed abbot, Turold, with a hearth troop of only 160 men, arrived just too late, pursued them and joined the ring of steel that was now forming around the fenland approaches to the Isle of Ely.

Meanwhile, King William was ordering 'castles' (small, local burghs) to be built right across the northern shires in order to prevent any further movements of brigands or invaders. He also ordered all religious houses to be investigated for treasure; their own and also safe deposits made by laymen, which he then used to pay off his worst mercenaries. Simultaneously, he astutely manoeuvred the papal legates who had been sent to him to remind him of the Divine favour he had been shown and to ensure that suitable acknowledgements in the form of rewards were offered to Mother Church, into an agreement whereby he could raise even more mounted troops from the conventual houses while increasing the numbers of such houses![3] He was nothing if not pragmatic, for mounted troops (miles) were expensive to hire yet these newly created hearth troops would be free of charge to the Crown.

With these matters arranged satisfactorily, he turned his attention to the Danes on Ely, offering their remnants a large reward (maybe this was actually the one offered before) to sail away home. They obligingly did so but their hasty repairs do not seem to have been sufficient for they sailed into a great storm, with heavy losses. Maybe this explains why the treasure did not arrive in Denmark. The Danes, one might suppose, would not be returning to England for many a long year, leaving only Hereward and his brigands holding the Isle of Ely, now as much their prison as their refuge, had they but known it. While local forces blocked the exit routes eastwards and southwards, King William briefly retired to do business in Normandy. He had many enemies over there.

This was the signal for Eadwine and Morcar to slip away from the English court, Eadwine to Scotland and Morcar to Ely. Others had the same idea and Ely now seems to have acted like a magnet for many undesirables. Well, it was a lesson of history that mopping up all troublemakers piecemeal successfully was usually impossible, so what was simpler than to encourage them all to go to one place of refuge, one that (they apparently thought) the king dared not, could not storm? Maybe they had been led to believe this? Nevertheless, there were strongly defended royal estates to the east of Ely, at Fordham, Freckenham and Chippenham, making a defensive front for Norfolk. We encounter their details in *Domesday Book*. There were also, presumably, other fyrdmen covering Cambridge, though the inhabitants of the 'two hundreds of Ely', of Haddenham, Cottenham, Waterbeach and Exning, were now anything but happy, certainly not sympathetic to the parasitic invaders in their midst.

By this time, King William (who returned to England in 1071) had become something of an expert in fenland campaigning, a recent memory that may have encouraged the Danes to depart. I think we can forget all the fanciful stories about building a causeway across the fens because, for a start, with the Danish fleet gone the English ship force could now sail into the Wash and right up to Ely and the port of Haddenham (Hill Row). Here, at Haddenham–Hill Row–Aldreth, there was an ancient causeway leading to Ely, whilst another ran from Stuntney, it is said. It might, of course, have been necessary to improve some sort of approach from Soham to Stuntney, across the Blackmoor, Turf and Barraway Fens, in order to land on 'Babylon' to the north. Nevertheless, either by using these pre-existing causeways or amphibious forces, William could have easily assaulted the Isle of Ely itself at any time, which is why I say he waited until 1071, anticipating a 'magnet' effect.

In fact, we are now told by the *Chronicle* that he called out the English ship and land forces to deal with this nest of criminals, so his force would have become overwhelming and partly composed of fyrdmen from the adjacent fenland areas. My guess at the tactics employed – it can only be a guess – is that crossbowmen and infantry in light craft followed the Ouse to Haddenham while light horse swam from Stuntney, accompanied by more boats, in order to make a pincer attack. Meanwhile, any exit from the north side and into the Wash would be sealed off by the English ship force riding to the north of the Isle of Ely. There was no need for Norman heavy horse, indeed the terrain was all against them, and stories of 'burning *the* causeway', as opposed to firing the reeds, are probably as fictitious as the need to build one when in possession of a ship force and two existing causeways.

With the Danish fleet gone, encirclement had (of course) become possible and the brigands had obviously been lulled into a false sense of security by the king's absence abroad. One also suspects that provisions were becoming scarcer on the island, with the ring of steel covering all routes into Cambridgeshire and Norfolk making raiding impossible. Brigands had been lured into this killing zone, yet with the desperate inhabitants undoubtedly yearning for vengeance on them and praying for royal intervention. We have no indications that William's attack was protracted by any serious resistance and Hereward would have been a fool to remain once he saw such forces gathering. He seems to have abandoned his men and escaped; now he simply disappears from history, as does Eadwine, said to have been killed by his own men.[4] Meanwhile, Morcar surrendered to King William. Justice on the surviving brigands was swift and terrible, repaying months of murder, rape, torture and theft endured by the local inhabitants with ghastly mutilations, after which the locals would have no difficulty in settling scores. When justice enables retribution it often makes for political capital among the masses, thus making William a 'just' king.

How do we know about this 'ring of steel' that trapped Hereward and his brigands within the Isle and 'two hundreds' of Ely? We have the evidence in *Domesday Book*. This source gives each of the twenty estates within these hundreds three valuations, one for the present (1086), one 'when received' (presumably 1070–71) and one that was historic, 'in the time of King Edward' (1066). Predominantly these valuations tell us that they had been richer in 1066 than they subsequently became, with some distressing figures for 1070–71. However, three entries record higher values in 1086; three places had not been disturbed but had profited!

So we see that Stuntney (a very profitable eel bed fishery) and the other two places, though only a short distance across the fens from Ely itself, adjoined the royal estate at Soham and its neighbour Wicken (in the adjacent Staplow Hundred) and neither of these places came to harm. Here, we can say, royal forces drew the defensive line. On the western side of the double hundred, on the other hand, at Haddenham, Hill Row and Linden End, the port for Ely, they were badly mauled (according to their valuations) but to the south of them, protected by a belt of intervening marshes, were the hundreds of Northstow, Papworth and Chesterton. Here at Rampton, Over, Willingham and Cottenham we again see prosperous estates unaffected by Haddenham's troubles. Thanks to well-defended vills to the south of the peripheral marshes, on the south and east of the double hundred, we can see where the rebel occupation was contained and, one can say, cynically maintained until the time was ripe. The economic evidence, the statistics, provides the truth.

Next, King William led his ship and land forces north to Scotland, in 1072, entering the Forth, and King Malcolm came to treat with him, gave hostages and promised to be his vassal. It was a circumspect preparation. The following year, so the *Chronicle* says, William led both 'English' and 'French' forces overseas, where the 'English' in particular did great damage in Maine, helping to suppress a revolt against Norman rule. In 1074, the king was again campaigning in Normandy and England was deceptively peaceful, for a while.

It seems to me that we can reject a great deal of the 'received wisdom' concerning the (so-called) 'Harrying of the North' as dramatic licence built on totally unsecured propaganda invented by the Church, in the person of Orderic Vttalis, flamboyant declarations that he could never have verified at the time. We have already seen the history and topography of the Humber estuary and its lack of immediate resources for campaigning armies and this would necessitate foraging over much wider and more generously provided areas, resulting in widespread hardship for local populations, especially at the hands of mercenaries. Yet the misery was not inflicted vindictively and the effects were more complex than a blanket misfortune, though still *les grande misères de la guerre*.

In fact, on the northern edge of Lincolnshire in 1086 we see that a very fenny and marshy area had actually increased its arable (ploughed) land over the 1066 record, supporting a reasonable level of population who were, no doubt, as much 'fen tigers' as farmers. In the East Riding of Yorkshire, just as much a fenny wilderness as Lincolnshire at this date, some historians have created 'wasted' (despoiled) settlements by observing the lack of ploughs and ignoring the ancient topography in order to declare that all traces had been *deliberately* eliminated. Economically, such wastes of marsh and waters were valuable enough to be recorded in *Domesday Book* in spite of their lack of ploughlands and terra firma, but modern man has forgotten the economic value of such wastes.

Darby and Maxwell drew attention to the caution that should be exercised when proposing King William's sole responsibility for apparent economic changes,[5] while Bishop argued that the 'wasted' or vacant upland settlements of Yorkshire were actually the result of post-1070 settlers moving down into the more profitable, now abandoned, lowland vills.[6] This would make sense if the foraging forces who operated before, during and after 1068–70 had stripped the more accessible settlements, driving their inhabitants into the hills or even southwards. It would also considerably diminish the area said to have been 'harried'. 'Certain areas of the East Riding had a considerably higher concentration of settlements than the average ... the greatest concentration of settlements was to be found in Holderness,'[7] yet Holderness was very boggy and somewhat deficient in ploughs. It would surely have been the most susceptible area to foraging, by either side, whilst its economy was obviously as dependent on fen resources as on arable. I think we can propose that our picture painted by 'received wisdom', whether that of Yorkshire or of Hereward's Ely, has been seriously distorted for dramatic and propaganda purposes.

Notes

1. For payment of the fyrd see Hollister, op. cit. (1962), pp.29, 32, 44 and 79, while for the synthesis of English and Norman forces see pp.144–145.
2. Q.v. Douglas, op. cit. (1964) part IV.
3. Wright (2020), pp.46–49.
4. *The Anglo-Saxon Chronicle.*
5. H. Darby and I.S. Maxwell, *The Domesday Geography of Northern England* (CUP 1962 & 1977), pp.448-53.
6. T.A.M. Bishop, 'The Norman Settlement of Yorkshire' in *Studies in Medieval History Presented to F.M. Powicke* (OUP, 1948) pp.2–4.
7. Darby and Maxwell, op. cit., p.177.

Chapter Thirty-Eight

Fresh "Bones" for the Kingdom

The next threat, one might say predictably, came from among William's own nobles and, once again predictably, it almost certainly involved resistance to payment of the geld, the payment of land tax. Even for the writer of the *Chronicle*, the cloven hoof slips out as he spins the tale for no one with wealth welcomed this uniquely English specie taxation, whether Church or laity. In fact, the Church's hostility to such taxation (for good doctrinal reasons) has, in my opinion, biased *all* the surviving accounts of the so-called 'Norman Conquest' of England and blackened King William's achievements with bitter spite – for the simple reason that churchmen wrote such records under the direction of their superiors and their superiors lived (and thought) as great lords. All lords hated taxation.

The Breton lords in England had borne their share of the fighting and hardships and felt themselves to be something more than members of a province-by-conquest of Normandy. Whether they had grievances stemming from the award of estates in England is difficult to say but, like everyone else, they objected to being heavily taxed rather than being left to enjoy the fruits of their labours. No doubt they were happy to see campaigns supported by mercenaries (including Englishmen) but few contemporaries seem to have understood that Crown revenues had to be spent on such means of defence. What they did, however, understand was the need to recruit English support themselves if they were to have any hope of success against King William and his English fyrdmen.

Ralph de Gael, Earl of Norfolk, was the son of a lord who had served the indulgent and negligent King Edward in 'the good old days' of indulgent Breton kingship and who then joined with William of Normandy and so improved his pelf. In spite of this, he was not happy. He now secretly succeeded in interesting the Earl of Hereford, Roger de Breteuil, son of William fitzOsbern and his brother-in-law, in a coup. There was also Waltheof, Earl of Huntingdon, son of Siward of Northumbria, another earl who could remember 'better days' under the late King Edward (of blessed memory). One of St Cuthbert's miracles, as related by Simeon of Durham, actually *tells* us that the geld was the underlying reason for Waltheof's treason, this 'unjust tax' resulting from King William's 'cupiditas'.[1]

Just for good measure, Earl Ralph sent secret emissaries to William's enemies, to Denmark (of course) and also to King Phillipe of France and to Count Robert of Flanders and, obviously, to other lords in Brittany who could start diversionary actions. The whole plot has been nicknamed 'the bridal of Newmarket' for its supposed nativity at the bride-ale of Exning in 1075. Once again, Bishop Odo was, to begin with, circumspectly out of the way and King William was in Normandy but the new Archbishop of Canterbury, Lanfranc, seems to have got wind of the plot and someone certainly reported it to William even before anything had happened.

Lanfranc told the king that it would be foul shame if loyal vassals could not deal with such an internal uprising for him and, just to underline that this was *not* at all an English uprising (as some historians have claimed), he called on Wulfstan, Bishop of Worcester, and Æthelwig, Abbot of Evesham, to mobilise their troops and block Earl Roger's progress as he sought to join with Ralph, for Roger had raised his western lands behind him. Now William de Warenne, Richard fitzGilbert, Geoffrey de Coutances and Bishop Odo (Earl of Kent), with the folk of that land, moved into the field in order to prevent Ralph from moving south. Outmanoeuvred, the gallant Earl of Norfolk then abandoned his wife and Norwich castle and fled, but the Countess was allowed to depart for Brittany. Cnut of Denmark, son of Sweyn, arrived too late with perhaps 200 ships (8,000 men?), obviously now in difficulties to raise more, so he went to the Humber to ravage the coast there and also to plunder St Peter's Church at York, and so added to the damage already done. Poor pickings for his men, which may have had some bearing on later events? No, he did not linger.

It is self-evident that a speedy response had prevented the development of a serious problem and, equally, that a unified English resistance to treasons and invasion could now be expected. What was, however, ominous was that (once again) the threat to the country had come from 'French' rather than 'English' sources. King William returned at Christmas 1075, bringing with him the surrendered and contrite Earl Waltheof, who seems, in the end, to have taken no part in the rebellion but who had, obviously, failed to give due and loyal warning. Earl Roger was deprived of his lands and made a perpetual prisoner. Other Bretons were more harshly dealt with but Waltheof was imprisoned pending a final decision by the judges, which sounds as though his case was given some independent consideration, rather than being punished vindictively and summarily. Executing Earl Roger would have appeared too harsh to William's 'French' lords, for men of his status were generally better treated than their social inferiors, but the English custom was to treat men equally and so, on the last day of May, Waltheof was beheaded. He died as, indeed, he had lived, by English custom for, you will recall, from the Law of Alfred onwards the emphasis had always been on loyalty to one's social superiors for *all* degrees of Englishmen and especially to the king, who was (of course) next to God.[2]

Now the king ordered his castle-building programme to increase, though the revenues from the geld were falling, and in particular he ordered stone castles of impregnable design to be built at London (the 'White Tower') and Colchester. Both had the same plan but the behemoth at Colchester was far larger, far more ambitious, and included an earth and timber annex, a burgh, that would accommodate an army. Such structures were, of course, built to impress but they also denote strategic thinking alongside evolution in design and purpose.

Both London and Colchester were towers built in areas where stone was not naturally abundant, where the indigenous material was timber. They were, therefore, expensive projects. Colchester could reuse material from the Roman ruins of Colonia Claudia and London seems to have used some similar resources, but the interesting feature at Colchester is the annex. In effect, Colchester was a burgh, a fort designed to hold a field force ready to march anywhere in Anglia or towards the lower Wash, or even onto London, but appended to it was an impregnable tower that would resist attack even when the field force had gone. Perhaps the annex was also intended as a refuge for the valuable spinners and weavers on the Essex–Suffolk border in the event of invasion.[3] Maybe the White Tower was similarly designed with burgh and tower but, if so, all traces of the annex disappeared long ago as the site was developed. Both of these fortresses were on rivers and both commanded networks of roads. They were clearly designed to protect England's commerce and especially London from attacks on the eastern seaboard, and both were royal castles.

Elsewhere, 'castles' had been built of indigenous materials. There were pre-Conquest 'castles' at Rayleigh and Clavering, on the Marches and at Hen Domen as well as the older burghs (some of these 'cankered by peace') and there were remaining Roman fortifications, such as Pevensey and Portsea. However, now the general emphasis was away from the sheltering of field forces, or even of refugees, to a new tactical model, the flying column, a concept made possible by a new reliance on heavy cavalry and campaigns of movement. Such columns only needed staging posts and so small-garrison strongpoints were now an adequate strategic model, though often held not by the Crown but for the Crown, by a seneschal deputed by a magnate. Their small local garrisons could act as police forces and also as bullion guards for the precious royal revenues (collected locally). These are the structures that we now increasingly and commonly refer to as 'castles' and which underwent significant development during the succeeding century as their seneschals realised their usefulness for personal security.

Many of these early 'castles' were still merely burghs or ringworks in appearance but others began to adopt a model that appears to have developed first in England from the stone or timber towers of early churches, the use of a tower structure on a mound, the (so called) 'motte-and-bailey' castle.[4] Where stone was the local material it was used because it was available as well as strong but, as yet, the idea of a stone tower on an earth mound does not seem to have developed, for neither London nor Colchester were towers on mounds. The stone towers generally sat on natural rocky eminences or even took the form of the Presence Chamber built by William at Chepstow.[5] It was in timber-building shires that the motte castle became important, offering greater potential resistance than any simple burgh or ringwork and constructed rapidly. Now, thanks to royal foresight, there were 'castles' of one sort or another covering and guarding the north, the east and also the Welsh borders; 'castles' covering those road and river routes that might be used by invaders or rebels hoping to penetrate freely inland.

King William was now increasingly distracted by the defence of his French possessions and by the need to combat that curse of any medieval king, an ambitious son. So it was that in 1079 King Malcolm of Scotland, spying a chance, attacked Northumbria, burning, looting and slaving up to the Tyne, but he did not go beyond it for England was now covered by a network of garrisons on established lines of communication. Unfortunately, King William, short of money for this new extension to the military infrastructure, now sold the earldom of Northumbria to Bishop Walcher of Durham, a most unwise choice of lieutenant. By 1080, the avaricious bishop had been murdered and King Malcom felt reassured enough to sweep south once again.

Notes

1. Kapelle (1979), pp.134–5.
2. Morris says the same (pp.70–271), though he seems to attribute this respect for native law and due legal process to Norman brutality.
3. Q.v. Wright (2014), pp.373–380.
4. Wright (2019), pp.39–42 and (2020), pp.49–51.
5. Wright (2020), pp.97–98.

Chapter Thirty-Nine

Crisis, Attrition and Oath

In the summer of 1080, King William sent his half-brother, Odo, Earl of Kent and Bishop of Bayeux, to 'pacify' Northumbria, which he seems to have done with his characteristic enthusiasm for brutal war. Indeed, it is possible that some of the damage traditionally attributed to 1069–70 should be reassigned to this 1080 campaign.[1] Why did the king not lead this army himself? Well, he had (like former monarchs) realised that in England when one border required pacification opportunists on other borders would become active, so he personally led another army into Wales to settle a dispute between two kings there and to impress them (and the region) with his military might. At Chepstow, he had built an impressive stone 'presence chamber' as the core of his castle, for in warfare, demonstrations of strength may be as effective as slaughter and they are often more economical in the long run. It was later to develop into a massive castle complex and it survives today.

Having been reconciled with his rebellious son Robert, King William now also sent him into Scotland with another army. Perhaps this was to make a point to King Malcolm of Scotland but it is also possible that William was testing the supposed loyalty of son Robert and brother Odo (both of whom he now had reason to suspect) by placing them together whilst holding another army himself, in readiness, south of the border. However, events seem to have passed off without any such indications so William returned to Normandy, but was he really secure and did he believe himself to be secure? Whilst he had been campaigning on the southern Marches of Wales, brother Odo may indeed have been plotting in Cheshire with Earl Hugh 'the fat' of Chester, who held the northern Marches. Anyway, in 1082 we suddenly find Odo and Hugh together and each with their respective military forces, foregathering on the Isle of Wight in order to create an army, for this was the traditional jumping off point for armies destined either for France or (what is most important) to intercept an invader arriving from France – and William was in France!

Historians have explained this coalition as a preparation to 'go on Crusade', but it was done without the king's permission or knowledge and it was done whilst he was fighting enemies in France and so on the wrong side of the Channel to prevent it.[2] I have suggested (elsewhere) that William had, by now, suspicions about his half-brother and so I believe that he had now given him opportunities to seek out disaffected equals and to contact foreign rulers – a, by now, familiar model for political change – but, what the plotters did not know, the faithful Archbishop Lanfranc was watching developments on the Crown's behalf.[3]

King Cnut (IV) of Denmark was now plotting with Count Robert of Flanders to assemble an enormous fleet (by now he needed help) and William's son, Robert 'Curthose', was also to be drawn into this plot. Well, the upshot was that William returned to England, late in 1082, and arrested brother (bishop and earl) Odo in person, when no one else dared to, and immediately consigned him to the impregnable tower of Rouen with orders that he should *never* be released!

As I have observed before, it would be impossible to keep the formation and equipping of such an invasion fleet secret, in which case putting two and two together, that is Odo and Hugh's army *and* the Continental confederacy preparing against him, it would be a simple matter for William to deduce intentions and likely outcomes. I also believe that King William had received further information concerning his brother and other magnates from within his own administration. I have written about it elsewhere and it concerns the falling returns from the geld and the lack of Crown revenues.[4] The royal response to this suspicion of widespread treason – for to withhold taxes *was* treason in itself – was, I believe, to already set the administrative wheels 'grinding fine' among earlier records (kept at Winchester), in preparation for a great survey, in truth an audit, the one known to us today as *Domesday Book*.[5]

The year 1083 seems to have been one in which King William was carefully studying all intelligences reaching him from several quarters and also ordering 'castles' and defences to be put in order. Famine had struck in 1082 but in spite of this the king ordered a 'mickle geld', late in 1083, of 72 pence on the hide. This was a desperate attempt to raise royal revenues and, of course, bound to failure as no one actually knew what it was possible to raise; there had never yet been an audit and there had been so many tax evasions over the years. It was so very easy to claim that some land or another no longer existed where it had once been recorded, or to commute it to rent and so avoid land tax altogether. So in 1084 we may imagine the desperate efforts of royal clerks to 'balance the books' ahead of impending invasion, which, by some accounts, may have been intended to be larger than even William's fleet of 1066 had been. Nevertheless, it is possible that William was himself already actively recruiting, sequestering and negotiating ahead of his enemies.

So it was that in 1085 William returned to England with an enormous force, one requiring ships of its own, and maybe he had also been buying up chandlery in order to diminish international supplies. As I have said before, wars are not won by battles but by clever strategy and strategy includes economics and material. It was obviously King William's intention to sequester as many assets as he could that might be of value to his enemies, simultaneously providing a massive military presence in England with which to intimidate any attackers.

Once these assets were safely in England, it became a war of attrition; of who could hold their forces together for the longest period of time, paying them and providing for them until the other side finally capitulated or, in the case of the confederation, became desperate enough to attack. Clearly England would groan under such a burden and, equally, the maintenance of discipline among idle, mercenary soldiery was going to be a major problem, but it was a calculated risk and a clever strategic concept.

Billeting was arranged 'to each (landholder) according to the amount of his land', just as with the collection of the geld.[6] Moreover, if this strategy was successful it would serve as a paradigm for the future, provided that the economic resources could still be found. Meanwhile, the confederate fleet forming in Limfjord grew restless with the autumn, many men needing to return home to see to their harvests and now short of both food and money. King Cnut called a halt to preparations, possibly in need of mercenaries and the money to pay them but also in order to deal with a threatened German invasion of his territory, which he suspected had sympathies with elements within his court – and we might even suspect had something to do with King William. Certainly intelligences providing such information seem to have reached King William, for he now began to prepare instead for anticipated needs, that is for future economic resources, both money and provisions, whatever might be needed yet again, whilst simultaneously standing down the present burden of licentious soldiery.

Large numbers of mercenaries were swiftly paid off and sent home, and King William prepared a special Christmas Council at Gloucester. Here he called not only a Synod but also the Great Council of his realm, and it is at these deliberations that he appears to have persuaded all the important landholders that a series of surveys was necessary in order to determine resources; I have suggested that he secured their co-operation by promising rights of inheritance and clear titles to property once these surveys were completed.[7] No doubt some of these nobles anticipated pulling the wool over official eyes for good! Equally important, he called a consultative meeting of his Witan, almost certainly composed of Englishmen (as it was a uniquely English constitutional body) and quite separate from either the Great Council or the Synod, a Witan to advise and reassure him concerning the execution of this enormous audit.[8] His loyal (royal) servants had prepared a very clever paradigm, which the king seems to have needed validated before ordering its final commission.

In the first half of 1086, King William sent out survey teams under commissioners (legati) in order to collect new information by which to audit the older geld records already available in his chancery at Winchester. By Lammas the information was with his clerks and ready for conflation, and so he called a great meeting of all landholders, both the great and the small, on Salisbury Plain and there he made his offer of tail male inheritance of all estates, now according to the revised records, *provided* that every man owing military service, landholders *and* their hearth troops, swore fealty *directly* to the Crown. In future there were to be no legal loopholes whereby fealty sworn to an intermediate lord excused those of his subordinates who only followed their orders. Now *all* fealty was, first and foremost, to the Crown. We call this 'feudalism', though it was, in truth, the practical application of English law.

This was not only a clever act of generalship, it was also the creation of a true 'feudal system', rather than a comital one, the holding of any estate or 'fief' *as of the Crown*, even when it was a subinfeudation of some great lord's estates and therefore not strictly 'in capite'. Henceforth, there were to be no dissentient voices when *le roi le vult*, there would only be, in English law, traitors. What the King of England commanded would be done, loyalty to the king was next to loyalty to God, as King Alfred had declared. In effect, we see the concept of the Divine Right of kings, which had come to pass (like all things) because God willed it.

With this great act of homage accomplished, King William led this concourse to Wight and thence to a campaign in France, a campaign that resulted in his untimely demise. But he was not the only one, for Cnut (IV) had already been murdered by his own rebellious soldiery. Nevertheless, King Cnut (IV), like King Edward of England, was subsequently honoured as a saint, 'Cnut the Holy', while William was reviled by the Church. His gifts to Holy Mother were set at nought because of his demands that she should contribute her share to the defence of the kingdom. Perhaps we should excuse this as economic illiteracy on the part of unworthy academics?

Notes

1. Trevor Rowley, *The Man Behind the Bayeux Tapestry* (2013), p.116.
2. Ibid., pp.134–135 and 139–140.
3. Wright (2020), pp.8–9.
4. Ibid., pp.90–96 and also (2014), pp.156–162.
5. Wright (2014) and (2020).
6. The *Peterborough (E) Chronicle*: this proves that the geld was a land tax and that the principle involved was land assessment.
7. Wright (2020), pp.102, 106 and 114–116.
8. Wright (2014), pp.319–323.

Chapter Forty

The Power of the Crown

We have now travelled a long way from the Anglo-Saxon kingdoms and we have seen how successive waves of raiders and invaders destroyed both their world and the security of these kingdoms. We have seen how co-operation, confederation and cohesion helped them to fight back. We have seen that the Danish invaders developed a successful strategic paradigm that the English kingdoms then took for their own model and so turned the tables on them. Moreover, under Alfred it was demonstrated that an active and aggressive kingship was the key to employing this strategy and we subsequently saw that weak and craven kings allowed such advantages to slip away from them as political factions and individual greed replaced group identity and responsibility. These are the broad outlines we have discovered and sometimes, just sometimes, the records allow us to glimpse details.

Tactically we have little enough information to glean from chroniclers with no military appreciation and even less interest, clerics who began by promising Divine intervention, who then progressed to blaming its failure on the 'wickedness' of the secular population and finally, around the millennium, themselves, and for personal safety began to evolve into a 'Church militant' modelled on secular aristocrats, so that they could survive. Such writers had no idea how a king might need to think, much less the problems he faced, and were probably not interested anyway. That said, the few hints at tactics we have or can deduce do enable us to see that combats were fought with a careful eye for the advantages of terrain, they were not just disorganised slogging matches. The fault of many historians in the past, when analysing these battles, has been to ignore the topographic changes consequent upon later industrial and agricultural developments and so look upon a modern landscape as the site of the battle. They have also, often, paid little attention to the communications available at the time or the composition of forces.

Most important to our review of strategies has been the network of communications, the realisation that adequate highways existed, that byways were followed, that rivers provided routes and could also often be the best routes for pedestrians following their banks. Too often the historian's mental picture (I have seen as much reproduced in documentaries) of military movements has been a simplistic 'cross-country' ramble and scramble by pedestrians encumbered with armour. Now that we have seen so much emphasis on being 'horsed', we can at last appreciate how forces *could* move with speed, even when not travelling by boat, and arrive in fighting condition. We also see that for much of the time Vikings sought the security of numbers, of mass safety, avoiding dense cover where guerrillas could operate more securely, trusting to roads and rivers and avoiding the unknown.

Organisation for war was also important and the organisation of resources particularly so. Technology played its part, as we have seen in the relative constructions, designs and consequent seaworthiness of shipping, with adaptation of design finally effecting a tactical revolution. Most interesting to my mind has been the realisation that Danish ships were probably built with inland travel in mind, so they were less seaworthy but, alternatively, easier to manoeuvre and portage on rivers. English ships, however, were designed to be both seagoing and fighting vessels, and it just might be that their design then influenced Scandinavian construction, just as ship burials themselves possibly travelled from England to Scandinavia. In England we then saw major changes in land warfare after the millennium with the importation by sea of Continental practices.

Predictably, the earliest Anglo-Saxon defensive measures took the form of reactive policing. As such, they were largely ineffective, especially when outnumbered by concerted attacks. The best defence is, always, to prepare for war. With the establishment of burghs, however, such bases were established, bases able to accommodate forces, to shelter people and to sustain local defence, places that also formed refuges and grew into trading centres, so aiding economies.[1] Combination and co-operation allowed defensive forces to become more proactive, seeking and pursuing enemies (when well led and systematically supplied), while the subsequent establishment of numerous small burghs, or as we term them later on, 'castles', together with mounted flying columns, intensified the protection of major routes. Finally, as developed under William, the ability to sequester an enemy's military resources provided real and proactive prevention.

Long-term strategic changes inevitably involve social change. The United Kingdom's desperate isolation early in the Second World War created both structural changes in administration and social unification; there was a strong and political emphasis on levelling the class structure of society in order to incentivise the masses. The conclusion of hostilities did not automatically cancel out these attitudinal modifications, they had been too widely adopted and accepted to be relegated, and the erosion of older class structures continued to work. We should, perhaps, look for such subtle changes and social shifts in the change from Anglo-Saxon to English kingdoms, a social 'levelling up'.

It seems to me that the ancient Anglo-Saxon kingdoms had relied on rigid social hierarchies and attitudes, structures closely aligned to the mindset of Scandinavian adventurers, that is Danes and 'Vikings'. Poul Anderson has expressed the loyalties of such military aristocracies as follows: 'Love, loyalty, honesty ... were only for one's kindred, chieftain and close friends. The rest of mankind were foemen or prey.'[2]

Such was the mindset of kingdom communities of the seventh and eighth centuries in England and such, I think, continued to be the social concept of the Danish and Viking invaders. However, in England as the kingdoms coalesced and became larger units, in order to meet the threats of both united and of sometimes separately operating 'forces', two things happened. First of all, love and loyalty had to be extended beyond the immediate leader or king and, although it was difficult to eliminate this self-interested 'hearth troop' loyalty, it became increasingly obvious that security lay in general unity and united responses. Secondly, the need for manpower, warrior power, caused an extension of privileged status, so that all who had some form of 'free tenure' could be impressed into the fyrd. Slaves, of course, could never join the general fyrd, so a tension surely arose between the economic value of slave production (to sustain the fighting forces) and slave freedom and release within the lower levels of society, resulting in the creation of serf and bordar (as we later call them) tenants. Of course, such relatively 'free' tenants were then economically incentivised to produce more than slaves did, which would also encourage moves towards manumission.

The 'Viking' armies, however, were always composed of freemen, however minor their level in society, though maybe not without injections of renegades and criminals, and as ship sokes they had no reason to look beyond their clan or crew association. They had no property in England or families to lose (until they joined the Danelaw) and therefore depended on the notice of their leader for favours and justice. It is much more difficult to advance such self-interests when part of an enlarged body of warriors, a combined array, but on the other hand, the lack of overall cohesion (even when bands co-operate) can become a structural weakness in combat.

Serendipity, it seems, created the means by which all efficient defensive preparations could finally be sustained, for the accident of the geld 'tribute' made further developments possible, but only by eventually changing attitudes. Initially the geld attracted an influx of alien, Continental, peoples with their own political structures and then in the new millennium the older Anglo-Saxon attitude to loyalty was further undermined by attempts at introducing Comital – that is Norman French – politics with their basic 'loyalties of convenience'. Thanks to the political turmoil created by such attempts, a final cohesion became possible with the realisation that England was not just a 'loose congeries of the *gens anglorum*' formed from the *gentis anglorum* but a single kingdom with a single kingly power sustained by an English legal system and an unique, English, taxation. Paradoxically, this came about when a Norman king rejected his previously accepted Norman-French polity in favour of English institutions and concepts.

This could not have been possible without a thorough absorption of the scattered Danish (Danelaw) settlers into an English identity and it seems likely that the differentiation into 'French' and 'English' legal camps accelerated or fully catalysed this process. The determination shown by the Anglo-Norman forces of 1069–70, and 1071, to put an end to the invading army trapped in the Humber was not only a tribute to leadership and unity, I think it also emphasises for us the bitter hatred felt by *all* English dwellers for the murderers and slavers they so readily termed 'Danes'. Of course, what they meant was Vikings, 'pirates', not their now settled and absorbed neighbours on the east side of the kingdom; both English and Danish Englishmen saw the destroyers of families as detested outlaws. The persistence of myths linking flayed hides of Danes to church doors tells us the strength of feeling and that such condign punishment was seen as divinely sanctioned.

What we see most clearly with the advent of William of Normandy is the differentiation between 'French' and 'English' law and his respect for the English Coronation Oath. If we need this 'Anglicisation' confirmed we have only to look into *Domesday Book* to see that the whole administration of the kingdom hinged on and functioned by *English* units of length and area measurements, a political adoption also displayed in chancery by the continued Norman use of English writs, though these were writs now in the Latin language (in order to accommodate and facilitate both 'French' and 'English' comprehensions) rather than in English (or French) alone.[3] Had there not been such a thorough appreciation of the 'status quo ante' *nothing could have functioned* in the new polity. The idea of a 'Norman Conquest' destroying everything 'Saxon' was always a nonsense. It would have inevitably resulted in chaos and anarchy.

So it is that we witness King William's relegation of the comital Norman-French system of very loose (and even convenient) loyalties to authority, the system so often misrepresented as 'feudal', in favour of an English emphasis on supreme loyalty to the Crown, a new presentation of an old system that was finally, *and in fact,* feudal, for it relied on the individual 'fief', whether large or small, being secured by loyalty given directly to the king above all other intermediate lords. This development, secured by the audit we now call *Domesday Book* and presented at the Salisbury Plain ceremony of fealty, minimised the risk of treacherous alliances being formed with foreign powers by greedy magnates retaining private armies, and it surely reassured the few surviving English landowners of the king's commitment to uphold the laws and customs of England. We see this most obviously demonstrated in the readiness of fyrdmen to turn out and join 'Norman' forces. It was a system completely different from Continental polities and it conferred peculiar strength on the new Anglo-Norman kingship. It is tempting to see in this comprehensive overview of contractual relationships, which could condemn subordinates for obeying their lord's actions and orders and impose collective or associative guilt, the influence of the Venerable Bede's *Da Domesday* treatise. Was this the determining contribution to the formulation of true feudalism I wonder?[4]

Of course, this conversion to a central loyalty was not effected overnight, but the evidence of its efficiency is there. In abolishing the opportunities for magnates to aggrandise themselves, it not only constrained the comital ambitions of 'Frenchmen', it also spelled the end of the ealdormanic system of government and its replacement (in part at least) with shrieval powers dependent on the king. Its strengths were that a command to resist an enemy, even as an arrière-ban, now came with the full force of royal command, whether personally led or not, and the ultimate penalty for failure or treachery became the English death penalty. It also relied on a new tactical mass of 'miles', knights, sergeants, and king's thanes, that group now destined to evolve into shire knights and squires, whose territorial privileges could now be seen to rely on their loyalty *first and foremost* to the Crown. Their security was not now an ultimate appeal *only* to their (granting) overlord as a form of sub-regulus, but, in law, their ultimate 'good lord' was now the king and this made all the difference to fealty. The humblest of knights or sergeants could now appeal a grievance against an overlord to the king's justice, a process we see evidenced in the twelfth century. That was the first step in equality for *all* men before the law.

So, after covering three centuries of struggle and, at times, calamity, can we discern any simple structural picture? I think we can. If you will bear with me and recall what we have explored already, I think we can present a broad developmental picture.

Initially we might say that the first waves of raiders were 'reiving', they were 'lifting' whatever they could, though instead of cattle they were focusing on slaves. Then, as loot became less plentiful, they began to place more emphasis on slaving, though the very fact of participation in a successful venture also conferred status when the participants returned home. Success tempted some to remain 'in the field' in order to exploit this licence and profitability, and we must always bear in mind that the returns from any venture had to cover the enormous expense of ships and warlike outlay as well as turning a profit.

As resistance increased, due in part to uniting of defence forces, so it became necessary for the pirates also to bond together in groups of raiding forces and acknowledge (temporary) overall leaderships. At this point it became desirable to exploit any weak links that could be found in the English kingdoms; aristocratic rivalries and ambitions. Treachery was made easier under weak and cowardly English kings and terror became a weapon with which to demoralise opposition at all levels.

With unified defence came economic muscle and, given capable leadership, demographic resources. As a consequence, invasions had to become more ambitious until they at least resembled national-style conflicts. Now the object was not to merely milk England of treasure and useful peoples but to completely subsume the economy. However, by permitting a new settlement zone, the Danelaw, King Alfred can be said to have fractured the aim of his Danish opponents, for its inhabitants would increasingly identify with the English peoples in order to ensure their own security and newly acquired status.

The resources required for such invasion fleets ensured that conflicts became dynastic, with the aristocracies of either side being drawn into the self-serving political maelstrom. Then came a glittering prize in the form of a mountain of silver, the ultimate temptation to invade. Nationalism played no part, it did not yet exist, nor would it for centuries to come. Indeed, even a national identity was far in the future for most European peoples.

Perhaps English unification, once completed (and it took time) made regional conquests, which had been the practice in earlier days, impossible. Instead it became 'all or nothing'. It was no longer possible to select a territory or to operate a 'domino effect'. Finally, added to this comprehensive defence capability was the political restriction of local magnates, men who no longer exercised individual powers but who now only had power *under* the Crown. This was now the English feudal system, which covered all but the wilder borderlands with Scotland and Wales for centuries to come.

Notes

1. Q.v. Wright (2014), pp.287–290 and drawing on *Winchester Studies I ... an Edition and Discussion of the Winton Domesday*, Barlow, Biddle, von Feilitzen and Keene (ed. M. Biddle, OUP, 1976); and Heather Swanson, *Medieval British Towns* (1999).
2. Poul Anderson, *Hrolf Kraki's Saga* (N.Y., 1973) xix.
3. Q.v. F.M.Stenton, *The Latin Charters of the Anglo-Saxon Period* (Oxford, 1955), especially pp.90–91.
4. Bede's *Ða Domesday*.
5. Q.v. Douglas (1964), p.293; Barlow (1970 and 1979), pp.146–147; also M.E. Harmer, *Anglo-Saxon Writs* (1952) in general.

Chapter Forty-One

Anglo-Norman Security

For the magnates, both lay and clerical, who had formerly ridden out with enormous hearth troops, the financial emphasis was now on subinfeudation, for this would ensure that the crippling burden of the land tax (which fell upon them) was diminished by granting small portions of their massive estates to their knights, sergeants and squires (as the miles/ milites now became) in the form of 'manors', for which the subinfeuded manorial (free) holder would be liable to pay a minor share of the overall tax burden. Therefore, permanent hearth troops, as opposed to retained fighting men who could be called on in need and given set (feudal) duties, now became an expensive luxury, for without land such men had no tax obligations, while their magnate, as lord, still had to clothe, feed, house and pay them for their constant attendance – as well as paying the land tax in full.[1]

William's sudden death in 1087 saw the release of brother Odo and the succession of son William ('Rufus') to the English throne. Son Robert received Normandy and son Henry money. Relying on the consequent confusion and on the hunger of the larger magnates for an extension of opportunistic 'French-style' (comital) vassalage to England, Odo now plotted with Robert and other ambitious Normans to destroy William 'Rufus' in 1088. The 1086 conversion to central and comprehensive loyalty was not effected overnight, because it was not automatically acknowledged by the Norman magnates once King William had so opportunely died.

Bishop Gosfrith and Robert de Mowbray therefore ravaged Bristol and Bath and Berkley Harness was laid waste. Robert in Shropshire joined with Welsh raiders and ravaged and burnt Worcestershire, until bested by archbishop Wulfstan's troops. In the north, bishop William of Durham did all the harm he could. Earl Roger ravaged Norfolk and others Leicestershire and Northamptonshire, whilst Odo destroyed all the lands of the king and of the archbishop in Kent and triumphantly retired to his 'castle' at Rochester to gloat. Once again, England was being torn apart by ambitious and greedy nobles who refused to acknowledge the Crown or the rule of English law.

What happened? Well the English fyrds turned out en masse to aid their king. They marched on Rochester and also took Tonbridge 'castle', while the king himself, with an Anglo-Norman force, also closed in on Rochester, only to find that Bishop Odo's nerve had failed him and he had fled to Pevensey 'castle'. Meanwhile, Robert 'Curthose's' Norman fleet was intercepted in the Channel by an English ship force and defeated. William 'Rufus' was his father's son.

Odo now entreated for a truce and promised, in return, to surrender Rochester, but when William agreed and sent an escort with the surrendered Odo, in order to receive Rochester, the garrison there rescued the bishop and imprisoned the king's men. Now King William 'Rufus' took a great Anglo-Norman force to Rochester and besieged it and when it surrendered Odo was banished overseas. Following this the king sent forces to Durham and the bishop there surrendered, gave over his bishopric and went overseas in turn. In this way, with English fyrdmen, was the Norman throne secured for William II.

This tells us, as we already know but is so rarely admitted, that the English had *not* been deprived of their weapons. It also tells us that the professional cadre (the select fyrd) was still intact and efficient and that the respect for English law that William I had always shown had reassured English society. The much-paraded legal 'difference' between 'Englishmen' and 'Frenchmen', so regularly claimed as evidence of English 'oppression', was nothing of the sort and when later chroniclers claimed that the English were inferior they were only chewing on sour grapes.[2] Of course, they were not deigning to notice peasants, rather the objects of such spiteful asides were the former select fyrdmen who were now acting as miles, knights and sergeants, who were now on a par with French miles. There were 'king's thanes' and 'king's almsmen' entered in *Domesday Book* in 1086 with substantial holdings, though many historians try to airbrush them out because they do not, yet, commonly adopt French names. In fact, it seems very probable that the comprehensive picture of shire knights and squires that we encounter in the twelfth century was substantially formed by such English warrior families who had integrated with the new order in the years following the (so-called) 'Conquest' and then continued to be assimilated during the succeeding half century.[3] By adopting a French praenomen, one became a 'Frenchman' rather than a king's thane.

With such resources behind him and such a record of sibling perfidy as a warning, it is no surprise to read of King William II's now vengeful campaigns against his brother, Robert, in Normandy. Whilst he was away fighting in Normandy in 1091, King Malcolm of Scotland again took the opportunity to ravage the north but, after a rapid reconciliation with Robert, William called out both the English land and ship forces and marched north later in that same year. This was a mistake insofar as the ship force was caught in awful weather just before Michaelmas, and badly damaged. Yet in spite of this setback, when Malcolm saw the Anglo-Norman army he agreed to become William's vassal rather than fight.

The royal army then took Carlisle, over in the Strathclyde west, a strategic covering of the Solway Firth and River Eden route (otherwise available to Irish Vikings), but by 1093 King Malcolm was yet again ravaging northern England and this time Earl Robert of Northumbria trapped Malcolm and killed him *and* his son and heir with him. Duncan, who by this act became heir to the Scottish throne, was himself next displaced by a usurper but finally won his throne – with the help of the Anglo-Norman army. We also learn that in 1094 King William called out 20,000 English troops for service in France, men who brought with them a useful £10,000 for their sustenance. Keeping the money, he sent them home. I think that instead of criticising this as 'avarice' we might here discern the origins of the 'scutage' payments that were to provide an alternative to military service in the next century and beyond by using default payments to hire smaller but more professional forces. William II, it seems, was a man ahead of his times and innovators are never understood by those who feel threatened by change. Once again we see a total inability among contemporary chroniclers to link the raising of money with the defence of the realm, the monkish presumption (or prelate calumny) being that cash was destined for luxuries and pleasurable pursuits.

In this same year, 1094, there was much raiding by the Welsh and finally King Duncan of Scotland was murdered by his own people. In 1095, true to tradition, Earl Robert of Northumbria also became defiant and, yet again, an Anglo-Norman army marched north, this time to best the earl's forces, besiege and capture him. After Michaelmas, the king was in Wales and there he now penetrated as far as Snowdon, but his forces could not bring their enemies to a pitched battle. Desultory fighting continued in 1096 and 1097 but when it all proved wasteful the king withdrew his forces and (pragmatically) ordered 'castles' to be built all along the borders. Pacification by overall conquest had to await Edward I and his comprehensive castle programme.

So the fusion of English and foreign forces in support of a Norman dynasty continued to provide troops, not only for border protection but also for conflicts in France, this in addition to providing numerous garrisons at home. In 1097, the king gave the ætheling Edgar troops with which to invade Scotland. When 'Rufus' was murdered and brother Henry ascended the throne of England, Robert of Normandy threatened his own invasion, causing the new King Henry in his turn to gather forces at Pevensey.

Now the 'Conqueror's' accord was put to a real test, for many barons wished to support Robert 'curthose', no doubt yearning for the freebooting comital world they still experienced when in France, but the English bishops now despatched their own 'knights' to support the new king and a treaty was eventually agreed. The threat was finally disposed of in 1106 when, after invading Normandy with an Anglo-Norman army, Henry defeated and captured his brother and with him some powerful Norman lords. The troublemakers were 'bagged' and a lesson delivered.

The civil war that followed Henry's reign, the war between Stephen and Matilda, was in no way a 'French' versus 'English' conflict. Rather it was a last attempt by the aristocracy (of either party or faction) to rid themselves of the burdens of fealty and of taxation; it was their hope of a Continental-style disintegration of central power and authority. Opinions varied (then as now) as to the late King Henry's merits, some saying he had been just and maintained the laws and others that he was avaricious, harsh and cruel, but on his death law and order certainly broke down and so civil war intervened. Maybe it was nostalgia for the good order of Henry's reign that caused Walter Map to present him in such glowing terms, or maybe it was the rose-tinted spectacles of age looking back on his own youth? Anyway, the contrast between Map's descriptions of Henry's court and those of the chroniclers and other sources once again stand as a warning against accepting particular contemporary accounts at face value.[4] What followed Henry I was 'The Anarchy' and that created no apologists, only bitter wailing and gnashing of teeth.

Historians speak of the baronial armies that now emerged as 'mercenaries' but I wonder how many of these men were former select fyrdmen, or how many 'mercenaries' were refugees from the harsh famines and murrains that had marked King Henry's reign, and now joined one side or another, even as foot soldiers if not as 'knights', in order to avoid starvation? Yet when King David of Scotland invaded with a vast army, earl William of Aumale put him to flight at the Battle of the Standard (at Northallerton) in 1138. Though in 1140 the baronial alliance triumphed and captured King Stephen at Lincoln, for all the ensuing chaos major foreign invaders were loath to interfere until Henry of Anjou brought an army to England, after Matilda had died, in order to promote her claim (and his, as her son) and Stephen and Henry then reached an accord. The upshot of this, as we all know, was the founding of the Plantagenet dynasty in 1154 with the crowning of Henry II as King of England.

Of course, it is always difficult to isolate a single gestation in a long course of evolution and such an evolution is the process we have been following on the battlefield and in parallel with the unification of regions and Anglo-Saxon kingdoms. We can therefore see inception and we can see completion but the critical moment, even supposing one ever exists or existed then, escapes us. We see exactly the same process in the parallel evolution of English law, first of all regional and then employing ethnic unifications that finally evolved into a body of equitable law by which to encompass *all* men in all parts of the kingdom.

So it was that in the tenth century, in the Marches of Wales, on the Wye below Hereford, a body of twelve men composed of six Englishmen and six of Welsh race was constituted, a 'joint bench', the origins of a jury. This was, in Professor Stenton's words, 'a habit of mind fully competent to undertake the experiments which were to issue in the Anglo-Norman jury'.[5] We see the same processes at work in the eventual integration of the Danelaw with England proper, with solidarities at first requiring parallel systems, in order to promote harmony, but which ultimately fused. The concept of the *finalis concordia* (commonly called the 'feet of fines'), as Stenton observed, was certainly familiar to the Witan of Edgar and Æthelred, long before it was actually recorded (in structure and records) at the end of the twelfth century as the 'Feet of Fines' series. So we see that mechanisms of all kinds seem to be evidenced long before we have them on permanent record simply because they were evolving during the long process of consolidation that accompanied the emergence of English and then Anglo-Norman security.

So it was that King William I willed that all should have 'the law of King Edward in lands and in all things ...' but finally came around to moderating the harshness of some aspects of English law – such as substituting mutilation for the death penalty in general – though with such notable exceptions as eorl Waltheof providing instructive examples. The evolution of the jury is also a contentious subject as arguments tend to focus on discovering a single and unparalleled genesis, yet for all its origins the final promotion and adoption do appear to ultimately belong in the Norman sphere.[6] By the time of Henry I we see a 'new and highly individualistic legal system', so that despite the collapse of the machinery of government in Stephen's reign we do afterwards finally arrive at what has been termed 'the Angevin leap forward' in law that certainly built on earlier Anglo-Norman foundations.[7] And underpinning the regulation of law and order we see a true and English feudalism that, within a short period of time, came to be administered by sheriffs as royal representatives, men who were local justices and minor landholders, the very country knights whom we suspect of having ancestral links to the select fyrds.

Notes

1. Wright (2020), pp.99–100 and 129.
2. Henry of Huntingdon, *Historia Anglorum*.
3. Wright (2020), p.13; also D.M. Stenton, *English Justice Between the Norman Conquest and the Great Charter, 1066–1215* (1965), pp.31–32 and note 23.
4. Walter Map, 'De Nugis Curialium' in 'Anecdota Oxoniensia' (ed. M.R. James, 1914) and James in *The Honourable Society of Cymmrodorion*, Record Series no. ix.
5. D.M. Stenton, *English Justice Between the Norman Conquest and the Great Charter, 1066–1215* (Jane Lectures, 1963), 1965, p.7.
6. F. Liebermann (ed.), *Die Gesetze der Angelsachsen* (1903–1916), p.488.
7. Stenton (1965), p.26.

Chapter Forty-Two

The Communal Achievement

Of course, even by 1100 we are far too early to be talking in terms of nationalism, but what we can see is that by the accession of Henry II, Bede's 'English peoples' have become thoroughly united in a kingdom, a kingdom called England. We can say that by then the divisions of the Tribal Hidage were no more and we were on course to be Chaucer's 'fair field full of folk', both collectively and linguistically. Of course, that is because at some point in this twelfth century the general voice itself moved from Old English (and other languages) to Early Middle English, the (so called) 'Second Continuation' of the *Peterborough Chronicle* tells us as much. At least 'in southern England the passage from Old English to Middle English had begun before the middle of the 11th century'. [1] Now, c.1150 there was a common tongue, a common vehicle for communication (apart from Latin) and one we believe was increasingly commonly used by those who were not peasants, though the Chancery (with civil service conservatism) still preferred to use French.

What is astonishing is that all these subtle changes to a common and joint identity survived the wasteland of The Anarchy, so that after it they were still deep rooted enough to discover a common goal in the reinstatement of one monarch, Henry II. It seems to me that this bond and unification was achieved in large part by the development of efficient and co-operating military forces composed of several former ethnicities, though the general misery of civil war was also a unifying influence. By 1154, men could look back to the Norman kings and maybe before (though legal memory at this time only acknowledged a span of ninety-nine years) to say that *that* had been a time of secure and regulated government, royal government under the law and that it was needed once again.

The Anarchy itself showed how such resources could be misused and then exhausted, but simultaneously, it also underlined that they could, once again, be deployed under a strong king in order to maintain the proper defence of a kingdom's security. And security from foreign invasion and from criminal acts, after all, is the first and foremost benefit sought when creating any community, the most important political promise of them all. It is very difficult to achieve in the absence of true unity, which is why such a promise figured in the English Coronation Oath. King William I took this oath and took it seriously and, whatever the hysterical misrepresentations made by spiteful religious chroniclers, he certainly kept it during the succeeding twenty years of his reign.

Some historians speak of an 'English nation', a unified whole, before 1066 but I think this is an error. If nations exist as products of their members' beliefs, perhaps more importantly in the past as products of the beliefs of aristocratic minorities (in the absence of democratic structures), then pre-Conquest England was *not* entirely united, it still retained independent identities in regions such as Northumbria and on the Welsh Marches, even in the West Country.[2] This was not entirely due to conflicting ambitions between earls, men who might lay emphasis on historic sub-kingdoms in order to serve their own political ends, but also because of Franco-Breton aspirations to change the whole (balanced) political structure of England to a comital model. Nevertheless, England and the Danelaw were by 1086 some thirty-four shires united as one kingdom under the law against all comers and other ethnicities.

As with modern politics and parties, ordinary inhabitants in given areas of the pre-Conquest kingdom had shaped their views and resources according to the directions given them by their own political (aristocratic) leaders. For them there was no direct oath of loyalty to the Crown, not as yet, only a presumption and predisposition to show loyalty to the Crown as to their own and local 'good lord', whenever that was possible. Under active kings like Alfred and Edward the Elder, especially during overt or patent invasions, unity became apparent and loyalty to the de facto king was emphasised but, then as now, covert and political subversions made social and political elements much less receptive to widescale cohesion and then inactive, negligent and cowardly kings sapped both the will to resist and any belief in unity. They devalued the institution of kingship by allowing self-serving noble factions to form and usurp royal power. Men like Harold and William had been the royal nuclei around which some sort of collective identity could form once again, and after the 'Conquest' (as we call it) a gradual integration of 'English' and 'French' elements reinforced this feeling with the emergence of an identity separate from either of these ethnicities and so unique in Europe. The sniping at English 'inferiority' that we sometimes encounter in the contemporary writings of some French authors only evidences their insecurity in the face of a growing communal (if not common) identity.

So it was that the twelfth-century monk of Ely who wrote a 'life' of Hereward by producing a document, one might even call it a novel, which entirely distorted the few earlier witnesses and accounts, turned him from a brigand into a chivalrous hero. Why did he do this? In the first place, the ancient rivalry between Ely and Peterborough would encourage such a metamorphosis of the man who had sacked Peterborough and, in the second, it allowed the storyteller to reach a satisfactory conclusion by reconciling Hereward and King William. Thus the moral of this tale (or romance) was not 'English resistance' but the accord subsequently reached between the 'English' and the 'French' elements in twelfth-century society. Had this author flown in the face of contemporary religious chroniclers and his Church's tradition, by praising William, his story would never have been accepted by his superiors, for in the twelfth century, as in the eleventh, William and subsequent kings were flying in the face of Divine will by taxing Mother Church and kindly abbots and bishops, who supervised and edited such writers, were not prepared to collectively forgive such contempt for their holy predecessor's guidance. One had to be careful how one attacked royal policies but equally one also had to observe religious dogma when writing authorised 'histories'. Life outside the cloister, even *in* it if you did not follow authority, could be cold and hungry.

When Henry of Huntingdon narrated the Battle of the Standard in 1138 he, most tellingly, conflated his 'French' barons with an English unity, referring to a 'gens Anglo-Norman'. Ailred, abbot of Rievaulx, spoke of peoples united once again in a single English identity when writing *c*.1160.

It seems that the respect that William I had shown *ab initio* for the differences between 'English' and 'French' laws and customs had encouraged a growing mutual respect throughout society. Campaigning against invaders by Anglo-Norman forces (as the *Chronicle* testifies) reinforced this perception that the English were *not* a conquered race, disarmed and subjugated to foreign laws and systems but equals. No, I very much regret to say that such false constructs of ethnic superiority were subsequently created by nineteenth-century historians who misread the surviving evidence, apparently in an attempt to foist the new 'nationalism' and a national identity onto the remote past, men supporting the class system, men playing at contemporary politics and men selling stories.

In reality, an English Witan appointed William, the evidence for this is unequivocal, and after bitter experience of his own coterie and of Norman morality, it was William who eventually created a *truly* feudal system in order to secure the throne of England. Feudalism was *not* imported in 1066 any more than castles, knights and chivalry were, such things belong in novels.[3] Along the way and afterwards this new and truly feudal system, this system firmly based on the 'feudum' and 'fief' held as of the Crown, helped surviving English military sub-tenants to transform it and themselves and create a substrate in society by themselves adopting 'French' names, thus transforming select fyrdsmen into shire knights by the twelfth century. This metamorphosis was completed by the thirteenth century when ostensibly French-speaking landholders, both large and small, seem to have adopted a form of Middle English as their *lingua Franca*. Moreover, the marital reciprocity of the smaller landholders had already been noticed in the *Dialogues of the Exchequer*, c.1170, so willing English–French alliances were nothing new.

So I conclude by observing that not all battles are fought, let alone won, on a bloody field. I agree that a series of bloody battles, which must have seemed endless to contemporaries, transformed the Anglo-Saxon kingdoms into a more or less unified military machine, one operating by land and sea, between the eighth and the end of the eleventh centuries, but this was not all. The necessary political battles accompanying such upheaval required the whole kingdom to adopt a common identity in an age when, paradoxically, even economies were local and loyalties often opportunistic.

It was this battle to enforce legality and to focus supreme loyalty on the Crown that eventually created Medieval England, and this was only achieved after so-called conquest and its consequent social changes had finally been accepted. This took time and was not easily accomplished when magnates promoted their own selfish ends. It therefore owed a good deal to battles necessarily fought in secret, because they involved the king's personal stratagems, a man whose motives were never divulged to anyone else and so never recorded in any chronicle. That this could come about is a tribute to the growth of mutual respect manifested during a rapid political fusion of two cultures with very different polities and which might otherwise have clashed with disastrous consequences. Instead we might say that all battles came, well at least relatively speaking, to a satisfactory conclusion because they resulted in internal peace and a durable concord that could finally resist pressures from outside the kingdom and furthermore provide foundations on which to build in the future.

So we can say that the conflicts we have been reviewing were not ends in themselves, rather they were platforms on which to ultimately build successive social cohesions that then led to the unification of what had once been individually vulnerable kingdoms. It seems that our traditional and false picture of this period, the early medieval period's historical presentation of received wisdom and group thinking, has always been founded in an aristocratic and imperialist vision, that is on a vision of a succession of *unions fait de la force*. No doubt this was an easier explanation than a process of unification.

Such a 'conquest' construct essentially relies on the use of force by external and 'superior' societies in order to impose law, order and stability on social and political inferiors, the all-pervading concept that 'might is right'. In the received progression we have reviewed, therefore, this then, supposedly, culminated in the colonisation of backward 'Saxon' peasant communities by a race of 'Norman supermen', a very appealing doctrine to our recent class-conscious ancestors. The application of such a vision of history to a vision of empire that would 'improve' large areas of the world then becomes understandable and is excusable as the civilising influence of a 'world policeman'. This vision of historical 'progress' was then equally applicable to the Roman Empire, the Norman Conquest and the Pax Britannica, and to this day it continues to recommend itself to great power blocs.

In point of fact, I submit, we have witnessed a rather different historical progression. Motivation undoubtedly came from the need for security and gave emphasis to co-operation and even co-ordination, so the means to the end were inevitably military but their aspect changed in order to accommodate changing circumstances. Time after time, resources and leadership drove progress towards cohesion and stability, and these were then most noticed afterwards by their absence in weak administrations and in weak individuals; absence emphasised the value of such things. I think that the events we have unfolded have also helped us to understand unstated, undeclared, policies that were never recorded because they were never divulged to the writers of chronicles, who were not likely to have understood them anyway.

Both a series of events *and* serendipity helped to cement progress towards stability and security, a combination of the unpredictable with the inevitability of gradualness. It was neither brutal force nor a 'master race' philosophy that finally unified kingdoms and created the means and machinery for one will and one conception to triumph, instead it was co-operation, pragmatism and determination that provided the means of security.

With time, and because kingdoms were inevitably class structures, this fusion into a single entity inevitably favoured aristocratic and imperialist philosophies and these were then developed to form our received wisdom, in order to explain how much and just how it had been achieved. Political success also creates personality cults that, in order to become coherent historical accounts, need to become more than catenations of 'worthies', they need to be seen as embodying some collection of values and qualities that larger than life figures jointly possessed. All too often, ruthless power is the easiest explanation to offer, though it is a false god.

If we admit that we have created leadership cults in order to justify our perceived political achievements then perhaps, in a democratic age, we now need to move away and to look more closely at our history of social cohesions? Although individuals and their personal qualities have figured so prominently in our review of events, surely the ultimate achievement was communal and it was also greater than the mere sum of the parts.

Notes

1. Stenton, op. cit., 1955, p.24, citing Erkwall, *Early London Personal Names* (1947), p.197.
2. Q.v. Wright (2020); also Wright (2014), pp.360–362 discussing Cornwall.
3. Wright (2020), pp.1–7 and 13–14.

Index

Æbbe 59
Ælfgar 152–4
Ælfgifu (of Northampton) 133, 141, 162
Ælfgyfu 162
Ælfheah 115, 123, 132–3
Ælfhelm 128, 141
Æflæd 111
Ælfnoth 154
Ælfric 122, 124, 127, 136, 154
Ælfsig 135
Ælfsige 111
Ælfstan 122
Ælfhryth 103
Ælfweard 82
Ælla 20
Ælmær 132, 140
Æscwig 122
Æthelbald of Mercia (Ismere Charter) 2, 15
Æthelberht 15, 67
Æthelflæd 74, 77, 79
Æthelhelm 54
Æthelhere 59
Æthelhun 11
Æthelnorth 54
Æthelnoth 143
Æthelred 16–7, 21–2, 25, 48, 54, 74, 103, 105–6, 116, 118–9, 122–4, 126–7, 129–30, 133, 138–9, 140–1, 143–4, 149–150, 159–160, 162, 225
Æthelstan 13–14, 41, 45, 82, 89–92, 96, 130, 153
Æthelward 143
Æthelweard 123
Æthelwig (Evesham) 208
Æthelwold 72–3
Æthelwulf 11, 13, 15, 21, 64, 73
Æthere 45
(R.) Aire 91–2, 95, 100, 197
(R.) Avon 52–3, 75
"Acled/Aclea 13
"Ageland" 198
"Ash Ships" 58–9, 61, 112, 129
"Assendun" 140–1, 143
Akeman Street 140
Aldred 146, 154

Alfred xi, 17, 20–2, 25, 33–5, 37–9, 40–2, 44–8, 51–2, 55–59, 60–1, 64–9, 70–1, 74–5, 79–81, 84, 86–8, 97, 101, 103, 105, 117–118, 133, 144, 209, 214–5, 220, 227
Aller 41
Alney (Apperley) 140
Anderida 178
Andover 123, 149
Anglia 9, 11, 15–16, 19, 33, 36, 41–2, 44–5, 51, 55–8, 68, 73, 78–9, 82, 100–102, 108, 127, 132–133, 138, 141, 152, 209
Anglo-Saxon Chronicles 9
Anlaf 74, 90, 93, 95
Anwynd 33
Appledore 45–6, 48
Archers 53, 173, 181–2
Archil 192
Ash Valley 58
Ashdown/Ashe 22
Asser 36, 54
Athelney 38, 40, 67
Athulf 74
Axholme 91, 95, 194–5, 199
Aylesbury 78
Aylesford 140

(R.) Blackwater ("panta") 51, 74, 108, 112–113
"...by" names 81–2
"Bridal of Newmarket" 208
Bradbury Rings 39–72
Baldwin 145–146, 159
Barnsdale 91–93
Barton-upon-Humber 95
Basecg 22
Basing 22
Basques 173
Bath 40, 69, 133, 221
Battle 45, 178
Battle Hill 178–179, 181
Battle of Hastings 164
Battlesbury 41
Bayeux Tapestry 159–162, 173, 175, 178–179, 181–182, 185, 190
Beachy Head 58, 178
Bede 3–4, 68, 219, 226

Bedford 77–78
Bedfordshire 132–139
Benesing 74
Benfleet 47–48
Beorn 145–146
Berghred 28
Berkhampsted 187–188, 190
Berkshire 15, 22, 128, 130–132, 187
Berkshire Downs 22, 128
Bermondsey 140
Bernwood Forest 78
Billingsly 153
Black Mountains 75, 77, 153
Bleddyn 155
Bondir 6
Bosham 145–146, 160
Bratton Camp 41
Brecon Beacons 77, 153
Brendon Hills 9, 75
Bretons 180, 208
Bretwalda 9
Bridgenorth 57, 74, 153
Bridgwater 10–11
Brihtric 130
Bristol 9, 11, 53, 75, 98, 155, 221
Britford 159
Brithwulf 13
Brixton Deveril 40
"Bromsbyrig" 74
Brownsea 33
Brunaburgh 91
Buckinghamshire 131–132, 139
Burghal Hidage 68–69, 84, 87, 102
Burhred 17
Buttington 54
Bryhtnoð 109, 111–114, 116
Bryhtwold 113
Byrtsige 73

(R.) Colne 47, 130
(R.) Churn 53
Caldbec Hill 179, 181
Cambridgeshire 33, 132, 204
Canterbury 9, 13, 101, 130, 132, 135, 148, 150, 187, 208
Canvey Island 47–8
Caradoc 157
Carhampton 9–11
Carlisle 223
Carucates 86, 100–101, 117
Castleford 93, 100, 167
Cenulf 73
Ceolwulf 34, 75
Ceorl 13
Cerne Valley 39
Channel 9, 11, 13–4, 16, 35, 47, 51, 56, 59, 108, 133, 145, 160, 162, 169, 174–5, 187, 190, 194, 211, 222

Cheltenham 52
Chepstow 210–11
Cheshire 78, 82, 105, 211
Chester 24, 55, 74, 124, 139, 153, 155, 211
Chichester 56
Chilterns 78, 130
Chippenham 35–6, 39, 41–2, 51, 53, 72, 203
Christchurch 72
Cirencester 42, 53, 143
Clydog 79
Cnut 11, 113, 133, 136, 138–141, 143, 159, 162, 174, 186, 208, 213
Cnut IV 212, 214
Coinage 116–7, 120
Colchester 24, 78, 79, 81, 209–10
Colchester Castle 209–10
Comital System 214, 217–19, 221, 223, 227
Conan II 161
Constantine II 82, 90, 93
Copford 85
Cornwall 9–10, 105, 123, 191
Coronation 165, 218, 227
Cosham 139
Council of "Clofesho" 2
County Hidage 135
Cranborne Chase 39
Cricklade 139
Crossbows 173, 181–2, 184, 195, 204
Cuckhamsley Hill 128
Cumberland 98, 124

(R.) Dearne 92
(R.) Dee 55
(R.) Derwent 93, 169–70
(R.) Don 91, 95, 194, 197
"Dingesmere" 91, 94–5
"Domboc" 64, 67
Damnonians 9–10, 68, 191
Dane's (Devil's) Bank 91
Danelaw 45, 58, 65–6, 68, 71, 74–5, 78–9, 82, 85–6, 89, 94, 97, 100–102, 108, 117–18, 126, 159, 217–18, 220, 225, 227
Danes 7, 10–11, 13, 15, 17, 19–22, 25, 30, 33–6, 38–9, 40–2, 45–8, 52, 54–59, 64–5, 68, 73–5, 77–80, 84, 85–6, 88, 96–8, 100–02, 105, 111, 123, 126–7, 131, 144, 191, 194–5, 197–8, 201–03, 217–18
Danevirke 5
Dartmoor 10, 123–4, 134
Dartmouth 146
David 224
Dean 124–5, 134, 140
Deira 21, 82, 97
Dengy 109
Derbyshire 28, 33, 134, 158, 197, 200

Devil's Dyke/Ditch 72
Devon 9–10, 13, 36, 47, 52, 55–6, 59, 105–6, 123–4, 140
Ditch-Marsh 194
Dives-sur-Mer 175
Domesday Book 12, 87, 100–1, 109, 117, 125, 136, 157–8, 166, 194–5, 197, 199, 200, 203–5, 212, 218, 222
Doncaster 24, 91–2, 194, 5
Dorset 11, 39, 105, 123, 127, 139
Dover 46, 148–9, 150, 160, 187, 190
Duncan 223
Dungeness 150
Durham 3, 82, 97–8, 191–2, 207, 210, 221–2
Durlstan 34

"Ethandun" 41, 44
Eadhelm 100
Eadnoth 191
Eadred 98, 100–1
Eadric ("the Wild") 195, 201
Eadric (Streona) 128, 130–1, 139–41
Eadsige 125
Eadwig 100–1, 103
Eadwine 82, 154, 158, 187, 189, 191, 203–4
Eadwold 73
Ealdred 188
Ealhere 14
Ealstan 11
Eamont Bridge 82
Eanulf 11
Earliest raids 3–5, 9–11
East Hendred 128
East Lyng 38
East Thurrock 85
Eastbourne 186
Ecgbriht 77
Ecgbryht 9–10
Ecgbryt's Stone 40
Eddisbury 74
Edgar 101–103, 152, 158–9, 187–89, 191–2, 223, 225
Edington 40–41
Edith 128, 146, 149, 151–2, 158, 160, 187
Edmund 19, 48, 90, 96, 98, 100, 138–141, 152
Edward 11, 138–9, 144–6, 148–152, 154–155, 157–165, 174, 165, 174, 177, 188, 192, 204, 207, 214, 223, 225, 227
Edward ("the Elder") 72–5, 78–81, 82, 86–9, 101–3
Edward "the Exile" 152
Edwin/Eadwin 82, 154, 158, 166–7, 187, 189, 191, 203–4
Ely 33, 72–3, 75, 111–12, 114, 144, 202–6, 227

Emma (Ælfgyfu) 127, 141, 143–4, 162
Emporia 8, 11, 13, 17, 32
Emporos 8
Engelfield 21
English Ships 31, 45, 48, 61, 65, 105, 145, 160, 216
Eohric 73
Eric 30, 99–100, 141
Ermin Street 53
Ermine Street 24, 33, 57, 90–3, 95, 111, 140, 167, 195, 202
Essex 9, 14–5, 33, 46–7, 55, 72, 78–79, 108–9, 111–12, 119, 122, 130, 132, 140, 143, 150, 209
Eustace 148–9, 160–2, 173–4, 183–5, 188, 190
Evesham 53, 143, 208
Exeter 24, 33–5, 47, 51, 56, 125, 127, 190–1, 195
Exmoor 9–10, 40, 75, 123, 134, 150, 192
Extents 102, 117–8
Eystein Orre 170

(R.) Foulness 95, 194
(R.) Frome 33, 40, 100, 123, 139
"Five Boroughs" 96, 98, 101, 139
"Force" – see Great Army
(Wentwood) "Forest" 157
Fareham 124
Farndon 82
Farnham 46
Feet of Fines 225
Fir 60
Flaying Alive 85
Fleam Dyke 72
Florence of Worcester 153, 158
Folkestone 108, 150
Fordham 103
Foremark 28–9, 33
Forest of Dean 134, 140
Fortifications 17, 38, 78, 209
Fosse Dyke 26
Fosse Way 24, 35, 38, 40, 133, 139, 140
Foulness Island 15, 50–1
Fræna 122
Frekenham 203
Friðegist 122
Fulford 166, 175, 186
Fulham 42, 44
Fyrds 88, 141, 149, 159, 192, 221, 225

"Gafol" 112, 115–6, 118, 133
"Great Army/Force"7, 16, 29, 33, 74–5, 122
"Great Ship Force"10, 15
Gainsborough 24, 26, 92, 138, 195
Galtres/Gantres 169
Geld 70, 115, 117–9, 141–2, 155, 158, 186, 191, 207, 209, 212–14, 217

Geoffrey (Coutances) 208
Gifford 48, 184
Gjellestad Ship 61
Glasbury-on-Wye 154
Glastonbury 41
Gloucester 24, 53, 75, 153, 157, 213
Gloucestershire 140, 149, 157
Goda 106
Godfred 16
Godgifu 160
Godwine 122, 143–6, 149–52, 157, 160–1, 191–2
Goodwin Sands 14
Goole Moor 91, 95
Gorm the Old 6
Gosfrith 221
Gospatric 191–2
Graveney Boat 60
Great Council 139, 143, 213
Greenwich 133, 140
Grimbold 73
Gronhaug Ship 60
Gruffydd 145–6, 152–5
Gunnislake 10
Guthrum 33, 41–2, 45
Guy (Amiens) 184
Guy (Ponthieu) 160, 174, 184
Gwent 157
Gyfelliog 75
Gytha 190–1

(R.) Humber 16, 27, 33, 55, 91, 194–5, 197–8, 201, 205, 208, 218
"Hægelisdun" 19
"Hæstingas" 132, 177–8
"Hamwic" (Southampton) 10, 15
"Healfdene"/Halfdan 33–34, 36, 74
"Heimskringla" 166
"Helga Æsk" 60
"Hugh" 127, 211–2
Hack-silver 4, 25, 27, 65–6, 84, 112, 116–7, 136
Haddenham 72, 75, 203–5
Hadleigh 45, 48
Hadstock 85, 140, 143
Hæsten 46–8
Hampshire 15, 22, 40, 122–4, 127–8, 130, 132, 157, 187
Handfast Point 34
Harald 105–6
Harald Hardrada 154, 160, 166–7, 169–70
Harebryht 11
Harold (Godwineson) 143–4, 145–6, 149–55, 157–67, 169, 171, 174–5, 177–9, 184, 199, 227
Harold (Harefoot) 143–4, 162
Harold Klak 7

Harthacnut 143–4
Hatfield Forest 91
Hayling Island 125
Hearth-Troops 2, 11, 29, 35, 38, 135–6, 148, 150, 172, 182, 192, 202, 214, 217, 221
Heath Wood 28–9
Helmsley Gate 169
Hen Domen 209
Henry (III) 145
Henry I 148, 224–5
Henry II 224, 226
Hereford 75, 152–4, 207, 225
Hereward 202–4, 206, 227–8
Hertfordshire 47, 132, 187
Hides 86–8, 129, 135
Hingston Down 10
Hoar Apple Tree 179, 181
Holderness 198, 206
Holme 73, 93
Hook Norton 75, 77
Horik I 7
Horses (use of) 42, 138, 172–3, 175, 177, 180–1, 183, 186, 196
Hraold 75
Hugh (Chester) 127, 211–2
Hundreds 100, 203–5
Huntingdon 78–9, 207, 228
Huntingdonshire 132, 139
Hutha 14
Hythe 47, 150
Hywel 79

(R.) Idle 91, 194
"Iglea" 40
Icknield Way 24, 55, 57, 72, 128–9, 140
Idwal 79
Iley Oak 40
Immigration 24
Industries 8, 45, 119, 134
Ine 54, 67, 118
Ipswich 108, 130
Irish Sea 28, 47, 153
Irish Vikings 13, 16, 92, 106, 143, 223
Ivar (Boneless) 19–20

Jarrow (Monk Wearmouth) 3–4, 6
Judith 146
Jury 71, 225

(R.) Kennet 24, 53
Kennington 128
Kent 8–9, 11, 13–5, 36, 46, 74, 78, 105, 115, 119–20, 122, 124, 130, 132, 139–40, 177, 187, 190, 208, 211, 221
King's Thegns 89, 111, 113, 135, 143, 158
Kingdom of the Isles 6, 124–5

Kit Hill 10
Knowlton Henge 39
Kola 125
Kvalsund 60

(R.) Lea 56–8, 74
(R.) Limen/Lympne 45, 108
Land's End 16, 123, 150
Lanfranc 208, 212
Launceston 123
Leicester 74–5, 78–9, 98
Leicestershire 28, 111, 221
Leofgar 154
Leofric 143, 149, 152, 154
Leofwine 149
Leominster 145
Liber Eliensis 109, 111, 114
Lifing 133
Limfjord 213
Lincolnshire 26–7, 33, 81–2, 91, 95, 118, 138–9, 158, 166, 194, 197–8, 200–1, 205
Lindsey 11, 16, 27, 52, 55, 73, 122, 136
Lindisfarne 2, 4, 6
Llangorse Lake 77
Local Knowledge 18, 20, 24–5, 27, 40, 42, 46, 51, 77, 88–9, 91, 93, 123, 129, 131, 152, 166, 177, 181
London 13, 24–5, 45–8, 52, 57–8, 65, 70, 72–4, 97, 105, 115, 122, 130, 133, 139–41, 143, 150–1, 177–179, 186–7, 209–10
Lucumon 59
Lydford 123
Lyng 38, 68–9

(R.) Maran 74
(R.) Mole 130
"Magensæt" 140
Macbeth 152
Macredun/Morden 22, 39
Mærieswein 191–2, 201
Magnus 144–5, 154, 160
Maine 205
Malcolm 98, 143, 191, 205, 210–11, 222–3
Maldon 74, 77–8, 108–9, 111–12, 116, 123, 153
"Malfosse" 185
Manna 78
Manchester 79
Manningtree 146
Map (Walter) 224
Marsh camps 26–7, 46–50, 56, 112
Mathilde 191
Matilda 224
Medway 9, 11, 46, 123, 140
Meon 125
Mercia 2, 9, 13, 17, 19, 26, 30, 33–6, 42, 44, 48, 52, 54–5, 64, 67–8, 72, 74, 77, 79, 85, 87, 90, 99, 101, 128, 139–41, 154–5, 158
Mersea 16, 74, 90, 97–8, 153
Mersea Island 55–6
Middlesex 132, 187
Millenium 215–7
Milton Regis 46, 48
Minehead 9, 75
Minerals 9, 119
Monasteries 2–3, 10, 19, 67, 87, 123
Morcar/Morcær 139, 158–9, 166–7, 189, 191, 203–4
Morden Bog 39

(R.) Nene 33, 73, 111
(The) Narrows 11, 52, 130, 143, 150, 161, 190, 194
(The) Needles 34
Neatham 158
New Forest 39
Newmarket 72, 208
Norfolk 55, 118, 203–4, 207–8, 221
Norman Horse 183
North Foreland 13–4
North Riding 199
Northamptonshire 77, 111, 132, 135, 139, 221
Northamptonshire Geld Roll 135
Northey Island 108–9, 112
Northumbria 1–2, 9, 16, 20–21, 26, 32–4, 44, 47, 51–2, 55, 58, 72, 74, 79, 82, 90, 97–8, 100–01, 111, 122, 128, 139, 141, 152, 154–5, 158–9, 191–2, 207, 210–11, 223, 227
Northwich 74
Norwegian Vikings 9, 11, 154, 166–7, 198–9
Norwich 127, 208
Nottingham 7, 25, 79
Nottinghamshire 27–8, 158, 194

(R.) Orwell 140
(R.) Ouse 1, 72, 77–8, 93, 95, 131, 166–7, 170, 204
Odal Rights 6
Odda 36, 149–50
Oderic Vitalis 199
Odiham 157
Odo (Bayeux) 172, 174, 183–4, 188, 190, 208, 211–2, 221–2
Offa 27, 64, 67
Offa's Dyke 54
Olaf 90, 93, 95–8, 100, 106, 115, 122–3, 143
Old Harry Rocks 34
Ordheh 54
Organisation for War 216
Orosius 61, 68

Osbeorn 194
Osbern Pentecost 150
Oscytel 33
Oseberg Ship 6, 7, 60–1
Osric 11, 15
Ohter 74–5
Ohthere 61
Owain 90
Oxford 74, 78, 81–2, 127–8, 130, 133, 139, 159
Oxfordshire 111, 131–2

(R.) Parrett 11, 38–9, 54–5
(R.) Piddle 33
"Parks" 39, 53, 157–8
"Passage to Paradise" 67
"Proverbs of Alfred" 65
Padstow 105
Pallig 124
Papal Legates 67, 202
Passenham 78
Peak District 97–8
Peddar's Way 24, 111
Pegwell Bay 14
Penselwood 40, 140
Peterborough 19, 73, 135, 202, 226–8
Pevensey 132, 145–6, 150, 175, 177, 186–7, 195, 209, 222–3
Pewsey (Vale) 24, 53
Phillipe (France) 188, 208
Pilton 69
Pine 60–62
Pinhoe 125
Piquet Hill 41
Poole 33
Porlock Bay 9, 75, 150
Portaging 51, 53–4, 58, 62, 216
Portchester 69
Portland 11, 105, 123
Portsea 125, 209
Portskewet 157
Portsmouth 125, 139
Pucklechurch 98
Purbeck 33–4

Quentovic 11, 14, 46

(R.) Rother 45
"(The) Raven" 36
"Read's Island" 95
Rægnald 98
Ragnar Lodbrok 20
Ralph 149
Ralph (de Gael) 150, 152, 207–8
Ralswick Boats 62
Ramsey 111
Ransoms 29, 32, 75, 84, 126, 132, 163, 201

Rayleigh 48, 209
Reading 19, 21, 22, 24–5, 126, 128–9
Reculver 9, 14
Repton 28–9, 33, 46, 50, 92, 143
Rhiwallon 155
Riccal 166–7, 170
Richard (fitz Gilbert) 208
Ridgeway 127–8
Rippon 106
Robert 150–1, 172, 188
Robert (Curthose) 211–12, 221–2
Robert (fitz Wymarc) 177
Robert (Flanders) 208, 212
Robert (Mortain) 197
Robet (Mowbray) 221
Robertsbridge 45
Rochester 11, 44, 48, 85, 106, 123, 221–2
Rogaland 60
Roger 206–21
Roger (de Breteuil) 206–208
Roman Ridge 91–3, 167
Roman Rig 91
Romney 11, 45, 150, 186–7
Romney Marshes 11
Roskilde 60
Roydon 56–8
Ruddlan 80, 155
Rule of St Benedict 1
Rune Poem(s) 62, 170
Rye 45, 186–7
(R.) Severn 35, 51–5, 57, 74–6, 123, 143, 146, 153, 157
(R.) Somme 160
(R.) Stour 45, 146, 150
(R.) Swere 77
"Saga Farmann" 62
"Scergeat" 74
"Sermo Lupi..." 102, 107, 124
"Seven Boroughs" 139
"Ship List" 174
Salisbury 22, 127, 159, 214, 218
Salisbury Plain 22, 41, 100, 214, 218
Sandwich 13–4, 108, 128–30, 133, 138–9, 144, -6, 150
Sawbridgeworth 56–8
Scandinavian Place Names 20
Scotland 6, 82, 86, 90–1, 98, 143, 152, 166, 191, 201, 203, 205, 210–11, 220, 222–4
Scots 80, 90–4, 98, 154, 199, 200–1
Scratcbury 41
Scurfa 74
Scutage 223
Selwood 54
Selwood Forest 40
Shaftesbury 67, 143
Sheppey 9, 13, 15–6, 46, 150

Index   237

Sherston 140
Shoebury 15, 50–1
Shrewsbury 54–5, 98, 153, 195
Shropshire 74, 129, 134, 139–40, 221
Sidrac 21
Sigeferth 139
Sigelm 73
Sigulf 73
Sihtric 82
Simeon of Durham 207
Siward 149, 152, 207
Skuldelev 60–2, 129
Slavery 21, 31, 64–6, 84, 87–8, 96, 144, 153, 201
Snowdon 223
Somerset 9–10, 40–1, 106, 139, 191
Somerset Levels 38, 41
South Cadbury 40
South Foreland 14, 130
Southampton 10, 15, 59, 68, 105, 122, 127–9
Southwark 151, 187
St Albans 57, 73
St Brice's Day 126–8
St Frideswide's 127
St Valery 175
Staffordshire 6, 10, 28, 116, 118, 139, 197–8
Staines 47–8, 130
Stamford 79, 81, 165, 167
Stamford Bridge 167–9, 177, 185
Steepholme 76
Stephen 224–5
Stigand 146, 187
Stockton 169
Strands 46, 48
Strathclyde 33, 80, 90, 98, 223
Strood 46
Stuntney 203–4
Styrkar 170
Surrey 9, 13, 15, 78, 132
Sussex 9, 15, 68, 122–3, 130, 132, 177, 186–7
Sutton Hoo 6, 10, 60–1
Swannage 34
Swein (Estrithson) 160
Swein (Godwineson) 145–6, 149, 152, 154
Sweyn 105–6, 122, 124, 127, 133, 136, 144–5, 192, 194, 201, 208
Swindon 53, 72
Synod 213

(R.) Tame 27, 98
(R.) Taw 192
(R.) Tamar 10, 123
(R.) Thames 9, 11, 13–5, 20, 22, 24, 33, 42, 45–8, 50–6, 72, 101, 108–9, 122–3, 128–31, 133, 139–40, 149–50, 159, 188, 194
(R.) Tove 77–8
(R.) Tovy 123
(R.) Trent 26–9, 33, 79, 92, 95, 98, 194–5, 197
(R.) Tyne 4, 33, 210
Tadcaster 166
Tamworth 27, 74, 76, 97–8
Taunton 10, 39
Tavistock 10, 123
Teignmouth 124
Teignton 124
Tempsford 78, 131
Tenterden 46
Tettenhall 74, 89
Textile Production 81, 108, 134
Thanet 9, 11, 13–6, 46, 101, 105, 108, 120, 160
Thelwall 79
Thetford 19, 25, 55, 73, 81, 100, 127, 131
Thored 122
Thorkell 130, 133, 143
Thorne Moor 91
Thralls/Thralldom 3, 21, 31, 65–6, 85, 97, 101
Thundersley 48
Thurcytel 77, 131
Thurferth 78
Thurkil 141
Tiddingford 73
Tin Mining 8, 10, 119
Toglos 78
Torksey 26–8, 31, 48, 50, 81, 92
Tostig 146, 151–2, 154–5, 158–9, 165–7, 170
Towcester 77–8
Tribal Hidage 87, 101, 129, 226
Tribute 16–7, 24, 26, 31, 33, 65, 90, 106, 112–6, 118–9, 122, 125, 129, 132–3, 135, 138, 140–2, 144, 150, 153, 163, 165, 186, 188, 201, 217–8, 229
Tonbridge 221
Turold 202
Tewkesbury 52, 140

(R.) Usk 146, 157
Uhtred 139
Ulfegeat 128
Ulfcytel 127, 130

"Vita Ædwardi Regis" 161–2, 164
Valley of White Horse 38
Vikings ("Ship Men") 6, 8, 10–1, 13–4, 16, 26, 30–2, 42, 46, 55, 66, 78, 81–2, 85, 90–2, 93–4, 105–6, 111–5, 123–5, 127–8, 130, 132, 143, 154, 167, 170, 198, 202, 216–8, 223
Virgilus 73

(R.) Welland 78–9
(R.) Went 95
(R.) Wharfe 166
(R.) Windrush 52
(R.) Witham 26–7
(R.) Wye 157, 225
(The) Wash 24, 33, 72, 75, 111, 166, 194, 202, 204
"Wasta" 200
"Wicganbeorg" 13
"Wigingamere" 77–8
St Wystan (Wgstan) 5, 25
Waltheof 201, 207–8, 225
Wales 9, 54–5, 77, 86, 98, 123, 134, 145, 152–3, 155, 195, 211, 220, 223, 225
Wallingford 68, 128, 133, 187
Walcher (Durham) 210
Walton Naze 146, 151
Wantsum 13–4, 108, 130, 150
Wapentakes 95, 100
Wareham 33–4, 39, 69
Warwickshire 111, 139
Watchet 75, 106, 123
Waterways 15, 24, 42, 52, 60, 63, 70, 74, 129, 178
Watling Street 24, 55, 57, 74, 98, 133, 153
Weald 119, 124
Wedmore 41
Welland 78–9
Welsh 54, 74–7, 79–80, 82, 98, 145–6, 152, 154–5, 157–8, 190–2, 195, 197, 210, 221, 223, 225, 227
Walland Marsh 45, 150
Wentwood Forest 157
Wessex 9, 11, 13, 15–6, 20–2, 25, 33–7, 39, 41, 44–7, 51–2, 55, 58, 64, 67–8, 74–6, 79, 82, 85, 87, 90, 101, 118, 123, 128, 139–40, 159, 187
Westbury 40–1, 152
Westminster 85, 165, 188
Weymouth 127
Wherwell 149
White Tower 209
Whittlesey Mere 73, 111
Whitwell Gap 96

Wight 34, 59, 123, 125, 128, 130, 133, 143, 150, 160, 165, 211, 214
Wihtræd of Kent 8
William (of Durham) 221
William (fitz Osbern) 190, 192, 195, 207
William (Rufus) 221–3
William (Warenne) 208
Duke/King William I 106, 157, 160–2, 165–6, 171–2, 177, 182–3, 191–2, 195–9, 201–8, 210–14, 218, 221–2, 225, 227–8
William of Poitiers 164, 177, 185, 190, 199
Wilton 22, 127
Wiltshire 22, 40, 127, 132, 139, 158
Wimbourne 72
Winchester 15, 22, 25, 59, 68–70, 81–2, 87, 97, 101, 115, 129, 133, 143–4, 146, 151, 186–7, 190–1, 212, 214
Winchester School 87
Wintersetl 19, 27–8, 33–4, 38, 50, 56, 63, 109, 115, 126–7, 136, 140, 194, 197–8
Witan 148–9, 160, 164, 187–9, 213, 225, 228
Witham 26–7, 74
Wool Street 24, 79, 111, 140
Worcester 57, 126, 144, 153, 158, 208
Worcestershire 221
Wulfballd 105
Wulfead 10, 59
Wulfleah 128
Wulfnoth 130
Wulfsige 111
Wulfstan (& Ohthere) 61
Wulfstan (Bishop of Worcester) 96, 98, 100, 102, 106–7, 124, 126, 159, 208
(Archbishop) Wulfstan 221
Wyre Forest 153

Yeovil 39–40
Yingalinga (Dynasty) 16
York 16–7, 19, 24–5, 45, 55, 79, 82, 90, 92, 96–8, 100–1, 139, 158, 165–7, 169, 171, 188, 191–2, 194, 197–9, 208
Yorkshire 74, 95, 97, 118, 158, 192, 194, 197–201, 205–6